Healthy Food for Healthy Kids

A Practical and Tasty Guide to Your Child's Nutrition

Bridget Swinney

M.S. Nutrition, Registered Dietitian

Meadowbrook Press

Distributed by Simon & Schuster
New York

Library of Congress Cataloging-in-Publication Data

Swinney, Bridget, 1960–
    Healthy food for healthy kids: a practical and tasty guide to your child's nutrition /
Bridget Swinney.
        p. cm.
    ISBN 0-88166-336-0 (Meadowbrook)–ISBN 0-671-31725-3 (Simon & Schuster)
    1. Children–Nutrition. 2. Food preferences in children. 3. Cookery. I. Title.
RJ206.S95   1999
613.2'083–dc21   99-23788
                                                            CIP

Coordinating Editors: Liya Lev Oertel, Christine Zuchora-Walske
Copyeditors: Nancy Campbell, Christine Zuchora-Walske
Production Manager: Joe Gagne
Production Assistant: Danielle White
Cover and Interior Art: Jone Hallmark

Text © 1999 by Bridget Swinney, M.S., R.D.

Published by Meadowbrook Press, 5451 Smetana Drive, Minnetonka, MN 55343

www.meadowbrookpress.com

BOOK TRADE DISTRIBUTION by Simon & Schuster, a division of Simon and
Schuster, Inc., 1230 Avenue of the Americas, New York, NY 10020

The contents of this book have been reviewed and checked for accuracy and appropriate-
ness by professionals in the field of nutrition. However, the authors, editors, reviewers, and
publisher disclaim all responsibility arising from any adverse effects or results that occur or
might occur as a result of the inappropriate application of any of the information contained
in this book. If you have a question or concern about any of the information in this book,
consult your health-care professional.

03   10 9 8 7 6 5 4

Printed in the United States of America

Dedication

For Nicolas and Robert,
my favorite taste testers.
On a scale from one to ten,
you're a million!

Acknowledgments

First I must thank my family–Frank, Nicolas, and Robert–who for two years put up with my recipe testing (and the resultant messy kitchen) and my long hours at the computer.

Thanks to my colleagues, family, and friends who offered both technical and practical review: Peggy Connor, R.N.; Jacquie Craig, M.S., R.D.; Kathy Cross; Sandra Eardly, Ph.D., R.D.; Connie Evers, M.S., R.D.; Wendy Gregor, M.S., R.D.; Glenda Herman, M.S., R.D.; Beatriz Leyba; Ann Litt, M.S., R.D.; Elvira Johnson; Candi McNany; Marna Moreland; Maureen Murtaugh, Ph.D., R.D.; Colleen Paradise; Joanna Reagan, M.S., R.D.; Christine Reinarts, M.S., R.D.; Sue Reitzel; Norma Robinson, R.D.; Amy Tracy; Jane Stephenson, R.D.; Gene Swinney; and Judith Swinney.

Special thanks to Marilyn Rotwein for providing nutritional analysis of recipes and for being so supportive!

Thanks to family and friends–especially Frank, John, Alicia, and Sue–who offered pep talks, baby-sitting, and other helpful measures during the final stages of the book.

Thanks to those who agreed to share their recipes with the readers of *Healthy Foods for Healthy Kids:* Minerva Al-Tabaa, an expert in Middle Eastern cuisine; The Colorado Dietetic Association, publisher of *Simply Colorado;* Madhu Gadia, author of *Light and Luscious Cuisine of India;* Kim Pierce and Barbara Gollman, authors of *The Phytopia Cookbook;* Brenda Ponichtera, author of *Quick and Healthy Recipes and Ideas* and *Quick and Healthy Volume II;* Sue Reitzel, for sharing her family recipes and ideas; and Debbie and Sandy Russell.

Thanks also to Pamela Wiggins, IBCLC, author of *Breastfeeding: A Mother's Gift* and *Why Should I Nurse My Baby?* for allowing me to reprint a section from her book and to The Food Allergy Network for permission to use their materials.

To all my taste testers, thanks for your discriminating taste buds: Michael and Marcus Atkinson; Katie, Cristian, and Ben Barrera; Mrs. Daw's Pre-K class at Saint Mark's Methodist Day School; Den Four of the Lindbergh Scout Pack–Albert Ahumada, Frank Apodaca, Nicolas Blando, Marco Leyba, David Navar, Timmy Navar, Sammy Showery, Scott Superville; Sean Fraser; Miss Karen's preschool class at Saint Mark's Methodist Day School; Norman Leyba; Kendra Melendez; Melissa Ogren; Mykle Mary and Zoe Reitzel; Sofia and Lorraine Rojas; Shelby Seifers; and the students of Mrs. Slaughter's first-and-second-grade class at Lindbergh Elementary School. Thanks also to the taste testers' parents who gave their feedback. And last but not least, thanks to Nicolas and Robert, who tasted every recipe in this book, plus a lot more that didn't meet their standards!

At Meadowbrook Press, thanks to Bruce Lansky and Liya Lev Oertel for their patience and enthusiasm while I was writing *Healthy Food for Healthy Kids*. Thanks to Liya and Christine Zuchora-Walske for cutting the "fat" from the manuscript while keeping all the best parts. Thanks to Christine for pulling the book together with a tight deadline. Thanks to the talented Jone Hallmark for the cute-as-a-bug cover art and inside graphics, and thanks to Danielle White for the easy-to-read typesetting.

Contents

Section I

The Whys and How-Tos of Healthy Eating

Section II

Feeding Your Child

Introduction

Hello! Chances are, you have bought this book because you are interested in your child's health and eating habits. Congratulations. You have taken an important step toward maintaining your child's present and future health.

Now more than ever, we have reason to be concerned about our children's eating habits. Obesity among children is on the rise due to decreasing activity levels and to high-fat and high-calorie diets. In addition, we have learned that eating habits formed in childhood affect a variety of chronic diseases. Heart disease, for example, develops slowly and can begin in childhood.

You–whether you are a parent, grandparent, guardian, day-care provider, or teacher–may have substantial influence (positive or negative) on a child's eating habits. Yours is an important, though often frustrating, job. You have to compete with peer pressure and a barrage of commercials for junk food and fast food. And you know it takes a vast commitment of time and energy to get your kids to eat right!

So take a deep breath and follow me into the world of kids' nutrition. I hope not only to answer all your questions about nutrition, but also to give you a kitchen toolbox filled with menus, recipes, and ideas that are kid-tested and parent-approved.

Happy, healthy eating!

Bridget Swinney

Section I

The Whys and How-Tos of Healthy Eating

CHAPTER ONE

The Parents' Ten Commandments of Healthy Eating

Don't you wish your kids came with an instruction book? I know I did. I quickly learned that parenting is a continuous on-the-job training experience. (And just when you think you've got it figured out, everything changes!) Fortunately, you can educate yourself about parenting issues to help you tackle the challenges.

This book was written to give you guidance, inspiration, and practical ideas on an important aspect of parenting: feeding your kids. To help you establish positive eating habits in your children, here are ten helpful rules. Follow them, and mealtime will be more pleasant (for you and for your kids) as well as more healthy. These rules are the foundation for the rest of this book.

Commandments in Brief

1. Thou shalt not force or bribe thy child to eat.

2. Thou shalt set a good example by eating at least five fruits and vegetables and drinking three glasses of milk per day thyself.

3. Thou shalt make mealtimes pleasant.

4. Thou shalt encourage thy child to help in meal planning, preparation, and cleanup.

5. Thou shalt back off when mealtime becomes a power struggle.

6. Thou shalt accept food jags as phases that will eventually pass.

7. Thou shalt accept the fact that thy child is an individual and thus will dislike certain foods. (And there may be many!)

8. Thou shalt not give up on introducing thy child to new foods. Thou shalt realize it sometimes takes ten tries to get a child to accept a food.

9. Thou shalt use this division of responsibility for eating: As the parent, thou art responsible for deciding when to eat and what to serve. Thy child is responsible for deciding how much (if any) he will eat.

10. Thou shalt give thy child a multivitamin -mineral supplement if he is a picky eater.

▼

Commandments Explained

1. *Thou shalt not force or bribe thy child to eat.* A parent's bag of tricks usually includes a few threats or bribes. These may range from "You'll stay at the table until you finish those green beans!" to "Chocolate cake for everyone who finishes his carrots." As a parent of a skinny six-year-old who eats like a bird, I find this commandment particularly challenging. It's easy to get exasperated, throw out the rule book, and start bribing.

However, research shows that children are born with good control of their food intake. They eat when they are hungry and stop when they are full. It is adults who teach kids they must eat at mealtime, even if they aren't hungry. Kids who are forced to eat lose their natural ability to control their food intake. In other words, hunger is no longer what makes them eat. Experts on child psychology tell us that this loss of control can lead to eating disorders like anorexia and bulimia or lifelong overeating problems. So leave those bribes and threats in the bottom of your bag of tricks and select a more positive approach instead.

Quick Tip: When your child demonstrates an eating behavior you like, let him know that you like it.

2. *Thou shalt set a good example by eating at least five fruits and vegetables and drinking three glasses of milk per day thyself.* If you expect your child to "do as I say, not as I do," prepare for disappointment. Kids model adult behavior, whether it's eating, exercising, or bad manners! So the best way to get your kids to eat healthily is to do so yourself. Start with the simple goal of eating five fruits and vegetables and drinking three glasses of milk a day. Many of the important vitamins and minerals we all need are found in fruits and veggies. Drinking milk is the key to lifelong strong bones, but milk is now too often replaced by sodas and other sweet drinks. If you and your children can achieve this goal, your family is on its way to long-term good health and good eating habits!

Quick Tip: Keep a bowl of fruit on the table as a tempting and easy snack source. Milk doesn't always have to be plain; chocolate milk sometimes goes down easier.

3. *Thou shalt make mealtimes pleasant.* Is your dinner hour the time you lecture Johnny for getting into trouble at school or nag your spouse for leaving a mess in the sink? Does your dinner "hour" take only ten minutes? Do you find it hard to concentrate on each other because the TV is blaring in the next room?

If you said yes to any of these questions, your family mealtime may need an attitude adjustment. Try setting a few ground rules: No TV during meals. No toys at the table. No lectures, arguing, or nagging. No answering the telephone.

I once read an interesting story about a family's dinner ritual. At each dinner, every member of the family had to relate something he learned that day. Such positive mealtime rituals stimulate conversation and learning.

For some, family dinners have fallen victim to our busy lifestyles. Between work schedules, sports, and music lessons, some families have a hard time sitting down to a meal together. Meals may be "grab and go" or eaten as individuals instead of as a family. Mealtime is important for developing social skills, so try to have meals together anytime you can. Remember: dinner doesn't have to be your main meal. If you can gather your whole family only at breakfast or lunch, great! And if you happen to eat a meal out, try to apply the suggestions above to make the meal enjoyable for all. If cooking time cuts too much into eating time, use leftovers creatively or look for quicker recipes. (See "Meal-in-a-Flash Menus" on page 358.)

Quick Tip: Bring your dinner with you to a soccer game or swim practice and have a family picnic.

4. *Thou shalt encourage thy child to help in meal planning, preparation, and cleanup.* Those who help make a meal have a vested interest in eating it! Offering lots of choices can make the experience more pleasant for everyone and can help defuse power struggles. For example, have your child choose a cup and decide what fruit to serve. Choices not only help foster children's self-esteem by giving them a role to play; they also remove some burden from you! Here are a few ways kids can help with meals:

Meal Planning

Even a two-and-a-half-year-old can answer whether he wants to have peas or corn for dinner. Once a month, I let one of my children pick what we have for lunch or dinner. The choice is never made without careful consideration! We usually end up eating macaroni and cheese; nonetheless, the exercise of planning a meal develops thinking skills and makes a child feel good about his contribution to the meal.

At the grocery store, you can let each child choose something new to try, pick a food for dinner, or even plan a meal, depending on the age of the child. Grocery shopping with one child at a time may work best. The grocery store is also a great place for teaching shapes, colors, nutrition, comparison shopping, and math.

Cooking

According to Connie Evers, author of *How to Teach Nutrition to Kids* (24 Carrot Press), "It's true that cooking with your child may add to the time, mess, and confusion initially. But eventually, you will appreciate both the extra set of hands and your child's growing self-sufficiency."

It's a tradition in our family for my husband to make crepes with my youngest son, Robert. When Frank calls, "It's time to make crepes!" Robert comes running, regardless of what other fun activity he is doing. At five, Robert can crack eggs, pour milk and vanilla, and help hold the hand mixer. Not only does Robert feel special for helping; he's also involved in a memorable tradition. Traditions provide stability.

Another reason to get your kids "cooking" early is that children are becoming increasingly responsible for their own meals and snacks. A 1991 Gallup survey found that eight out of ten kids sometimes cook or make their own breakfast, and 87 percent said they cooked or made some of their own meals. The earlier you get kids started in the kitchen, the more interested and educated they will be when it's time to cook on their own.

Quick Tip: At age seven, your child can probably learn to read food labels. Teach your child what to look for on labels when deciding what to buy.

Helpful Hints for Cooking with Kids

- Keep in mind that the younger the child, the longer it will take to make something with him. Start with something simple and fun. Making a simple sandwich or muffins from a boxed mix is easy, and a child can quickly enjoy the fruits of his labor.
- Incorporate a variety of skills in the kitchen. For younger children, teach number and letter recognition, counting, adding, and subtracting. With older kids, you can delve into more complicated subjects such as chemistry (fermentation), microbiology (how bacteria grow in food left at room temperature), math (hands-on fraction work by doubling or halving a recipe), reading (five- and six-year-olds can help read a recipe), and social studies (explore other cultures by making ethnic foods, learning the names of the foods in different languages, and incorporating ethnic food customs).
- Stress safety in the kitchen. Always wash hands well with soap before cooking and after using the restroom, coughing, or blowing your nose. Don't taste batter or dough containing raw egg or raw meat. Teach your children to use a separate cutting board for raw meats and foods that won't be cooked. Don't leave milk, meats, or eggs at room temperature. Take special care in teaching your child safety rules for cooking with a microwave, oven, or stovetop.
- Find work that your child can be in charge of: measuring dry ingredients, cracking eggs, stirring batter, shaping cookies, or pouring wet ingredients. Be sure to give your child jobs that are age- and skill-appropriate. If a job is too difficult, it may spoil your child's fun.

Mom, Can I Help? Suggested Jobs According to Age

1- to 2-year-olds can:

- dump in premeasured dry ingredients and help stir
- help shape cookies and other dough
- tell you when the timer goes off
- help decorate cookies or put on finishing touches like cheese, raisins, or icing
- hand you an egg or other ingredients

3- to 4-year-olds can:

- help measure ingredients
- help crack eggs and mix ingredients
- shape cookies
- help pour batter into a pan
- hold a mixer with you (his hand under yours)
- arrange food on a serving plate

5- to 6-year-olds can:

- help read a recipe
- learn how to measure and mix dry ingredients
- crack eggs and learn how to separate yolk from white
- learn how to safely use mixer or wire whisk
- stir eggs into a flour mixture
- set a timer

7- to 8-year-olds can:

- read a recipe out loud
- follow most of a recipe with your help and supervision, except placing things in or pulling them out of an oven

9-year-olds and up can:

- follow a recipe without help

• Don't be surprised if, in the middle of cooking, your child decides that he wants to go play outside or draw a picture. Your child's attention span for cooking will vary according to his age.

Cleanup

If you teach your children to clean up at an early age, their future husbands and wives will thank you! A child as young as two years old can bring his own plate to the sink (provided the plate is nonbreakable). As children get older, they can handle more responsibility. Nicolas, my six-year-old, was just put in charge of helping clean and wipe the table. Sponging off the table is his favorite part. To my delight, a few days after he started this job, he said, "Boy, the table sure is messy today!" From now on, I bet he

will think about his own neatness at the table. When you assign your children chores, just make sure they can handle the responsibility and that you show them a few times how to do it correctly. "Catch" them being helpful and comment on the specific act: "Thanks for taking your plate to the sink without being asked." Your attention reinforces the behavior you want to encourage.

5. *Thou shalt back off when mealtime becomes a power struggle.* This commandment is easier to preach than to follow. Little people know our hot buttons, and if eating is one of yours, your child will continually push it. Food often inspires heated conflicts between children and their parents. Though eating is certainly important, it must be ruled by your child's internal control, not the time of day

or your expectations. When eating becomes a source of conflict, your relationship with your child suffers, and your child may develop a negative attitude toward food. See commandment nine.

Quick Tip: Before you get into a battle with your child over his peas, ask yourself, "Is this really important?"

6. *Thou shalt accept food jags as phases that will eventually pass.* Your four-year-old has wanted to eat only macaroni and cheese meal after meal, day after day, for the whole week! Should you buy stock in Kraft? Not to worry: This too shall pass, more than likely. Food jags are normal, so don't make a big deal out of them. If the food is healthy, let your child have it, and offer other foods at the same time.

Quick Tip: Put a twist on your child's food jag. Add lean ground meat or chicken breast to the mac and cheese.

7. *Thou shalt accept the fact that thy child is an individual and thus will dislike certain foods. (And there may be many!)* Does it seem as though with every passing day, your child eats fewer and fewer things? Kids have food preferences just as adults do. However, sometimes it's hard to discern between true dislikes and food moods. Food moods are times when your child doesn't want to eat anything you want him to eat. In our house, we follow the "polite bite" rule. Everyone tries to eat at least one bite of the food in question. One bite is not asking a lot; it helps your child develop a taste for foods he would not otherwise eat; and it is the polite thing to do.

Recent research has uncovered why some people have a strong aversion to certain families of foods. Any broccoli, greens, and Brussels sprouts haters in your family? It could be that they are "supertasters." Supposedly, they have more taste buds on their tongue, so they perceive all tastes much more strongly. Though this might provide an excuse for not liking certain foods, there is no harm in tasting them a few times.

Quick Tip: Kids need to learn table manners. When your child is served a food that he doesn't like, teach him to refuse it politely.

8. *Thou shalt not give up on introducing thy child to new foods. Thou shalt realize it sometimes takes ten tries to get a child to accept a food.* So your child has tasted carrots and said he doesn't like them. So much for carrots! Well, wait just a minute. The fact that he doesn't like carrots the first time he tries them doesn't mean he won't love them the eighth time. Tastes develop over time, so the more often a child eats something, the more likely he will be to develop a genuine liking for it. It could also be that your child just likes his carrots raw instead of cooked or vice versa. For example, eleven-month-old Emma Claire doesn't like plain steamed carrot slices, but she will eat them in spaghetti or dipped in maple syrup, and she loves them with peas and potatoes in stew. So keep plugging away; your child may yet become a vegetable lover!

9. *Thou shalt use this division of responsibility for eating: As the parent, thou art responsible for deciding when to eat and what to serve. Thy child is responsible for deciding how much (if any) he will eat.* Once you know where your responsibility lies, the pressure is off! It's easy to slide into authoritarian ways—"Eat it or else!" However, this can not only damage your relationship with your child; it can also harm his natural instinct to control his food intake according to his hunger. (See commandment one.)

Ellyn Satter, a renowned child feeding expert who is a registered dietitian as well as a psychotherapist, developed the division of responsibility for food regulation. In her book *Child of Mine: Feeding with Love and Good Sense* (Bull Publishing, 1983), she gives an example of a girl who was very small for her age. No matter how adults tried to get the girl to eat more calories, she always ate the same amount. Finally, the adults figured that the girl was just destined to be small and was naturally eating the right amount.

10. *Thou shalt give thy child a multivitamin-mineral supplement if he is a picky eater.* Believe it or not, kids (and their tired parents) do make it through those picky-eating years. But to make sure your child gets all the nutrients he needs—and to provide you with a little peace of mind—give him a multivitamin-mineral supplement.

Be sure to pick an age-appropriate supplement for your child and read the directions carefully. For some brands, half a tablet is the suggested dose for two- to three-year-olds. Teach your child that a vitamin is not candy or a treat, but medicine. Make sure to keep vitamin supplements out of reach of children; iron overdose from multivitamins has killed several children.

Quick Tip: Giving your child a multivitamin-mineral supplement doesn't mean he needn't eat healthily, too.

Eating Habits and Good Health

Think for a moment about how you ate as a child. Unless you have worked very hard to change your childhood habits, chances are that the way you ate then closely resembles the way you eat now. Now you know what a great impact you have on your child's eating! Your child will spend her adult life either trying to change her eating habits or thanking you for helping her eat healthily in the first place.

It's true: the older we get, the harder it is to change. So the earlier you start children on the right eating track, the easier it will be for them to stay the course. Diet and health are intertwined, and poor eating habits help cause a variety of health problems such as obesity, heart disease, high cholesterol, high blood pressure, and cancer.

Obesity

Of the many people I have helped with weight control, one client stands out in my mind. "Ashley" was only in kindergarten, and she weighed 95 pounds. Her mother was wise to bring her in. Teasing from other kids and struggles with self-esteem make being overweight a nightmare. By encouraging Ashley to become more active and eat mostly "growing foods" (limiting junk), we were able to put a hold on her weight until her height caught up a bit.

Approximately 10 percent of preschool girls,[1] 14 percent of children six to eleven years old, and 12 percent of adolescents are overweight.[2] The National Institutes of Health define obesity as body weight 20 percent or more over the weight recommended for a particular age and sex.

Overweight is caused simply by an imbalance of energy: not enough physical activity to balance the food eaten. Genetics can also play a role. In our busy lives, convenience foods and fast food are taking over our snacks and meals. At the same time, computer games and TV are replacing playing outside for many kids. These changes have made Americans–both young and old– heavier than ever.

Overweight children are likely to become overweight adults. And overweight adults often have health problems as a result of their weight, such as heart disease, diabetes, high cholesterol, respiratory disease, cancer, and high blood pressure.

Childhood is marked by three critical developmental periods during which certain changes in body fat can increase the risk of later obesity. By understanding these critical periods, parents can help prevent future weight problems.

The Prenatal Period

Prenatal conditions may affect a child's weight later in life. For example, inadequate growth in the last trimester is associated with low birth weight, various health problems, and leanness. Children whose mothers have diabetes or require insulin during pregnancy, however, are more likely to be obese as adults.[3] Children whose mothers had gestational diabetes may also mature earlier. (See discussion of adiposity rebound below.)

About a dozen studies have shown a connection between birth weight and adult weight. In one study, infants weighing more than ten pounds at birth were four times more likely to be severely overweight at age seventeen than infants weighing less.[4]

Four to Six Years

The next critical period, called "adiposity rebound," occurs approximately between the ages of four and six, when body fat decreases to a minimum before increasing again into adulthood. Children who reach adiposity rebound at an earlier age appear to be heavier as adults.[5] It has also been suggested that diets high in protein and calories between ages four and six result in higher body fat at age eight.[6]

Adiposity rebound may contribute to later obesity for the following reasons:

1. This is often the time when kids become more independent and make many of their own food choices. A child whose parents have exerted too much control over her food intake may have trouble controlling the amount she eats. Overeating at this time can result in extra fat storage.[7]

2. Early adiposity rebound may be related to early maturing. And adolescents who mature more rapidly than average often have high levels of body fat in adulthood.[8]

Adolescence

The final critical period is adolescence, when body fat increases in girls and decreases in boys. In girls, increases in body fat during this period may have profound effects on obesity in adulthood.

Two Bananas a Day to Keep Fat Away?

The latest findings of the Young Women's Health Study show that adolescent girls who ate four servings of fruit a day had lower body fat and higher levels of HDL (good) cholesterol than those who ate less fruit. Four servings of fruit is equal to eating two bananas or one apple, one orange, one kiwi, and one peach.[9]

Research on Body Fat

Fat Preference

Children as young as three years begin showing preferences for high-fat foods.[10] A preference for high-fat foods is related to the amount of fat in the diet as well as body fat. Several studies have shown that children with higher body fat who prefer high-fat foods are more likely to have heavier parents.[11]

We Are What We Eat

Kids' calorie and fat intake seems to be related to body fat at age nine to ten years.[12]

Fit or Fat? It Makes a Difference

The increasing number of overweight kids may be due to our society's decreasing activity and increased time in front of the television, computer, and so on.[13] Regular exercise helps build and maintain healthy bones, muscles, and joints. It can also help control weight, lower blood pressure, and improve psychological well-being. Children who are active are more likely to stay active as adults, which lowers the risk of heart disease.[14]

What are some guidelines for healthy physical activity during childhood?

The American Heart Association recommends:

- regular walking, bicycling, outdoor play, and use of playgrounds and gyms;
- less than two hours per day of watching TV or playing computer games;
- daily school or day-care physical activity of at least twenty minutes a day;
- regular family outings that involve walking, cycling, swimming, or other recreational activities;
- modeling of healthy activity by parents, teachers, and caretakers.

Note: Emphasize fun and play rather than exercise, and plan enjoyable activities that match a child's skill level.[15]

? Questions You May Have

Q. Do all overweight children become overweight adults?

A. No. For many children, a temporary overweight period is just a transition before a spurt in height. A review of studies show that about one-third of obese preschoolers and about one-half of obese grade-schoolers become obese adults.[16]

Q. Do children inherit overweight tendencies from their parents?

A. The tendency to become overweight seems to be influenced both by being overweight as a child and by having one or more overweight parents. However, genes are not necessarily to blame. Obesity that "runs in the family" can be a result of similar home environments, bad eating habits, and/or sedentary ways.

Q. What should I do if my child is overweight?

A. Remember that your approach and attitude can either help or hurt your child. Keep in mind that not all overweight children become overweight adults; it's growth over time that's important. A drastic change on a child's growth chart, however, is a red flag that merits a closer look. If you feel a weight problem is starting, contact a registered dietitian or look for a children's weight control program called "Shapedown" that is family-based and usually conducted by hospitals.

Evaluate your child's eating habits—at home and away:

- Does your child consume high-calorie snacks or sweet drinks more than once a week?
- Is your child doing thirty minutes of moderate activity almost every day (such as walking, bike riding, physical education at school, skating)?
- If your child is in day-care, is she eating nutritionally balanced food there? Is she given ample time to play outside and be active?

- Does your child seem to eat just because she is bored, but not hungry?
- Does your child regularly snack in front of the TV?
- Has your child been given the opportunity to control her own eating? That is, does she follow her own appetite cues instead of finishing everything on her plate because she has to?
- Does your child eat a high-fat school lunch or snack on sweets or junk food after school?

By investigating your child's eating habits –while she is with you and away from you– you may be able to find the underlying cause of your child's weight problem. Though changing some environmental influences may be appropriate, putting your child on a diet is not an option! Trying to directly control your child's food intake can backfire. According to Ellyn Satter, author of *How to Get Your Kid to Eat, but Not Too Much,* "Children need to be able to trust their internal processes. Parents need to be able to relax and trust their children and those processes—not be police officers." Instead, she offers, parents should be positive, nurturing, and accepting of their children's bodies.[17]

Some lifestyle changes appropriate for the whole family include:

- Go on a family walk several times a week. Take up in-line skating. Hike at the park on the weekend. Take a long bike ride. Encourage your child to take up a sport like tennis, soccer, basketball, or karate.

- Encourage healthy between-meal snacks. As role models and food providers, parents should bring into the house only what they want their kids to eat.
- Limit TV watching and computer game playing. Get the whole family together to brainstorm fun, active alternatives.
- Make sure everyone drinks enough water. Often, simply replacing soda or juice with water can make a big difference in calorie intake. In fact, it has been suggested that adequate water intake can help control weight.[18]

Heart Disease

The evidence is in: Heart disease begins in childhood. Some risk factors for heart disease are obesity, high blood cholesterol, diabetes, high blood pressure, and inactivity. All of these problems can begin during childhood, and many carry into adulthood.[19] This has been proven by an ongoing study in Louisiana called the Bogalusa Heart Study. The study's twenty-plus years of research have shown that fatty streaks and lesions—the beginnings of plaque that can eventually block an artery and cause a heart attack—can be found in children. And the more heart-disease risk factors a child has, the larger the fatty streaks and lesions inside her arteries.[20]

Using Fats Wisely

Try to use mostly fats from the left column and limit those on the right. Read labels to find out what kind of fat is in the products you buy.

Better Fats	Worse Fats
canola oil	butter, coconut oil, palm and palm kernel oil
olive oil	
nut oils	shortening
soybean oil	stick margarine, light butter
tub margarine made from liquid oil	fat from meats, skin on poultry
high-fat foods low in saturated fat:	sour cream, heavy cream
avocado	foods high in saturated fat:
high-fat fish* (salmon, tuna, sardines, trout)	cheese
nuts*	whole milk
olives	coconut
wheat germ	high-fat meats (hamburger, hot dogs, bologna, ribs, sausage, bacon)

*Nuts and fish with bones present a choking hazard for kids under five years.

Fat—How Much Is Too Much?

After age two, children's fat intake can begin to equal that of adults—about 30 percent. Many studies have shown that children can benefit from a decrease of fat in their diet.[21] However, any good intention carried too far can result in problems. There have been several cases of infant failure-to-thrive due to parents restricting their babies' fat intake. Babies and children need adequate fat for rapid growth and development of organs that need fat, such as the brain.

Recent studies show that the type of fat

one eats may be significantly more important than amount of fat one eats. Diets high in saturated fat (the type found in meats and other animal products) and trans fats (made by processing liquid oil to make shortening and margarine) are much worse for us than a diet with the same amount of monounsaturated fat (found in canola oil, olive oil, avocado, nuts, and olives) and polyunsaturated fat (from corn, other vegetables, and fish). So watch how much animal fat, margarine, and shortening is in your family's diet and try to replace these with liquid oil and other monounsaturated fats. See the chart on the previous page for examples.

▼

High Cholesterol

High blood cholesterol is one risk factor familiar to most people. Should all children have their cholesterol tested? No. The National Cholesterol Education Program and the American Academy of Pediatrics recommend that children over two years have their cholesterol checked only if:

- one parent has high cholesterol (240 mg/dl or greater);
- a parent or grandparent had heart disease before fifty-five years of age;
- one parent's medical history is not known (especially if the child has other risk factors: high blood pressure, obesity, diabetes, or physical inactivity).[22]

If you feel that your child's cholesterol should be tested, discuss it with your pediatrician.

? Questions You May Have

Q. If my son has high cholesterol now, will he have high cholesterol as an adult?

A. Unfortunately some risk factors, like high cholesterol, tend to persist over time. The good news is that you can help your son develop heart-healthy eating and lifestyle habits now so that he lowers his lifetime risk of heart disease.

Q. What should I do if my child does have high cholesterol?

A. Kids over two years of age with high cholesterol should see a registered dietitian to make dietary changes that won't hurt growth. You will probably be asked to feed your child the "Step 1" diet from the American Heart Association (AHA). This is a balanced, healthy diet containing 30 percent or less calories from fat and less than 10 percent of calories from saturated fat. This diet is healthy for the whole family. In fact, the calorie and fat recommendations are the same that the AHA recommends for all children over two years of age.[23] Your child may also need to increase her activity level and keep an eye on weight.

▼

High Blood Pressure (Hypertension)

High blood pressure, a risk factor for heart disease and stroke, also can begin during childhood. There is some evidence that sodium intake during the first year affects blood pressure later in life.[24] And several studies suggest that higher sodium intake is related to higher blood pressure in children and adolescents.[25] When children are under stress, salt intake seems to cause blood pressure to increase even more.[26] Other nutrients may affect blood pressure as well. Calcium, magnesium, potassium, and fiber all appear to play a role in preventing high blood pressure in children.[27]

Don't worry, you won't have to memorize yet another set of dietary guidelines to keep your child's blood pressure at a healthy level! A healthy diet that has plenty of dairy products, legumes, fruits, and vegetables will contain the nutrients thought to help prevent hypertension. Cutting down on convenience and snack foods, fast food, processed meats, and salt used in cooking will keep sodium at a moderate level for the whole family. See Chapters Twenty and Twenty-One for a look at the shocking amounts of sodium in convenience foods and fast food.

▼

Cancer

It is estimated that an average of 35 percent of cancers are caused by dietary factors. Though genes play a role in cancer, environmental and lifestyle factors are believed to play a much bigger role. So even if a person has inherited a gene that would increase the risk of cancer, the lifestyle choices she makes can still make a difference in her overall risk. Following are some factors we can control:

Lifestyle Factors
• smoking
• diet
• sun exposure
• alcohol intake

Environmental Factors
• chemicals
• radiation exposure
• air and water pollution

Childhood cancer is rare; an estimated 8,000 American children ages birth to fourteen years are diagnosed each year. Causes are poorly understood, but radiation, secondhand smoke, and parental occupational exposures have all been blamed. Cured meats—such as hot dogs and lunch meat—eaten during pregnancy and childhood are also being investigated. Though diet may not play a huge role in causing juvenile cancer, it can play a major role in lowering lifetime risk of cancer. According to the

American Institute for Cancer Research:

- Eating right, staying physically active, and maintaining a healthy weight can cut cancer risk by 30 to 40 percent.
- A simple change such as eating the recommended five servings of fruits and vegetables each day could reduce cancer rates more than 20 percent.[28]

How Does Cancer Start?

Cancer is a long process that sometimes lasts for decades. Here is a very simplified explanation of the process.

The Initiation Phase

A substance that can start the development of cancer, called a carcinogen, enters the body by way of something we eat, breathe, or are otherwise exposed to. Normally, the body is able to deactivate the carcinogen. Occasionally, the carcinogen binds to DNA, the genetic material in the nucleus of a cell. The body will try to cut out the damaged portion of the cell so the cell can function normally. However, if the damaged portion is not removed before the cell reproduces, the damaged DNA structure will be passed on to a "daughter" cell. The damage is passed on from cell to cell until a tumor forms (see "Promotion Stage"). The cells with the damaged DNA are called "initiated."

Latency Period

This is the period between the initiation stage and the time when tumors appear. This period can last more than twenty years!

Promotion Stage

Most initiated cells lay dormant unless there is a "promoter" that encourages cell division. A known promoter is dietary fat, discussed below. Without cancer promoters, initiated cells never get to the disease stage. "Inhibitors" are factors that slow down or stop the cell division. Some cancer inhibitors are certain vitamins, minerals, fiber, and other substances called phytochemicals, which are found in food. Cancer promotion is reversible, which is why a healthy lifestyle, including a lifelong good diet, is the key to cancer prevention.

Dietary Factors Related to Cancer

Dietary Fat

According to the National Cancer Institute, diets high in fat have been linked to increased risk of various types of cancer.[29] Again, the type of fat eaten is important to cancer risk. Saturated fats and red meat have been linked with some types of cancer, while monounsaturated fats could play a role in prevention. Omega-3 fatty acids (found in cold-water fish like salmon) inhibit cancer growth in animals and seem to have a positive effect on the immune system.[30]

Overweight

Eating too much and exercising too little may be related to several types of cancer. For example, excessive childhood growth seems to cause girls to menstruate earlier, and early menstruation is a major risk factor for breast cancer. Eating more calories than one uses may be harmful throughout life. Obesity in later life also appears to increase the risk of several types of cancer.[31]

Vitamins, Minerals, Phytochemicals

Many vitamins and minerals have been associated with a decreased risk of cancers. Calcium may play a preventive role in colorectal cancer.[32] Antioxidants like vitamin C, vitamin E, and beta-carotene (just one of hundreds of carotenoids) may also reduce cancer risk. Below is a list of cancer-fighting phytochemicals, and their sources, developed by researchers at the University of Minnesota:[33]

Phytochemicals: Cancer Fighters from the Grocery Store

- citrus fruits: limonene, coumarins
- cruciferous vegetables (broccoli, cauliflower, cabbage): isothiocyanates, thiocyanates, dithiolthiones, flucosinolates, indoles
- flaxseed: lignans
- licorice: glyceritinic acid
- most fruits and vegetables: flavonoids, phenols
- onion, garlic, and chives: allium compounds
- plants, particularly soybeans and cereals: inositol hexaphosphate
- soybeans: isoflavones, protease inhibitors
- vegetables, including soybeans: plant sterols, saponins
- vegetables: coumarins

Healthy News for Kids

The American Institute for Cancer Research's bimonthly children's newsletter, the *good-news-letter,* provides kids with an entertaining reminder of how important healthy eating can be. Filled with puzzles, stories, interesting facts, and lots of suggestions for eating the right foods, the *good-news-letter* can be an important tool to help your kids make the right food choices for good health.

If you have a child between six and ten who would like to receive the *good-news-letter* every two months, call toll-free at 800-843-8114. Ask for the publications operator. While there is no charge for the *good-news-letter,* your donation of five dollars or more can help bring the newsletter to thousands of children across the country and support vital cancer research.

▼

How the Food You Eat Fights Disease

Our major diseases today—heart disease, cancer, diabetes, and osteoporosis—are all affected by our lifestyle. But those diseases don't happen overnight, and an occasional splurge is not what causes them. Rather, your frequent or daily habits—what you eat, what you drink, whether you smoke or drink alcohol, how much sun you're exposed to, whether you maintain a healthy weight, how much you exercise, and so on—over time contribute to or prevent disease. Healthy eating during childhood really can have big payoffs in adulthood.

What are some disease fighting components in food?

Antioxidants

When oxygen is used by the body, byproducts called "free radicals" are made. These free radicals can damage cells. That damage is thought to contribute to aging and other diseases like cancer and heart disease. Antioxidants are nutrients that protect the cell from damage by neutralizing free radicals. The majority of antioxidant research to date has dealt with beta-carotene, vitamin C, and vitamin E. Enzymes that act as antioxidants are made with zinc, copper, manganese, and selenium, so dietary intake of those minerals are also important. Research about antioxidants and disease prevention is growing.

Quick Tip: The best way to get your antioxidants is through food–not supplements. Eating a balanced diet containing a variety of plant foods is the key to long-term good health.

Phytochemicals

Phytochemicals are biologically active components from plants, now widely believed to have many beneficial effects on health, such as prevention of heart disease and cancer. There are thought to be thousands of phytochemicals found in all types of plant foods: whole grains, nuts, seeds, legumes, soy foods, fruits, and vegetables.

"Healthy" Bacteria

Yogurt with live active cultures can help the intestines stay healthy, which can help fight off "bad" bacteria. It is often recommended that children taking antibiotics also eat yogurt to help replace the beneficial bacteria often lost during antibiotic therapy.

Fiber

The fiber, or indigestible material found in whole grains, helps the digestive tract run smoothly and prevents constipation. This can help prevent cancer. Fiber also helps lower cholesterol and control blood sugar.

"Good" Fat

Recent research has revealed that a type of fat found in fish may help prevent heart disease and stroke. Omega-3 fatty acids, found in salmon, tuna, and trout, are also necessary for brain and eye development in fetuses and children up to two years. Omega-3 fatty acids are found in smaller amounts in flaxseed, soy, and canola oil.

Applying Science to the Dinner Table

Simple changes in family meals are not hard and can make a difference to your health. The good news is that you don't need a list of diet tips for every disease. Eating fruits and vegetables, for example, can reduce the risk of cancer, high blood pressure, and heart disease! If the tips below seem to be too much to swallow, work on one area at a time.

1. *Eat More Fruits and Vegetables.* One fact that all scientists can agree on is this: Eating fruits and vegetables reduces the risk of disease. For most types of cancer, persons with low fruit and vegetable intake have about twice the risk of cancer than those with a high intake.[34]

Have your family had their "five a day" today? The great thing about filling up on fruits and vegetables is that you are less likely to eat things like chips, cookies, and other less-nutrient-dense foods. Try to eat a variety of fruits and vegetables from day to day.

Five a Day
Do five fruits and vegetables a day sound like a lot of food? Here are a few easy tips for adding fruits and vegetables to your meals:

Breakfast
- Add mashed banana, dried fruit, or applesauce to pancake batter. Top pancakes and waffles with strawberries or other fresh fruit.
- Add dried fruit, peaches, strawberries, blueberries, bananas, or other fresh fruit to cold or hot cereal.
- Whip up a fruit shake. (See Chapter Fifteen for recipes.)
- Serve a fruit or some juice before serving anything else.

Lunch
- Add apple, raisins, pineapple, mango, or mandarin orange slices to chicken, tuna, or tossed salad.

- Serve a salad or raw veggies before meals. Use darker greens like romaine, leaf lettuce, or spinach for salads.
- Add sprouts, leaf lettuce, thinly sliced cucumber, finely shredded cabbage, spinach, or tomatoes to your sandwiches.
- Stuff leftover veggies or salad in a pita pocket with cheese for lunch.
- Buy ready-to-eat salads, carrots, broccoli, and so on. Now that's fast food!

Dinner
- Do a stir-fry for dinner. You can buy the vegetables cleaned, chopped, and ready to go, or use a frozen stir-fry mix.
- Zip up your spaghetti sauce with bell pepper, zucchini, carrot, or eggplant. Shred or finely chop the vegetables, and they will cook quickly. If your children are "vegetable spotters," you can use puréed cooked vegetables, and they'll be undetectable!
- Use puréed roasted red pepper or another vegetable as a sauce base.
- Start dinner with a vegetable-based soup like minestrone or gazpacho. (See Chapter Fourteen for recipes.)
- Make a fruit salsa to accompany your grilled chicken or seafood (recipe page 221).
- Make an appetizer of oven-fried zucchini sticks or eggplant slices (recipe page 180).

Dessert
- Serve a mixed fresh fruit salad for a great finish.
- Top angel food or pound cake with fresh or canned fruits.

- Make a fruit smoothie (recipe page 285).
- Try a fruit sorbet.
- Have a frozen yogurt layered with fruit.
- How about a frozen banana or frozen grapes?
- Serve fruit kebabs to top off a grilled dinner.
- Cook bananas with a little brown sugar. This dessert is sure to be a winner!
- Have a fruit fondue with yogurt dip or chocolate sauce (recipe page 213). Everyone needs to splurge sometimes!

2. *Discover the power of soy.* Soy foods are now well-known for their significant disease-fighting properties, including cancer fighting and cholesterol lowering. Soy protein also seems to have an effect on calcium balance in bone and on blood pressure. Good sources of soy protein include soy milk, tofu, and textured vegetable protein. In the recipe section, you will find ideas on how to incorporate soy into your family's diet.

Kid-Friendly Soy

Your kids' favorite foods are hot dogs and chicken nuggets; how can you possibly entice them to eat soy? Morningstar Farms and Worthington Foods make it easy to sneak soy past the pickiest of eaters with corn dogs, veggie burgers, and grillers (sausage look-alikes). Made of soy protein and grains, they taste very close to the real thing. They also make Recipe Crumbles, which can be substituted for ground beef in chili, soups, burritos, and more.

3. *Serve fish at least twice a week!* Many kids love the fish that is best for them—salmon, tuna, and trout—since they are mild-flavored. Take care with fish that have bones, since they are a choking hazard for children under five years old.

4. *Limit saturated fat intake.* The harder a fat is at room temperature, the more saturated fat it has. Animal fat, found in meats as well as eggs, milk, butter, stick margarine, shortening, coconut oil, and palm oil, contain a significant amount of saturated fat. The major source of total fat and saturated fat among preschool children is whole milk.[35] Thus, simple changes like offering 2-percent or 1-percent or even skim milk after age two and choosing lean meats and low-fat cheeses are usually enough to keep saturated fat intake down.

Trans fats—fats made by processing vegetable oil to make shortening and stick margarine—are just as bad as animal fat. This has led some health professionals to recommend their patients eat butter instead of margarine. While the jury is still out on which is best, whatever you use on your bread, use as little as possible! Use liquid oil for cooking and baking when possible.

Make sure that your main source of fat is monounsaturated fat (found in canola oil, olive oil, nuts, nut oils, and avocado) and omega-3 fatty acids (found in fish).

5. *Go meatless.* Eat a meatless meal at least once a week. Kid-friendly vegetarian meals are easy: macaroni and cheese, veggie burgers, bean burritos, pasta with marinara

sauce and cheese, baked beans with sliced soy hot dogs.

6. *Remember: Whole grains are best.* Offer whole grains daily to increase dietary fiber. Oatmeal, whole-wheat bread, and whole-grain pancakes, waffles, and cereals are easy ways to get whole grains on the table!

7. *Make family fitness a priority.* While eating healthily goes a long way toward preventing diseases, regular activity is also important. Make fitness fun by taking walks in the neighborhood every evening, playing toss, kickball, tag, or even a friendly game of badminton or tennis. Even babies can participate when carried in a backpack, front carrier, jogging stroller, or child seat on a bike. (Don't forget helmets.)

Cooking Tips to Cut Saturated Fat	
Instead of:	**Use:**
whole milk	low-fat or skim milk
heavy cream	skim or low-fat evaporated milk
sour cream	lite or fat-free sour cream or plain yogurt
shortening	liquid oil
butter or stick margarine	tub margarine or light butter (use applesauce, mashed bananas, or prune purée in cakes, brownies, or cookies)
bologna	turkey bologna, lean ham, or roast beef
burgers	95% lean ground meat, ground turkey, chicken breast or veggie burgers (also available in crumbles for cooking)
1 whole egg	2 egg whites
cheese	reduced-fat cheese

Establishing Healthy Habits

Some Tips on Establishing Healthy Habits

Before you had children, you may not have given much thought to how you ate or how your eating habits influenced those around you. But as a parent, you know that you influence your kids' diets from the very beginning of their lives. Not surprisingly, mothers often have the most influence. A recent study conducted in England showed that kids' fruit-and-vegetable intake was influenced by their mothers' nutritional knowledge, how frequently their mothers ate fruit, and whether their mothers believed that eating fruits and vegetables could help prevent cancer. The study also showed that kids' candy consumption was influenced by their mothers' taste for candy.[1] Here are some suggestions to keep in mind as you help your family establish healthy eating habits:

1. *Set a good example.* This is a very simple rule, but it's the most important one. If you want your children to eat healthy meals and snacks, you should, too. Try not to bias your child's developing tastes with your own food preferences. If necessary, eat a food even if you don't like it–or at least follow the polite bite rule!

2. *Have healthy foods available, and don't forget to offer them.* If you keep fresh fruit on hand all the time, that is probably what you and your family will eat regularly. Maintain-

ing a supply of healthy snacks is especially important for households with infants and small children, who need to eat often.

3. *Let your child help choose foods at the store and at home.* Since he was three years old, my son Robert has enjoyed helping pick out fruit at the store. This boosts his self-esteem, gives me an opportunity to teach him about shopping and nutrition (as well as counting and colors), and gives him an opportunity to do his part for the family. My son Nicolas regularly chooses meals for the family, which makes him feel good, too. If children choose a particular food, they are much more likely to eat it!

4. *Accept your body, even if you are not happy with how it looks.* This is an important concept for children to learn. Their bodies will go through many changes while growing up. Teach your children that people come in all shapes and sizes. Very few women are naturally tall and slim like models, and even fewer men have physiques like football players!

5. *Practice your poker face.* Babies and toddlers are often smarter than we give them credit for. If a child knows that he will get lots of attention by closing his mouth just before the "airplane" enters, he will do it again and again just to see the reaction. My son Robert is quite a clown, and he knows that it's hard for us to resist his cute expres-

sions and humor. So practice your poker faces at dinnertime, Mom and Dad!

6. *Be flexible and keep your chin up.* So you spend hours cooking up a surprise for little Emma, and she spits out the first bite. It's better to laugh than cry! Try again in a few weeks; she might like it next time.

▼

The Food Guide Pyramid

You are probably already familiar with the Food Guide Pyramid, which was developed by the U.S. Department of Agriculture to guide Americans toward healthier eating habits. Following is a summary of the pyramid with important information about each food group. Keep in mind that the pyramid is meant for ages seven and up. (See Chapters Nine through Eleven for nutrition guidelines for infants, toddlers, and preschoolers.) The number of servings listed

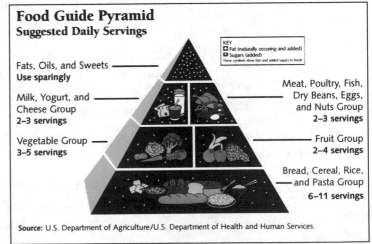

Food Guide Pyramid
Suggested Daily Servings

KEY
▢ Fat (naturally occuring and added)
▢ Sugars (added)
These symbols show fats and added sugars in foods

Fats, Oils, and Sweets
Use sparingly

Milk, Yogurt, and Cheese Group
2–3 servings

Vegetable Group
3–5 servings

Meat, Poultry, Fish, Dry Beans, Eggs, and Nuts Group
2–3 servings

Fruit Group
2–4 servings

Bread, Cereal, Rice, and Pasta Group
6–11 servings

Source: U.S. Department of Agriculture/U.S. Department of Health and Human Services.

apply to both adults and children, with larger servings for adults and smaller servings for children.

Grains

Six to Eleven Servings Per Day

If you are like most adults, you think of grains as fattening. Actually, the Food Guide Pyramid shows that grains and starches are the foundation of a healthy diet. Go for whole grains! Whole grains provide many health benefits because of their high fiber content. High fiber intake is associated with lower serum cholesterol, lower risk of heart disease, reduced blood pressure, enhanced weight control, better blood sugar control, reduced risk of certain forms of cancer, and

---

Fiber: Is Your Family Eating Enough?

Adults should eat twenty-five to thirty-five grams of fiber a day, and the average intake among adults in the U.S. is only fifteen grams. U.S. children are not eating enough fiber for good health and disease prevention, either. How much is enough? To determine the minimum number of grams of fiber a child should eat per day, add five grams to his age. A five-year-old, for example, should eat ten grams of fiber per day. It really doesn't take much planning or extra effort to eat ten grams. Three-quarters of a cup of corn bran cereal, one slice of whole-wheat bread, and an apple together contain about ten grams of fiber.

Source: Importance of dietary fiber in childhood. Williams, C.L. J Am Diet Assoc, 1995 Oct, 95:10, 1140-6, 1149; quiz 1147-8.

Fiber Boosters

On the left are typical kid foods, and on the right are substitutes that boost fiber intake.

food / grams of fiber	food / grams of fiber
½ cup applesauce / 1.5 grams	1 medium apple / 3 grams
3 pancakes / 1.4 grams	Aunt Jemima buckwheat pancakes / 5 grams
1 waffle / 1 gram	1 Nutrigrain waffle / 3 grams
1 cup Team Cheerios / 1 gram	1 cup Multigrain Cheerios / 3 grams
1 cup Frosted Flakes / <1 gram	1 cup Wheaties / 3 grams
¾ cup Cap'n Crunch / 0.8 grams	¾ cup Quaker Crunchy Corn Bran / 5 grams
1 cup Malt-O-Meal / 0.8 grams	1 cup Roman Meal apple-cinnamon multigrain cereal / 8 grams
1 slice white bread / 1 gram	1 slice whole-wheat bread / 2–3 grams
Taco Bell chili cheese burrito / 5 grams	Taco Bell bean burrito / 13 grams
1 cup white rice / 1 gram	1 cup brown rice / 3 grams
½ cup green beans / 1 gram	½ cup green peas / 3 grams
Doughnut / 0 grams	Bran muffin / 4 grams

A potato is a potato, right? Wrong! The nutrient content of a potato (or any vegetable or fruit) goes down depending on how it is processed, cooked, and stored after cooking. For example, a five-ounce baked potato with skin has twenty-six milligrams of vitamin C. Baked without skin, the content drops to twenty milligrams. When boiled with skin, the potato's vitamin C content drops further to ten milligrams. Frozen processed potatoes (such as Tater Tots, fries, and so on) vary from three to ten milligrams for a five-ounce serving. However, five ounces of French fries from a restaurant have 443 calories and twenty-three grams of fat, compared with 220 calories and no fat for a baked potato. The moral: All potatoes are not equal. Try to make your family's food choices count!

improved gastrointestinal function.[2] If you start your kids eating high-fiber foods early on, it will become a habit as they get older. Fiber is found in fruits and vegetables as well as in whole grains.

Fruits

Two to Four Servings Per Day

Vegetables

Three to Five Servings Per Day

Fruits and vegetables supply the majority of such vitamins and minerals as vitamin C, beta-carotene, iron, and folate in our diets. In addition to those vitamins, fruits and vegetables contain hundreds of phytochemicals, substances that have disease-fighting properties. We are still learning how phyto-chemicals fight as well as prevent disease. (See pages 21–22 for more information on phytochemicals.) Currently, only one in five children eats the recommended daily number of servings of fruits and vegetables. And nearly a quarter of all vegetables eaten by children and adolescents are French fries! Unfortunately, French fries are high in fat and salt and contain much less vitamin C than baked potatoes.

Milk, Yogurt, and Cheese

Two to Three Servings Per Day

The calcium found in milk and other dairy products is important for strong bones and teeth. Calcium helps the body perform other functions, too, such as coagulation of blood and contracting and relaxing of muscles. Calcium and other nutrients in dairy products may also decrease the risk of colon cancer, high blood pressure, and stroke. Adequate versus inadequate calcium intake in children may be responsible for a 5- to 10-percent difference in peak bone mass and a 50 percent difference in incidence of hip fractures later in life.[3] All children over eight years old should consume 1,300 milligrams of calcium per day, according to the recently updated Reference Daily Intakes (formerly U.S. Recommended Daily Allowances.)

Meat, Poultry, Fish, Dry Beans, Eggs, and Nuts

Two to Three Servings Per Day

You may be surprised to find the protein group in the middle of the pyramid instead of at the bottom. Most adults in the Western world eat too much meat, and our children are likely to pick up our eating habits. Yes, protein is important for growth–but in moderate amounts. Since fat almost always accompanies protein in meat, buy the leanest meat you can and serve a variety of animal and vegetable proteins. Introduce your child to dried beans and other legumes at an early age. Pinto beans, lentils, black beans, and chick peas are just a few legumes that may appeal to your child.

Fish is also a good growing food. In fact, for children under two years of age, the kind of fat found in fish like salmon, mackerel, and tuna is important for brain growth and eye development. Other less-prominent sources of this fat are flaxseed and flaxseed oil, soybean oil, and canola oil.

You may wonder how some favorite kids' foods like burgers, chicken nuggets, hot dogs, and fish sticks fit into the pyramid. They do contain protein, but many of their calories come from fat, so eat these foods only occasionally.

Fats, Oils, and Sweets

Use Sparingly

If you have school-age children, you have probably found junk food to be very popular with them. It's tough to keep your kids eating right when they are influenced by friends, TV advertising, and the availability of junk food everywhere! But don't despair: If you encourage healthy habits early on, those habits will stick with your kids–even if they do occasionally splurge on sweet or fatty foods.

A Word about Choking

The majority of childhood choking incidents are associated with food. Peanuts are the most common culprits. Other hazardous foods are hard, round items like grapes, popcorn, nuts, raisins, and hot dogs. Children may also have trouble swallowing peanut butter or accidentally swallow fish bones. Children under three are at greatest risk of choking, but care should be taken with the above foods until age five. Here are some ways you can reduce your child's risk of choking:

- Cut grapes and hot dogs into small pieces.
- Chop or grind nuts.
- Save popcorn and raisin snacks until your child is at least three years old.
- Mix peanut butter with mashed banana or applesauce to make it easier to swallow.
- When serving fish with small bones, separate the flesh with a fork or mash it to search for bones. For canned salmon, mash with a fork or grind in a blender before mixing into a recipe.
- Always supervise your child when he is eating. Make sure he is also well-supervised at day care.

Warning: At some day-care facilities, children are encouraged to not drink until after eating. This can be hazardous when a meal or snack includes peanut butter.

Despite the warnings always attached to this food group, it does perform a useful function in our diet. After all, fat and sugar make food taste good. But it's important to remember that fat and sugar are high in calories and low in nutrients–they're extra foods that should never supplant more

How Much Food Is in a Serving?

The Food Guide Pyramid recommends that people eat a certain number of servings from each food group. It also provides guidelines for adult serving sizes. Kids, however, need kid-size servings! Experts suggest that preschoolers should eat half the serving recommended for adults. Another suggestion is to serve one tablespoon of each food per year of a child's age.[a] The table below, modified from the U.S. Department of Agriculture's Child Care Feeding Program, provides recommended serving sizes for many common foods.

Food	Ages 1–3	Ages 3–6	Ages 6–12
Milk	½ cup	¾ cup	1 cup
Yogurt	¼ cup	¾ cup	1 cup
Cheese, natural	1 ounce	1½ ounces	2 ounces
Cheese food, cheese spread, or cottage cheese	2 ounces (¼ cup)	3 ounces (⅜ cup)	4 ounces (½ cup)
Bread	½ slice	½ slice	1 slice
Rolls	½ roll	½ roll	½ roll
Muffins (small)	½ muffin	½ muffin	1 muffin
Pasta, cooked	¼ cup	¼ cup	½ cup
Dry cereal	¼ cup	⅓ cup	¾ cup or 1 ounce
Saltine crackers	3 crackers	3 crackers	6 crackers
Graham crackers	1½ squares	1½ squares	3 squares
Vegetables or vegetable juice	¼ cup	½ cup	1 cup
Fruit or fruit juice	¼ cup	¼ cup	½ cup
Protein foods, lean meat, or fish	1 ounce	1½ ounces	2 ounces
Eggs	1 egg	1 egg	1 egg
Dried beans or peas (cooked)	¼ cup	⅜ cup	½ cup
Peanut butter or other seed butters	2 tablespoons	3 tablespoons	4 tablespoons

[a]The food guide pyramid. In L. Oesterreich, B. Holt, & S. Karas, Iowa family child care handbook [Pm 1541] (pp. 163–168). Ames, IA: Iowa State University Extension.

nutritious foods. A recent study showed that among the adults observed, nearly a third of their total calories came from fats and sweets. Eating many fats and sweets results in an overall diet that is higher in calories and lower in nutrients.[4] Most children cannot afford to waste their appetites on nutrient-poor foods. So make sure the extras don't take over your child's diet. Try to save fats and sweets for special occasions, or make them as healthy as possible. You might, for example, serve a milkshake instead of a hot-fudge sundae. (See Chapter Seventeen for healthy recipes.) For cooking, use a monounsaturated fat such as canola oil or olive oil instead of vegetable oil. For a spread, use low-fat tub margarine or light butter instead of stick margarine or regular butter. (For more information on which fats are healthiest, see Chapter Two.)

What's a "Normal" Meal?

At a typical meal, your five-year-old son might eat from two to three servings of pasta (three-fourths cup), one chicken leg (two ounces), two carrot sticks, half an apple, and one-half cup of milk. This is a well-balanced meal. However, a typical meal could also be half a cheese sandwich, one-half cup of fruit juice, and one-half cup of yogurt with fruit in it. This is also a balanced meal, though it contains several servings from two food groups and none from others. Because appetites vary among kids and between meals, it is important that you accept what is

normal for *your* child. Just keep encouraging healthy eating and try to balance your child's diet over a few days or a week instead of at every meal. Over time, your child will get the nutrients he needs.

Shopping Smart

Healthy eating starts with healthy shopping. Stocking your kitchen with healthy food will ensure that your family eats well—at home, anyway. (You can't control what your kids eat at friends' houses or at Grandma's.) To shop smart, you first need to assess your current habits.

Rate Your Shopping Habits

Answer yes or no to the questions below.

1. Is your refrigerator usually stocked with milk?

2. Do you buy low-fat or reduced-fat products and lean meats regularly?

3. Do you rarely buy snacks such as chips and candy?

4. Do you rarely buy hot dogs and lunch meats?

5. Do you buy diverse protein foods, including beef, pork, poultry, fish, cheese, and dried beans and peas?

6. Do you always have a supply of fresh fruits and vegetables?

7. Do you usually buy whole-grain breads and cereals?

8. Do you rarely buy meals-in-a-box?

9. Do the contents of your shopping cart resemble the Food Guide Pyramid?

10. Do you buy mostly fresh fruits and vegetables?

11. Do you seldom buy fried foods such as chicken nuggets, fish sticks, pot pies, and fried potatoes?

12. Do you buy reduced-fat milk, cheese, margarine, and sour cream?

How did you do? If you answered yes to . . .

. . . eleven or more questions, your family's food-shopping habits are great.

. . . between eight and ten questions, your family could improve its shopping habits.

. . . six or fewer questions, read the following information carefully!

Healthy-Shopping Tips

Most of us could use a few healthy-shopping tips. It's so easy to get into a rut, cooking the same things again and again, or to rely too heavily on convenience foods. Here are a few tips to help you maintain good shopping habits:

1. *Plan menus.* This is important. By planning ahead, you will have on hand what you need to eat consistently healthy meals. You will avoid impulse buying and feel less

inclined to call out for pizza! Keep a running list on your refrigerator, and add to the list as you come up with meal ideas or notice supplies dwindling.

2. *Arrange your grocery list by aisle to make shopping easy!* A well-organized list also helps thwart impulse buying. It makes shopping easier and faster, too!

3. *Make sure no one goes to the grocery store hungry or tired.* My husband can always tell when I've gone to the store hungry, because I usually come home with a few extras from the bakery! Tired kids—and adults—make for unpleasant and unwise shopping.

4. *Follow the U.S. Dietary Guidelines:*
- Eat a variety of foods.
- Balance your food intake with physical activity to maintain or improve your weight.
- Choose a diet with plenty of grains, vegetables, and fruits.
- Choose a diet low in saturated fat and cholesterol.
- Choose a diet moderate in sugar.
- Choose a diet moderate in sodium.
- If you drink alcoholic beverages, do so in moderation.

5. *Shop with your family's food priorities in mind:*
- Do you have specific dietary concerns? Read labels on packaged foods for information on ingredients and nutrition. (See sidebar: "What's on a Label?")
- Are you (and who isn't) trying to stick to a budget? (See sidebar: "Eating on a Budget.")

What's on a Label?

By now you are probably used to the Nutrition Facts Label, which was introduced in 1993. The following items must be listed on the labels of all packaged foods:

- Calories, fat, calories from fat, saturated fat, cholesterol, total carbohydrates, fiber, sugars, protein, vitamin C, vitamin A, calcium, and iron.

- Ingredients, listed in descending order by weight.

- Other nutrients if the food is enriched, fortified, or claims some other nutritional benefit. For example, if the front of a cereal box says "Good source of magnesium," its label must list the percentage of recommended daily magnesium intake a serving of the cereal provides.

Nutrition Facts
Serving Size 5 Cookies (31g)
Servings Per Container About 9

Amount Per Serving

Calories 160   Calories from Fat 70

	% Daily Value*
Total Fat 8g	**12%**
Saturated Fat 1g	**5%**
Cholesterol 0mg	**0%**
Sodium 90mg	**4%**
Total Carbohydrate 20g	**7%**
Dietary Fiber 0.5g	**2%**
Sugars 7g	
Protein 2g	

Vitamin A 0% • Vitamin C 0%
Calcium 0% • Iron 2%

*Percent Daily Values are based on a 2,000 calorie diet. Your daily values may be higher or lower depending on your calorie needs:

	Calories	2,000	2,500
Total Fat	Less than	65g	80g
Sat Fat	Less than	20g	25g
Cholesterol	Less than	300mg	300mg
Sodium	Less than	2,400mg	2,400mg
Total Carbohydrate		300g	375g
Dietary Fiber		25g	30g

Calories per gram:
Fat 9 • Carbohydrate 4 • Protein 4

Label-Reading Tips

- Vitamins and minerals are listed as a percentage of Daily Value based on Reference Daily Intake (formerly U.S. RDA). Vitamins and minerals listed are nutrients of which people often have trouble getting enough.

- Calories, fats, and other nutrients are listed as a percentage of Daily Value based on a 2,000-calorie diet. It's important to keep this in mind, because many people eat fewer than 2,000 calories per day.

- Health claims can be listed on a package if the food meets specific criteria. For example, if a food label claims "high in folic acid, which can help prevent neural tube defects," the food must be naturally high in folic acid. Food labels can also make claims about cancer, heart disease, osteoporosis, and hypertension.

- When used on food labels, the words below have very specific definitions:

Low-fat: contains 3 grams of fat or less per serving.

Lean and *extra lean* describe the fat content of meat, poultry, and seafood.

Lean: contains less than 10 grams of fat, 4.5 grams or less of saturated fat, and less than 95 milligrams of cholesterol per serving and per 100 grams.

Extra lean: contains less than 5 grams of fat, less than 2 grams of saturated fat, and less than 95 milligrams of cholesterol per serving and per 100 grams.

High in: contains 20 percent or more of the Daily Value for a particular nutrient in one serving.

Good source: contains 10 to 19 percent of the Daily Value for a particular nutrient in one serving.

Healthy: A "healthy" food must be low in fat, saturated fat, cholesterol, and sodium. In addition, if it's a single-item food, it must provide at least 10 percent of the Daily Value for one or more of vitamins A or C, iron, calcium, protein, or fiber.

Take advantage of food labels! They can be a big help in maintaining a healthy diet.

- Are you concerned about preservatives? Buy whole foods and avoid convenience foods and mixes as much as possible. For example, serve whole-kernel corn instead of creamed corn. Eat fresh potatoes instead of instant mashed potatoes.
- Do you worry about pesticides? Buy organic, shop at a local farmer's market or food co-op, grow your own vegetables, or buy a special product to get rid of more pesticide residues. You can also wash fruits and vegetables with very diluted dishwashing liquid. (See Chapter Eight for more information on pesticides.)
- Do you have food allergies in the family? Don't buy in bulk, as this can result in cross-contamination. Read labels carefully. (See Chapter Five for more information on allergies.)

6. *Keep variety and moderation in mind when planning menus.* Eating healthily means eating moderate amounts of a variety of foods. If you make a habit of serving three or four different foods at each meal, it won't be an effort to maintain variety and moderation; they'll be built into your family's diet.

7. *Do you like to decide each morning what you'll eat in the evening?* No problem—with a microwave for defrosting, you can make last-minute decisions. Here is a sample week-long menu for folks who prefer flexible, last-minute decision-making and quick preparation:

- Fish: three days a week (salmon, canned tuna, orange roughy, even frozen fish)
- Chicken: two days a week (chicken breast and leftovers)
- Vegetarian: one day a week (pasta and tomato sauce, black-bean soup and cornbread)
- Beef/Pork: one day a week (roast in Crock-Pot, stir-fry, fajitas)

Once you have a general idea of what you'll be eating for the week, then you can choose side dishes. By keeping a variety of frozen, fresh, and canned vegetables on hand, you'll always be able to make something that sounds good with a particular main dish. Below are some sample combinations.

Grilled Chicken
- Corn on the cob in its husk (grilled with the chicken)
- Zucchini or eggplant (These vegetables only need a few minutes, so add them to the grill when the chicken is almost done.)

Quick Tip: Use leftover grilled chicken to make a main-dish salad, or combine the leftover chicken with rice and vegetables to make into a one-dish meal.

Fish
- Brown-rice pilaf with mixed vegetables
- Broccoli with melted cheese and pasta
- Roasted potatoes and spinach salad

Quick Tip: If serving shrimp, broil shrimp and vegetables together on a skewer.

Beef
- Carrots and potatoes (cooked along with a roast)

Eating on a Budget

Children are expensive—and a family in which one parent opts to stay home may find itself adjusting to a budget crunch. Even after trimming luxuries from other areas of spending, a family often needs to reconfigure its food budget. The amount you spend on food can vary a lot—depending on how much you eat out, how many convenience foods you buy, how much impulse buying you do, where you shop, and whether you use coupons and/or saving cards. Here are a few tips to help you trim your food budget:

• Compare prices. Though larger sizes are usually cheaper than small ones, that is not always true. Store brands are usually cheaper than name brands. If you shop at wholesale clubs, do some in-depth comparisons to find out which of their items are cheaper as compared to the grocery store. Collect coupons and use them wisely. Even with a coupon, name-brand foods may still be more expensive than store brands and/or sale items.

• Avoid convenience foods whenever possible. Those best left at the store include meal "helpers" in a box, seasoned rice and pasta mixes, and prepackaged kids' meals. Infant juices are costly, as are some other foods marketed especially for infants. Note, however, that powdered baby formula is cheaper than ready-to-use formula. Foods that are worth the cost of their convenience include canned soup, spaghetti sauce, salad dressing, pancake or baking mixes, and frozen meal starters to which you just add meat.

• At home, store foods properly to avoid waste. Freeze leftovers immediately if they tend to just sit in the fridge until someone throws them away.

• Try to make the most of cooking time by preparing several dishes at once and freezing what you don't eat that day. For example, if you buy a seven-pound bag of chicken breasts, you can marinate and cook one-third for fajitas (freeze leftovers for sandwiches and salads), use one-third for chicken nuggets, and freeze the rest. Another time-saver: Buy ground turkey or lean ground beef on sale and cook it with garlic and onions. Freeze it in 1½-cup portions and add it later to pasta sauce or casseroles.

• Eat out as little as possible. Firstly, try to avoid unplanned meals out. When running errands, bring along a snack and juice to hold your child through till you can get home to eat lunch or supper. When you do eat out, you can still find ways to save money: Drink water instead of soda. Forego desserts. (Instead, bring some fruit to eat afterward.) Have kids share a meal if you know servings will be large. Order side dishes instead of more expensive entrées. Toddlers may not find much that suits them at a restaurant; sometimes an order of mashed potatoes or refried beans, along with a cup of milk and some fruit, is all a toddler needs. Don't forget some Cheerios and raisins for snacking while waiting for a table.

• Stir-fried vegetables (For extra convenience, use packaged frozen stir-fry medleys.)

• Corn tortillas, cheese, tomatoes, lettuce, salsa, Mexican coleslaw, and refried beans

Vegetarian

• With pasta and tomato sauce, a green salad

• With black-bean soup and cornbread, a carrot-and-pineapple or fruit salad

Convenience Foods

The price we pay for convenience is sometimes incredible! By planning ahead a bit, you can avoid many convenience foods. Before you buy a convenience food, ask yourself this: "Could I make the same dish without this product? Could I use another shortcut that would be cheaper and healthier?

On the other hand, some convenience foods not only save time; they are also healthier than their home-cooked counterparts! For example, Gardenburgers popped in the toaster are ready in five minutes and provide a tasty serving of whole grains and vegetables. Lean Cuisine makes a low-fat, family-size portion of lasagna that can be prepared in a fraction of the time it takes to make lasagna from scratch. (See Chapter Twenty-One for more information on convenience foods.)

Impulse Buying

If you plan a menu, make a well-organized list, and go shopping when you are not hungry or tired, you can avoid impulse buying.

Where You Shop

Shopping at warehouse stores like Sam's Club or Costco for some items can save you lots of money. However, not all products are cheaper at warehouse stores than at regular stores—especially if they're sold in quantities so big that they spoil before you can use them up! I find that to really save money, you must know how much things cost at the regular grocery store and be able to compare foods that come in different sizes.

Make a list of products and their prices per unit at both stores. And carry a calculator!

Coupons

Coupons save money only if you use them on products you normally buy and if a product is cheaper with a coupon than a similar product of another brand without a coupon. You can really save a lot by shopping at stores that redeem coupons at double- or triple-value. Mail-in rebates take time, but the savings can add up. Another good way to save money is by shopping at stores that offer a savings card for frequent shoppers.

▼

Nutritional Gold Mines

Ever wonder which foods are best for you? It's tough to narrow the list down to just a few, since all foods have some value, and there are many foods with a long résumé of health benefits. The foods listed below are some of the healthiest on the planet! Try to include them in your diet regularly. (And don't fret if your favorite food isn't on the list!)

Beans, Beans, the Magical Fruit!

The familiar children's chant about beans may seem silly, but it's right on target: Beans and soy products contain so many potent disease fighters, they're almost magical. They are an inexpensive source of vegetable protein packed with zinc, iron, folic acid, phytochemicals, and other B vitamins and trace minerals. Soy can be found in the form of tofu, soy milk, or texturized vegetable protein. (See Chapter Twenty-One for recommended brands and Chapter Two for information on kid-friendly soy.)

Quick Tip: Mexican food is a great way to get your kids to eat beans! Burritos, tostadas, nachos, and layered dips can all feature pinto beans or black beans. Use low-fat cheese and baked (not fried) chips to keep the fat down.

Go Big Green!

Leafy greens like spinach, romaine and leaf lettuce, and kale are full of carotenoids, folic acid, magnesium, potassium, fiber, and iron. Many kids will eat salad with ranch dressing. Remember that darker lettuces have more vitamins than iceberg lettuce.

Quick Tip: If your kids like lettuce on sandwiches, try a little raw spinach instead.

Berry Nice!

Blueberries, raspberries, cranberries, and strawberries are full of vitamin C, fiber, and disease-fighting antioxidants. A recent study showed that blueberries have the highest antioxidant score of any fruit or vegetable. You won't have to beg your kids to eat them, either.

Quick Tip: Berries can be lots of fun when served in a healthy dessert such as a fruit crisp or fruit smoothie. (See pages 285–286 for recipes.)

Sunrise, Sunset

Choose fruits with the color of the sun—cantaloupe, watermelon, carrots, sweet potatoes, and mangoes—and you will be the picture of good health. One serving of these foods often contains 50–100 percent of the Daily Value for vitamins C and A! One mango contains almost 133 percent of the Daily Value for vitamin C and 161 percent of the Daily Value for vitamin A for kids ages four to six. Mangoes are also full of carotenoids, fiber, and potassium.

Please Pass the Ketchup!

Cooked tomato products, such as tomato paste, spaghetti sauce, and ketchup, are chock-full of vitamins C and A, carotenoids, and other phytochemicals. Kids usually like foods with tomato sauce. And as a bonus, cooked tomato products contain carotenoids that appear to reduce the risk of prostate cancer in men.

Quick Tip: For a quick meal, cook frozen ravioli in spaghetti sauce on the stove or microwave—dinner's ready in ten minutes!

Great Grains

Whole grains contain not only fiber, but also trace minerals and phytochemicals not found in their processed counterparts.

Quick Tip: Some kid-friendly whole grains are oatmeal, granola, Nutrigrain waffles, whole-grain pancakes, Honey Puffed Kashi cereal, and Crunchy Corn Bran cereal.

Yo, Yogurt!

Yogurt contains the most calcium per ounce of all dairy products. It's appealing to most kids, and even those who are lactose-intolerant can usually eat it. Since yogurt is made with live cultures, it encourages growth of healthy bacteria in the gastrointestinal tract. This, in turn, helps protect against "bugs" that can cause stomach upsets and infections. Yogurt is often recommended during antibiotic treatment to prevent diarrhea and to help replenish bacteria in the intestine. Look for the words "live and active cultures" on yogurt labels.

Sounds Fishy!

Fish is definitely brain food—at least from pregnancy through the second year of life. Brain growth depends on omega-3 fats, which are plentiful in fish like salmon, trout, and tuna. Omega-3 fats may have other health benefits as well. Fish consumption in adults has been linked to reduced risk of heart disease. Fish are high in protein, zinc, and selenium, and most are very low in fat. Try to have fish a few times a week.

Quick Tip: Try serving kids mild-flavored fish like trout, sole, orange roughy, and shrimp. Look for baked fish sticks in the freezer section of the grocery store.

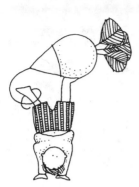

Just the Facts

If you ever get confused about nutrition, you are not alone. What's "good" or "bad" to eat seems to change daily! This chapter provides straight facts about growth, vitamins, hyperactivity, sugar, herbs, and fake foods.

Growth

Is My Child Growing Properly?

"Normal" growth is different for each child; it depends on her eating habits and the genes she has inherited. Regardless of a child's size at birth, she will eventually find her own individual growth pattern. Below are three growth scenarios. All of them are "normal."

* • Jill was only slightly above average in weight and height during first grade. She then shot up to tower over her second-grade classmates.
* • David was born three months premature. He weighed three pounds at birth. His size remained between the fifth and tenth percentile for children his age during the first eighteen months of his life. By the age of seven, however, he was growing in the fiftieth percentile.
* • Christian, age six, was an average-size newborn; he weighed seven pounds, eight ounces at birth. But by his fourth month, his growth slowed down to his genetic potential (his parents were both short), and he stayed at the fifth percentile for height and weight.

During every well-child visit, your child's height and weight should be plotted on a chart. Health-care professionals use growth charts for clinical assessment and for educating parents about their children's growth patterns as compared to a reference population. Ask to see your child's chart and discuss her progress with your physician.

Growth Alerts

Take a closer look at your child's growth if:

- Her weight or height has drastically changed from her normal pattern. This could be genetically programmed, but it could also signal a problem.
- Her appetite becomes consistently poor. Check her weight and height to make sure she is still growing normally.
- Her weight is increasing, but her height is not. During periods of growth, weight often increases before height. When you notice a weight increase, watch for a height increase. Keep an eye on your child's eating habits and activity to see if there may be another reason for her weight change.

To obtain a growth chart you can use at home to graph your child's growth, visit the National Center for Health Statistics (NCHS) website at www.cdc.gov/nchswww/about/major/nhanes/hanesrev.gov. Plotting weight along with height will help you understand your child's weight-to-height ratio. If you are concerned about your child's growth for any reason, ask your pediatrician to see your child for monthly growth checks. These are usually free, and they will help uncover potential problems—or at least ease your mind.

Your Child's Size

"Normal" Growth

Weight

- By four months: Birth weight doubles.
- By one year: Birth weight triples.
- During second year: Child gains slightly less than birth weight.
- After age two: Weight gain slows to a constant rate—about five pounds per year.

Height

- During first year: Height increases by 50 percent of birth length.
- By age four: Height is double that of birth length.
- By age thirteen: Height is triple that of birth length.

Factors That Affect Growth

- Birth weight and length
- Prematurity
- Genetics: parents' and grandparents' sizes
- Individual growth pattern
- Environmental factors

Brain Growth

One very important aspect of a child's physical development is brain growth. The brain begins growing before birth. It grows most rapidly during the first few months of a child's life. The brain is 75 percent developed at about two years and reaches adult size between ages six and ten.

Nutrition plays an important role in adequate brain growth. Studies have shown that early diet can have a lasting cognitive effect on children. Children who are diagnosed with protein or calorie malnutrition, for example, score lower on IQ tests years later. Such children also demonstrate behavioral problems such as lack of attention, poor memory, and easy distractibility.[1]

Brain-growth research has placed omega-3 fatty acids in the limelight. This type of fat has been shown to be essential to brain and retina development. It is supplied to a child in the womb and is also found in breastmilk. It is generally absent—or in short supply—in infant formula. Once an infant begins eating solid foods, you can offer her new sources of omega-3 fats, such as salmon. (See Chapter Three for more information on omega-3 fats.)

Genetics and Environment

Adults come in all shapes and sizes. So do children. Sometimes a person's size is determined mainly by genetics. Sometimes size is determined more by environmental factors. And sometimes a person's genetics and environment work together. For example, a genetic predisposition to short stature combined with an inadequate diet or a nutrient deficiency can stunt growth. In the same way, two naturally large parents with unhealthy eating habits are likely to produce overweight offspring. (See Chapter Two for more information on overweight.)

Why Isn't My Child Growing Well?

When a child doesn't grow according to her own normal pattern for several months, it's a good idea to investigate possible reasons.

Chronic or repeated illness, other medical problems, appetite loss, nutrient deficiency, and unsatisfied psychological needs can all affect growth. Discuss possible causes for the change in your child's growth with your health-care provider. Some common scenarios follow:

Too Much Juice

The following statement may seem self-contradictory, but it's true: Kids who drink too much juice tend to become growth-stunted as well as obese. In one study, 40 percent of the kids who drank the most fruit juice were also among the 20 percent who were the shortest in stature. In the same study, over 30 percent of the kids who drank the most fruit juice had weights above the ninetieth percentile. In a different study, two- and five-year-olds who drank more than twelve ounces of juice per day were more likely to be short and overweight.[2] Certainly not all juice drinkers will have growth problems, but juice consumption is something you should keep an eye on.

How could a beverage so often touted as healthy cause growth problems?

- Most juices provide only a few nutrients —mainly simple sugar and vitamin C.
- Juice often replaces healthier drinks and foods like milk and whole fruits, which contain more of the nutrients needed for growth.
- Drinking large amounts of juice may prevent the body from absorbing some carbohydrates, which in turn can cause diarrhea and stunted growth.[3]

Studies of infants and toddlers have shown that both tend to prefer sweets, so it is no surprise that given the choice, most children (of all ages) will choose juice over milk. Consequently, only 50 percent of children ages one to five meet the RDA for calcium.[4]

In one study, eight infants ages fourteen to twenty-seven months diagnosed with failure-to-thrive were referred for in-depth testing. Tests revealed that for all the infants, lack of growth was a result of excess juice drinking. All of the children had weights below the fifth percentile, and five of the children had diminished fat stores. The children's juice intake ranged from twelve to thirty ounces per day. Because they consumed so much juice, their food consumption was low, which prevented them from getting adequate protein, fat, and other nutrients.[5]

Drug Interference

Some medications, when taken for prolonged periods, can curb appetite or interfere with nutrient absorption. For example, Ritalin, a drug prescribed for Attention Deficit/Hyperactivity Disorder (ADHD), is associated with decreased appetite and decreased growth in height and weight.[6] If your child is taking prescription medication regularly, discuss nutrient interactions and changes in appetite with your health-care provider or dietitian.

Zinc Deficiency

Five to thirty percent of children around the world suffer from moderate zinc deficiency, which can affect growth hormones and result in reduced growth. Zinc deficiency may also affect thyroid hormones.[7] Good sources of zinc are shellfish, meat, poultry, whole grains, dried beans, and nuts.

Psychological Hunger

Nutrients and calories aren't the only elements necessary for adequate growth; a child's psychological needs must also be satisfied. Sometimes children who are offered plenty of food still fail to thrive because of psychological neglect or abuse.

▼

Vitamins

If you ask five different health professionals whether your child needs a multivitamin-mineral supplement, you will probably get five different answers. In an ideal world, your child would follow the Food Guide Pyramid every day and therefore would not need extra vitamins or minerals. But if your child is like most, she has picky days, food jags, sick days, and spells when she eats like a bird. When my kids go through these phases, I give them a daily multivitamin-mineral supplement. Remember: The availability of supplements should never be an excuse to eat poorly! Although multivitamins can help fill nutritional gaps, they do not contain the hundreds of healthy compounds present in food.

Which Multivitamins Are Best?

Iron deficiency (anemia) is a persistent problem all over the world. Kids are more likely to have trouble getting enough minerals like iron, zinc and calcium in their diet than they do getting vitamins like C or A. Be sure to give your child a complete multivitamin that contains minerals.

Individual Supplements

In most cases, you should not give your child supplements of individual vitamins, minerals, or herbs. Individual supplements can compete with other nutrients for absorption and can cause nutrient imbalances. Also, since children are smaller than adults, they are much more susceptible to vitamin toxicity. A few exceptions are listed below:

- Calcium: Calcium is vital for developing strong bones. If your child does not drink much milk or eat many high-calcium foods, you might consider giving her a chewable calcium supplement like Tums.
- Iron: If your child is anemic, your physician may prescribe an iron supplement for her.
- Fluoride: Investigate the fluoride content of your water. Ask your pediatrician or dentist whether the content is up to par. If it's not, your pediatrician or dentist may give you a flouride supplement.
- Vitamin B_{12} and Vitamin D: Children raised vegan may need these supplements as a result of avoiding all animal products.

(*Note:* Breast-fed infants may also need supplemental vitamins. See Chapter Nine for more information.)

A Matter of Taste

Okay, you've spent your whole lunch hour shopping for vitamins and you've forked over a small fortune to buy the best. One taste of it, and your child says "Blechh!"

This has happened to me. First, I encouraged my kids to try the vitamin a few more times. After all, I thought, one must acquire a taste for vitamins. When my kids reacted the same way again and again, I decided to taste the vitamin myself. After that, I decided that my kids deserved a medal for actually taking it more than once! When all those vitamins and minerals get packed into a pill with a pinch of sugar and flavor, the taste can be . . . well . . . yucko (to borrow a favorite word from my son Robert)! The moral: Don't expect your child to eat what you cannot. Try to find a vitamin that makes you both happy. Some health-food stores allow kids to taste-test vitamins to find ones they like. The same moral applies to those infant vitamin drops: I'll save you the unpleasant taste test and recommend that you mix the drops with formula, breast milk, or juice.

▼

Herbs

Americans spend billions of dollars per year on herbs. Some herbs do show great promise in improving the immune system and treating illnesses, but according to Jerald Foote, M.S., R.D., a nutrition consultant specializing in herbs, "Herbs are drugs, not magical healing compounds. They may be drugs derived from natural sources, but they are drugs, and have pharmacological effects on the body." Herbs can be harmful if used carelessly, just as drugs can. For example, a natural cold-and-flu remedy called Willowbark contains salycilic acid, the same active ingredient in aspirin, which should never be taken by children with viral infections due to the risk of Reye's syndrome.

Because herbal supplements are regulated as foods, they don't undergo the same scrutiny as conventional drugs. Herbal supplements don't always contain standardized amounts of active ingredients, and they may contain impurities. It's also important to remember that herbs have not been tested on children.

Do not give herbal supplements to your child unless you have discussed it with your child's health-care provider or a health professional who is well-educated in the use of herbs. Talking with a salesperson at an herb store is not enough!

▼

Hyperactivity

What Can I Believe about Sugar?

Here is what we know for certain about the health effects of sugar:

- Sugar can cause cavities. Regardless of the amount of sugar a food may contain, all foods with fermentable carbohydrates play a role in dental cavities. (See Chapter Seven for more information on dental health.)

The Common Cold and Early Childhood

If you feel like you are beating a path to your pediatrician's office, you are not alone! According to Barton Schmitt, M.D., professor of pediatrics at the University of Colorado School of Medicine, infants and preschool children average seven or eight colds per year. Science has identified at least two hundred cold viruses, and it takes a long time to build up immunity to all of them.

Cold rates triple in the winter, when people spend more time indoors breathing recirculated air. Smoking in the home can increase a child's susceptibility to colds, as well as to ear infections, sinus infections, croup, wheezing, and asthma. Dr. Schmitt recommends home day care for infants until the age of one; a child is exposed to fewer viruses and other respiratory irritants in her own home than at a day-care program with other children.[a]

There is no cure for the common cold, nor is there any way to prevent it besides keeping fit and staying away from cigarette smoke and germs. To keep your immune system in top shape for fighting colds and other illnesses, get plenty of sleep, eat a healthy diet including lots of fruits and vegetables, wash your hands frequently, and stay well hydrated. Note that the antioxidants found in fruits, vegetables, and yogurt seem to boost the immune system —one more good reason to eat them!

[a] Schmitt, B.D. When Your Child Has Frequent Colds, Contemporary Pediatrics, November 1995, Vol 12 no. 11. 101-102.

- Sugar is not an independent risk factor for diabetes or impaired glucose tolerance.
- Sugar is an "extra" food that may replace more-nutritious food (for example, soda and juice often replace milk), which may lead to a wide variety of health problems.

What Shouldn't I Believe about Sugar?

Following are a few statements I've heard from parents I know. Perhaps you've said similar things yourself:

- "Oh no–sugar! He'll be bouncing off the walls later."
- "She's eaten so much sugar, I'll never get her to sleep tonight."
- "Sugar makes him hyper."
- "She's all over the place; she must have had too much sugar today."

You may be surprised to learn that a common parental belief about sugar–that it causes hyperactivity–simply isn't true.

Parents are not the only ones who blame sugar for an increase in children's energy levels. In a study of Canadian teachers, 80 percent professed a belief that sugar consumption contributes to increased activity in normal children and to behavioral problems in hyperactive children. Fifty-five percent of the teachers suggested to parents that they limit their child's sugar consumption.[8] Studies of American teachers produced similar results. Sugar is widely believed to cause hyperactivity in children.

However, this relationship has never been scientifically substantiated. Twelve placebo-controlled, double-blind studies failed to provide any evidence that sugar, candy, or chocolate ingestion leads to unwanted behavior in kids with ADHD.[9] Another study examining the effects of sugar on children's behavior or cognitive performance found that sugar has no behavioral or cognitive

effect.[10] Therefore, diet-oriented treatment does not seem appropriate for children with behavioral problems.

But She Acts So Hyper . . .

"The research is all well and good," you may say, "but I could just swear that my child is extrahyper after birthday parties or after eating a lot of sugar." There are several possible explanations for your child's behavior:

- You expect your child to be hyperactive after eating a lot of sugar, so she fulfills your expectation. Your perception can be influenced by what you believe. In one study, a group of mothers who considered their sons to be sugar sensitive reported their sons to be significantly more hyperactive when they were told their sons had been fed sugar. The boys had actually received an artificially sweetened drink.[11]
- The environments in which your child eats sugar are conducive to activity. Put together kids, a party, and sweets, and kids may indeed start bouncing off the wall. However, sugar is not necessarily the culprit!
- Intake of any type of carbohydrate on an empty stomach has been shown to increase activity.[12] So if your child drinks Kool-Aid first thing in the morning– *zing!*–he gets a quick jolt of energy.
- The sugary food your child eats may also contain caffeine, which is a stimulant.
- Your child may indeed be part of a very small group of children who react to sugar.

Tips for Taming the Sugar Monster

You may have succeeded so far in keeping your child away from sweets, but when she starts school, watch out! Every holiday and celebration seems to revolve around sugar. Here are some strategies to help you and your child tame the sugar monster:

Beverages

Keep bottles of cold water in your car. This will help you avoid having to buy soda from a machine. At home, keep plain club soda or mineral water on hand and mix it with one-third or one-half glass of juice. Your child will get the bubbles she likes in a tasty juice spritzer without all the sugar most sodas contain.

Holidays

Just when you've finished the candy from one holiday, it's time for the next! What's a parent to do? Take stock of the goodies your child has collected (for example, in the neighborhood for Halloween or at school for Valentine's Day) right away and toss any that you don't want her to eat, such as jawbreakers or gum. Keep the rest in a special place from which your child can occasionally choose one or two. Make an agreement with your child to discard old candy when a new holiday rolls around.

Desserts

Every family needs to make its own rules about dessert. Our family rule is: "If you're too full for fruit, you're too full for dessert." You can sneak some nutrition into your desserts by serving dairy-based treats like pudding, yogurt, and smoothies or by serving fruit-based desserts. Try not to serve dessert every day—it's more fun if it's a special event!

Sweet Cereals

It takes an iron will to stroll down the cereal aisle with a kid in tow. There are so many less-than-healthy brands that kids adore! Nonetheless, I try to avoid buying popular kids' cereals—not only because they're sweet, but also because they're made with processed flours instead of whole grains. You may want to try a compromise: In our family, the children take turns picking out a cereal once a month. You might let your child sprinkle some sweet cereal on top of the cereal you would like her to eat. You could also choose a good whole-grain cereal and let your child sprinkle a teaspoon of sugar on it.

Cutting Sugar

You can cut sugar by one-fourth to one-third in most recipes. In some recipes you can substitute fruit or fruit juice for sugar. You can also lower your family's sugar intake by providing reduced-calorie condiments like pancake syrup. These cut sugar without using artificial sweeteners.

Diet and Behavior

Could other things besides sugar in your child's diet cause her to be hyperactive? Yes, it's possible. Below are some dietary factors that may be related to hyperactivity.

Caffeine

Many parents don't consider the caffeine content of the beverages and food their children consume. Caffeine could be causing your child's increased activity, especially if she is unaccustomed to consuming it.[13] It used to be easy to spot caffeinated drinks–they were all dark, like cola and coffee. That's not so anymore: Mountain Dew and Sunkist Orange Soda, among other soft drinks, contain caffeine. Chocolate and coffee-flavored yogurts and ice creams may also contain caffeine.

Fortunately, chocolate milk and hot cocoa–two favorite kid drinks–contain comparatively little caffeine. (See page 50 to determine the caffeine content of many popular drinks and desserts.)

Lead and Other Heavy Metals

Several studies have connected increasing concentrations of lead, arsenic, mercury, cadmium, and aluminum in hair to acting out, disturbed peer relations, and immaturity.[14] Further research has found a connection between increased lead levels in hair and physician-diagnosed ADHD. There appears to be no apparent safe threshold for lead. (See page 97 for more about lead.)

Anemia (Iron Deficiency)

If a child is anemic, he may display symptoms of hyperactivity or Attention Deficit Disorder (ADD) as well as irritability, poor concentration, and poor school performance.[15] Because various nutrient deficiencies may work together to affect behavior, it's important to have your child's overall health examined before diagnosing her deficiencies or behavior problems yourself.

Artificial Colors, Flavors, and Preservatives: The Feingold Diet

Twenty years ago, a pediatric allergist named Benjamin Feingold asserted that eliminating artificial colors, flavors, and other additives from the diet would help prevent and control hyperactive behavior. Many well-controlled scientific studies showed that most cases of hyperactivity were not related to additives in the diet.[16] In 1982, a Consensus Development Panel at the National Institutes of Health concluded that there was no scientific evidence to support the claim that additives cause hyperactivity.

More recently, the artificial sweetener aspartame has been tested to determine if it affects children with ADD. The study concluded that even at ten times the amount usually consumed, aspartame had no effect on cognition or behavior of kids with ADD.[17]

It is possible that a small number of children–from 5 to 10 percent–may benefit from trying an additive-free diet. Preschoolers seem to be more sensitive to additives than older children.[18] Be aware, though, that during some studies, children given either a specific additive or a placebo acted no differently. This suggests that any changes in the children's behavior were probably related to the attention the children were receiving.

▼

Fake Foods

Consumption of sugar substitutes has increased, yet so has the consumption of sugar. And the weight problem in America keeps growing. If people are using sugar substitutes to decrease their sugar intake and to lose weight, it's not working! So why teach kids to eat fake foods? It's better to enjoy the real thing in moderate amounts.

Are fake foods safe? All the sugar and fat substitutes you'll find on the market today have been tested for safety. Following you'll find safety information on a few new and well-known fake foods.

Caffeine Content of Beverages and Desserts

Beverage or Dessert	Serving Size* (in ounces)	Caffeine Content (in milligrams)	Beverage or Dessert	Serving Size* (in ounces)	Caffeine Content (in milligrams)
Coffees			*(Soft Drinks, continued)*		
Brewed coffee	8	135	Barq's Root Beer	12	23
Instant coffee	8	95	Mug Root Beer	12	0
Maxwell House Cappuccino, French Vanilla or Irish Cream	8	45–50	Lemon-lime sodas, caffeine-free colas	12	0
Decaffeinated coffee	8	5	Minute Maid Orange Soda	12	0
Teas			*Frozen Desserts*		
Celestial Seasonings Iced Lemon Ginseng Tea	16	100	Starbucks Frappuccino Bar	2.5 (1 bar)	15
Bigelow Raspberry Royale Tea	8	83	Healthy Choice Cappuccino Chocolate Chunk or Mocha Fudge Ice Cream	1 cup	8
Black tea, leaf or bag	8	50	*Yogurt*		
Snapple Iced Tea, all varieties	16	48	Dannon Coffee Yogurt	8	45
Nestea Pure Sweetened Iced Tea	16	34	Yoplait Cafe au Lait Yogurt	6	5
Green tea	8	30	Dannon Light or Stonyfield Farm Cappuccino Yogurt	8	0–1
Arizona Iced Tea, all varieties	16	15–30	*Chocolate*		
Lipton Soothing Moments Blackberry Tea	8	25	Hershey's Special Dark Chocolate Bar	1.5 (1 bar)	31
Nestea Pure Lemon Sweetened Iced Tea	16	22	Hershey's Milk Chocolate Bar	1.5 (1 bar)	10
Celestial Seasonings Herb Tea	8	0	Cocoa or hot chocolate	8	5
Soft Drinks					
Mountain Dew	12	55			
Cola drinks	12	41–47			
Sunkist Orange Soda	12	40			
Pepsi	12	37			

*Serving sizes are based on commonly eaten portions or on the amount of the leading-selling container size. For example, beverages sold in 16-ounce or ½-liter bottles are counted as one serving.

- *Sucralose:* This sugar substitute was approved by the FDA in 1998. It has been thoroughly tested for safety, and apparently there are no lingering doubts.
- *Saccharin:* This sugar substitute has been associated with cancer in lab animals that were fed large doses. Although the FDA recommended saccharin be banned in 1977, it has been kept on the market by congressional intervention.
- *Aspartame:* This sugar substitute, found in the well-known sweetener Nutra-Sweet, appears to be safe for most people. However, some individuals may have reactions like headaches or dizziness. Aspartame is not recommended for individuals with a genetic disorder called Phenylketonuria (PKU).
- *Acesulfame K:* The Center for Science in the Public Interest recommends that people avoid this, citing inadequate testing.
- *Olestra:* When the FDA was considering approval of this fat substitute, a huge controversy erupted in the scientific community. Physicians and scientists from the University of California, the University of Minnesota, Harvard School of Public Health, and the American Public Health Association

have all spoken against public use of Olestra. When Olestra is eaten with a meal that contains carotenoids, it prevents absorption of the carotenoids. (Carotenoids may help prevent heart disease and cancer.) For example, if you eat a meal consisting of a sandwich, carrot sticks, and Olestra-containing chips, the carotenoids in the meal (the beta-carotene in the carrots) will not be absorbed by the body. This is a problem if Olestra is eaten on a regular basis. Also, one study showed that when children were given a fat substitute for 10 percent of their fat intake, the children adjusted their diets accordingly and ate approximately the same number of calories per day as they normally would.[19]

Unless your child is overweight or diabetic, she has no reason to consume non-nutritive sweeteners regularly. Even if she is overweight, an occasional splurge on the real thing is far more likely to satisfy her sweet tooth than daily doses of artificially sweetened food. And because of the controversy over Olestra, it's best to cut the fat in your family's diet in other ways: Eat naturally fat-free chips like Baked Tostitos or Baked Lay's, or buy regular chips only occasionally—and enjoy the special treat!

Food Allergies and Intolerances

Since the late 1990s, there has been an explosive increase in allergies around the world. An allergy is a condition in which a person's immune system regards an ordinarily harmless substance as a dangerous "invader" and responds to it by producing antibodies that create unpleasant reactions, such as asthma, eczema, and hay fever. Food allergies, once viewed as a separate condition, are now known to be related to eczema (an inflammatory disease of the skin) and asthma. Dietary preventive measures are important for children who are at high risk for allergies.

Food allergies occur in about 4–6 percent of infants and in 1–2 percent of young children. Some food allergies are outgrown. However, allergies to peanuts, tree nuts, and seafood are likely to last a lifetime.

Allergies tend to run in families. Children with two parents who have allergies have a 40–70 percent chance of also developing allergies. One primary step in the prevention of allergies in high-risk children is to avoid introducing potentially allergenic foods (milk, eggs, wheat, peanut, soy, and tree nuts) until they are at least one year old. Peanut allergies appear to be on the rise, possibly due to an increase in peanuts' popularity.

Children with eczema, allergy to eggs, or a family history of allergies are more likely to develop an allergy to peanuts.[1] Peanuts are more likely to cause severe reactions like anaphylaxis than other foods. They are also more likely to cause a reaction with minimal contact.

Anaphylaxis is a sudden, severe, potentially life-threatening allergic reaction. It can be caused by food allergies,

---

The Most Allergenic Foods

The following foods cause most allergic reactions: eggs, milk, peanuts, tree nuts (such as cashews and hazelnuts), soy, wheat, fish, and shellfish. The most common food allergies—to milk and eggs—often disappear by the age of five.

---

insect stings, or medications. Although any food can potentially cause anaphylaxis, peanuts, nuts, shellfish, fish, and eggs are foods that most commonly cause a severe reaction. Symptoms can include hives, swelling (especially of the lips and face), difficulty breathing (either because of swelling in the throat or an asthmatic reaction), vomiting, diarrhea, cramping, and a fall in blood pressure. Symptoms can occur in as little as five to fifteen minutes and usually occur within one hour. Anaphylaxis must be treated immediately with adrenaline or epinephrine, or it can be fatal.

In general, food allergy symptoms include vomiting; diarrhea; cramps; hives; swelling; eczema; itching or swelling of the lips, tongue, or mouth; itching or tightness in the throat; breathing difficulty; and wheezing. Allergic symptoms can begin from one minute to one hour after ingesting the food. If you suspect your child has a food allergy, see an allergist for a diagnosis. Self-diagnosis can result in unnecessary food restriction and, in some cases, can be life-threatening. Skin-prick tests are usually the first method for allergy screening, but a controlled food challenge is the only way to make a final diagnosis.

The following steps can be taken to prevent or postpone food allergies in children:
- Breast-feed your child exclusively for the first year. This is the best way to postpone or prevent food allergies, as well as eczema and asthma. If breast-feeding is not an option, consider an extensively hydrolyzed formula or whey hydrolysate formula for infants at high risk for allergies.[2]
- If you or your spouse have food allergies, consider following an egg- or milk-free diet while you are nursing. No benefit has been shown for following this type of diet during pregnancy.[3] (See Chapter Nine for more information on breastfeeding.)
- Postpone the introduction of solid foods for six months and wait longer to introduce other highly allergenic foods:[4]
  –milk and soy: one year
  –eggs: two years
  –peanuts, tree nuts, fish, and shellfish: between three and four years

According to one study, the incidence of allergic symptoms like asthma, dermatitis, and wheezing can be increased by the following factors:[5]
- formula feeding the first week of life
- early weaning (less than four months)
- feeding beef at less than six months
- introducing cow's milk at less than six months
- parental smoking in the presence of babies
- day-care admission at less than two years

Chicken—An Unlikely Source of Peanut Oil

If your child has a food allergy, always be suspect about the food you eat away from home. Case in point: The fried chicken filets and nuggets at Chik Filet are fried in peanut oil. Who would guess? Kids who are allergic to peanuts also react to peanut oil. Luckily, the grilled chicken breast does not contain peanut oil. Most fast-food restaurants offer complete ingredient lists of their products, and some can be found on the Internet.

If your child is diagnosed with a food allergy, take the following precautions:

- Educate your child as appropriate for his age. A medical ID bracelet can help remind caregivers of a severe food allergy.
- Inform everyone who may come in contact with your child about his food allergy, including relatives, friends, neighbors, and babysitters; day-care directors, providers, and teachers; school nurses, office personnel, teachers, and principals.
- If your child has a severe allergy to food, make sure the proper antidote is available for use by the school nurse, teacher, and others who take care of your child.

▼

Managing Food Allergies at School

When your child spends time at school (away from you), it is vital to educate everyone—teachers, administrators, and other students—about your child's food allergy.

The Food Allergy Network offers the following advice:

Preschools have a unique situation because the children there are often too young to know how to avoid the foods to which they are allergic, and food is so much a part of their activities. Parents play a key role in this situation. They can take the lead and coordinate snacktimes and class celebrations with the teachers and other parents. Together, they can make sure that the food brought into the schools will be safe for all children or that appropriate alternatives are also available.

To minimize risks, some preschools allow only store-bought food with ingredient labels to be sent in for celebrations. Parents of the allergic children are responsible for reading those labels and determining whether or not their children can eat that food.

At the elementary-school level, parents are wise to meet with school administrators before school starts and carefully explain their child's food allergies, specify what foods must be avoided, and work together with the staff to manage class celebrations and field trips. Food-service staff can provide menus with ingredient lists so parents can select "safe" foods for their child.

Strategies for lunchrooms should be created that will keep the student safe while allowing the child to eat with friends. Many schools create peanut- or milk-free zones within the cafeteria. Others have a no-trading policy to avoid peer-pressured food exchanges that could be harmful for some.

With proper education, information, and a team effort among parents, students, and staff, food allergies can be successfully managed at school. For additional tips, including information about The School Food Allergy Program, contact The Food Allergy Network at 800-929-4040.

Shopping with Food Allergies

If someone in your family has a food allergy, you must always be aware of ingredients in foods. Since ingredients in products often change, read the label every time you buy a product. The Food Allergy Network publishes product alerts on its website (and via e-mail) that can notify you of products containing ingredients not listed on the label.

Shopping with a Milk Allergy

Milk and milk products are very common ingredients. Below is a partial list of ingredients that you should avoid for a milk-free diet.

- artificial butter flavor
- butter, butterfat, butter oil
- buttermilk
- casein
- caseinates (listed as ammonium, calcium, magnesium, potassium, or sodium caseinate)
- cheese
- cottage cheese
- cream

General Tips for the Family with Food Allergies

- Avoid buying foods in bulk; sometimes there is cross-contamination with other foods.
- Read food labels carefully. Information about cross-mixing with other foods is now listed (for example, wheat cereal that may have come in contact with soy).
- Avoid eating out. Eating out is risky for a person with a severe food allergy (especially with a nut allergy).
- Remember that medications and vitamins contain sweeteners, colors, and flavors. Over-the-counter medication and vitamins should have these things listed. Ask your pharmacist or pediatrician about ingredients in prescription medicines.
- Consult a registered dietitian on how to avoid and find appropriate substitutes for allergenic foods.

- curds
- ghee
- hydrolysates (listed as casein, milk protein, protein, whey, or whey protein hydrolysate)
- lactalbumin, lactalbumin phosphate
- lactoglobulin
- lactose
- lactulose
- milk (derivative, powder, protein, solids, malted, condensed, evaporated, dry, whole, low-fat, nonfat, skimmed, and goat's milk)
- nougat
- pudding
- rennet casein
- sour cream, sour cream solids

- sour milk solids
- whey (in all forms, including sweet, delactosed, and protein concentrate)
- yogurt

The following food products also may indicate the presence of milk:
- chocolate
- flavorings, including caramel, bavarian cream, coconut cream, brown sugar, butter, and natural flavorings
- high-protein flour
- lunch meat, hot dogs, sausages
- margarine
- Simplesse

Ingredient lists courtesy of The Food Allergy Network.

Shopping with an Egg Allergy

If your child is allergic to either egg white or egg yolk, he must avoid eggs completely. Eggs are used in many food products, so read labels carefully. Below is a partial list of ingredients that you should avoid for an egg-free diet.

- albumen
- egg (white, yolk, dried, powdered solids)
- eggnog
- globulin
- livetin
- lysozyme (used in Europe)
- mayonnaise
- meringue
- ovalbumin
- ovomucin
- ovomucoid
- ovovitellin
- Simplesse

Ingredient list courtesy of The Food Allergy Network.

Easy-to-Make Egg Substitutes

For Baked Goods:
You can make your own egg substitute to use in baked goods, such as muffins, cakes, and cookies. Each recipe below is equivalent to one whole egg.

1½ tablespoons water
1½ tablespoons oil
1 teaspoon baking powder

1 teaspoon baking powder
1 tablespoon water
1 tablespoon vinegar

1 teaspoon yeast, dissolved in ¼ cup warm water

For Other Recipes:

Use the substitute below in recipes where egg is used as a binder instead of a leavening agent. That is, this substitute will work in holding meatballs together but not in a cake.

Yield: 1 cup (approximately 5 eggs)

Mix 1 packet of unflavored gelatin with 1 cup of boiling water. Use 3 tablespoons of the mixture for each egg. Refrigerate leftovers for up to one week and microwave chilled mixture to re-liquefy.

Recipes courtesy of The Food Allergy Network.

▼

Information on Other Food Allergies

If your family has food allergies, the resources below can provide information about food labeling, recipes, and more:

Food Allergy Network

800-929-4040 / www.foodallergy.org

Food Allergy Network is a nonprofit organization established to increase public awareness about food allergy and anaphylaxis. Members receive a bimonthly newsletter and product alerts. A newsletter for kids is available by request, as are booklets, cookbooks, and videos.

The Food Allergy Network also publishes "How to Read a Label" cards. Each wallet-sized, laminated card lists the various ways a food group may appear on ingredient labels. The cards cost two dollars each and are available for milk, egg, wheat, peanut, soy, tree nut, and shellfish allergies. Other booklets, videos, and product alerts are available.

American Academy of Allergy, Asthma, and Immunology

800-822-2762 / www.aaaai.org

This searchable website contains a wealth of information about food allergies as well as other types of allergies and asthma. It also provides links to other allergy sites and a physician referral directory.

▼

Food Intolerances

An intolerance to a food is different from a food allergy. Though some symptoms can be the same—such as intestinal discomfort—food intolerances do not involve the immune system as allergies do. People may be intolerant to a food for several reasons:

- They may have an intestinal problem that mimics the symptoms of a food allergy.
- Their body may not make enough lactase, an enzyme required to digest lactose, the natural sugar present in milk. Lactase deficiency can cause diarrhea, bloating, and gas.
- Some people react to certain food additives, such as MSG and sulfites.

Because the symptoms of a food intolerance can be identical to those of a food allergy, it is important to see a board-certified allergist so that a diagnosis can be made.

▼

Managing Lactose Intolerance

If you or someone in your family has lactose intolerance, you are not alone. It is estimated that 80–90 percent of Asian-Americans, 75 percent of African-Americans, 50 of percent Hispanic-Americans, and 20 percent of European-Americans suffer from lactose intolerance.

Since milk is the main source of calcium in a child's diet, you may have to take special care to ensure that a lactose-intolerant child gets enough calcium. Here are some tips:

- Many people with lactose intolerance can drink a small amount (one cup or less) of milk, especially if it is with a meal.
- Many people can tolerate chocolate milk or whole milk because the presence of fat and cocoa slow down digestion and reduce symptoms of lactose intolerance.
- Reduced-lactose dairy products include yogurt, hard cheeses like cheddar or

Swiss, and ice cream. Non-dairy milk substitutes include soy milk, rice milk, and Vitamite.

- At the grocery store, you can find milk that has a reduced amount of lactose. There are also lactase enzyme drops (Lactaid) that you can put in regular milk to break down the lactose. The enzyme is also available in a tablet form that can be taken by mouth–appropriate for older children and adults.
- Look for fortified orange juice (Minute Maid and Tropicana) that provides as much calcium as milk does. Minute Maid also makes a calcium-fortified juice box.
- A small number of people are sensitive to the lactose found in small amounts in other products. They should read the label and avoid foods that have whey, lactose, nonfat milk solids, buttermilk, malted milk, margarine, and sweet or sour cream.
- For a list of calcium-rich foods other than milk, see page 66. (Vegan children rely on such sources of calcium, too.)

Vegetarian Eating

This chapter answers such questions as:

- *I don't plan to feed my infant meats. What other protein source can I offer?*
- *What are some vegetarian sources of vitamin B_{12}?*
- *Which is a richer source of iron—tofu or soymilk?*
- *Which foods are high in calcium?*
- *Must vegan children give up snacks?*
- *What's TVP?*
- *I don't understand protein combining. What are some examples?*

A meatless eating plan can be very healthy for infants and children if, like most well-rounded diets, it has balance and variety. In fact, a vegetarian diet more closely resembles the current U.S. Dietary Guidelines than does the typical American diet.

Often parents don't choose a vegetarian diet for their kids; their kids choose it themselves. Many toddlers and preschoolers don't like the texture of animal protein and refuse it, much to the dismay of their parents. Adolescents and teenagers often forego meat as much for social and environmental reasons as for the health of it.

Personally, I was happy when my son Robert chose to eat a mostly vegetarian diet until he was about eighteen months old. His diet was the same as that of other children his age, except that he ate beans and cheese instead of meat. To this day, much of his protein still comes from milk, cheese, and beans!

Vegetarian eating is a source of many myths. Here are a few of them:

Myth: Vegetarians don't have enough protein in their diet.

Fact: Not only do vegetarians generally have enough protein in their diet for good health; many nonvegetarians eat too *much* protein.

Myth: Vegetarians are more likely to suffer from iron deficiency anemia than meat eaters.

Fact: Though iron found in plant foods is not as well absorbed as it is from animal foods, vegetarians are not more likely to be anemic.

Myth: Vegetarians are unhealthy.

Fact: Many people would like to have the health records that vegetarians have. They generally have lower rates of heart disease, high blood pressure, type II diabetes, and osteoporosis than meat eaters.

Infants

Parents who choose a vegetarian diet for their infant will find it is not that different from the diet of a baby who eats meat:

- The vegetarian baby receives breast milk or formula.
- Cereals, fruits, and vegetables are offered at the appropriate times.
- Instead of adding meats to the diet at eight to ten months, the vegetarian baby is offered mashed tofu or beans without skins as a supplemental protein source.

- Infants weaned from breast milk before one year should be given baby formula—either cow-milk-based or soy-based.

As with babies who eat meat, breast milk or formula is still a major part of a vegan baby's diet; the other foods provide supplementary protein, calories, and nutrients.

Toddlers

Toddlers eat a diet that contains beans, tofu, cheese, and vegetables in place of meat, with special care given to iron intake and calcium-rich food. From one to two years, toddlers should have fortified whole soy-milk or whole cow's milk, not a low-fat milk.

Growth

You may be concerned that if your child doesn't eat meat, she may not grow properly. According to the American Academy of Pediatrics, the growth of vegan children is similar to that of meat-eating children if

Feeding Schedule for Vegan Babies, Ages 4–12 Months

Milk

*4–7 months**	Breast milk or soy formula
6–8 months	Breast milk or soy formula
7–10 months	Breast milk or soy formula
10–12 months	Breast milk or soy formula (24–32 ounces)

Cereal and Bread

*4–7 months**	Begin iron-fortified baby cereal mixed with milk
6–8 months	Continue baby cereal; begin other breads and cereals
7–10 months	Baby cereal; other breads and cereals
10–12 months	Baby cereal until 18 months, total of 4 servings daily (1 serving = ¼ slice bread or 2–4 tablespoons cereal)

Fruits and Vegetables

*4–7 months**	None
6–8 months	Begin juice from cup (2–4 ounces)—vitamin C source; begin mashed fruits and vegetables
7–10 months	4 ounces juice; pieces of soft or cooked fruits and vegetables
10–12 months	Table-food diet; allow 4 servings per day (1 serving = 1–6 tablespoons fruit and vegetable, 4 ounces juice)

Legumes and Nut Butters

*4–7 months**	None
6–8 months	None
7–10 months	Gradually introduce tofu; begin casseroles, puréed legumes, soy cheese, and soy yogurt
10–12 months	2 servings daily, each about 0.5 ounce; nut butters should not be started before 1 year

*Overlap of ages occurs because of varying rate of development.

Source: Reed Mangels, Ph.D., R.D., reprinted with permission from Vegetarian Resource Group.

adequate menus are planned.[1] However, poor growth has been observed in some children who follow a macrobiotic diet, which may be too low in fat, calories, zinc, calcium, vitamin B_{12}, and riboflavin to support optimal growth. Parents who choose a macrobiotic diet for their children should take care that it is nutritionally adequate.

Nutrients of Concern

Iron

Iron deficiency (anemia) is the most common nutritional problem of all children–whether they eat meat or not–and is most likely to occur between one-and-a-half and two years. Iron deficiency is not more common in vegetarian children. However, parents should be sure to give their child iron-rich foods. These foods include iron-fortified cereals and foods naturally high in iron, such as tofu, blackstrap molasses, beans and legumes (especially soybeans), bran flakes, sea vegetables, cream of wheat, textured vegetable protein (TVP), and tempeh. Nut butters, nuts, and seeds can be added to the diet when age-appropriate.[2]

Excessive milk consumption can increase the risk of iron deficiency because milk does not contain iron and can take the place of foods that do. Three cups of milk per day satisfy the calcium and protein needs of children.

Iron Absorption

Many plant foods are high in iron, but the iron is not absorbed by the body as well as the iron from meat. Iron absorption can vary twenty-fold at a meal, depending on what foods are eaten together. (See chart above.)

Iron-Rich Vegetarian Foods

The Recommended Dietary Allowance (RDA) for iron for children six months to ten years is 10 milligrams.

Food	Amount	Iron (in milligrams)
Sea vegetables	½ cup	18.1–42.0
Tofu	½ cup	6.6
Instant oatmeal	1 packet	6.3
Cream of Wheat	½ cup	5.5
Soybeans	½ cup	4.4
Garbanzo beans	½ cup	3.4
Navy beans	½ cup	2.5
Pumpkin seeds	2 tablespoons	2.5
Swiss chard	½ cup	1.9
Black beans	½ cup	1.8
Soymilk	1 cup	1.8
Cashews	2 tablespoons	1.0
Whole-wheat bread	1 slice	0.9
White bread	1 slice	0.7

Soy- and grain-based veggie burgers and meat replacers are also good sources of iron.

To Increase Iron Absorption:

- Eat vitamin C foods, citrus fruits, and other fruits and vegetables with meals. Five ounces of orange juice can increase iron absorption as much as five times. Foods high in vitamin C include citrus fruits, melon, mango, pineapple, berries, tomato products, cabbage, broccoli, cauliflower, peppers, spinach, and potatoes.
- Use iron or stainless-steel cookware. Iron from the pans can leach into your food, especially when you are cooking acidic foods like tomato sauce.

Vitamin B$_{12}$

Lacto-ovo vegetarians do not have a problem getting enough Vitamin B$_{12}$, which is found in milk and milk products. However, vegan children will need other sources of vitamin B$_{12}$ (which is naturally found in animal products). Vegetarian sources of B$_{12}$ are fortified soymilk, fortified breakfast cereals, meat analogs, and Red Star T6635 yeast (Vegetarian Support Formula).

Calcium

Although lacto-ovo vegetarian children consume more than the RDA for calcium, vegan children may not. Calcium-rich foods (listed at right) are necessary to achieve proper calcium intake in children who do not drink milk.

Vitamin D

Vitamin D is made in the skin with exposure to sunlight. Vegetarian children who live in sunny southern climates and have their hands and faces in the sun (for twenty to thirty minutes a day, two to three times a week) receive adequate vitamin D. The main dietary source is milk, and children who drink milk get adequate amounts of the vitamin.

Children who live in northern climates may not be exposed to adequate sunshine year-round, so they should make sure to get vitamin D from another source. Other factors calling for another source of the vitamin are dark skin, sunscreen, and pollution, which can all block ultraviolet light necessary to produce adequate vitamin D. It has been recommended that all vegetarian

Vegetarian Sources of Calcium		
The RDA for iron for children six months to ten years is 10 milligrams.		
Food	**Serving**	**Calcium (in milligrams)**
Firm tofu (with calcium sulfate)	2 ounces	125–380
Minute Maid Premium Calcium Orange Juice or Tangerine Juice	1 cup	350
Tropicana Pure Premium Orange Juice with Calcium and extra vitamin C	1 cup	350
Milk	1 cup	300
Rice Dream, vanilla, enriched rice milk	1 cup	300
Westsoy Plus soymilk	1 cup	300
Cheese made with soy, rice, or almond milk	1 ounce	20-300 (check label)
Blackstrap molasses	2 tablespoons	274
Cheddar cheese	1 ounce	204
Regular tofu (with calcium sulfate)	2 ounces	60–190
Collard greens	½ cup	175
Corn tortilla	1	100
Minute Maid Drink Boxes (orange, apple, cherry, grape)	6¾ ounces	100
Sesame seeds	1 tablespoon	85

children have a dietary source of vitamin D.[3] Vegetarian sources of vitamin D are milk (cow, soy, and rice) and fortified cereals.

Examples of Kid-Appealing Cereals Fortified with Vitamins B_{12} and D:
(Since formulations change from time to time, check labels periodically to be sure.)
- Cheerios–General Mills
- Corn Chex and Rice Chex (B_{12} only)–Ralston Purina
- Corn Flakes–Kellogg's
- Crispix–Kellogg's
- Frosted Mini Wheats (B_{12} only)–Kellogg's
- Kix (D only)–General Mills
- Oatmeal Crisp–General Mills
- Raisin Bran–Post
- Total–General Mills
- Wheaties–General Mills

Zinc

Zinc is a mineral important for growth and development and many other functions. Zinc, like iron, may be a problem for vegetarians because of poor absorption. Offer your child plenty of foods rich in zinc.

▼

Vitamin Supplements

The general advice regarding supplements found in Chapter Four also applies to vegetarian children. However, vegan children who do not eat fortified foods may also need supplemental B_{12}, calcium, and (if not exposed to adequate sunlight) vitamin D. Ask your health-care provider for an individualized recommendation.

▼

Protein

Protein intake of most vegetarian children either meets or exceeds recommendations. However, because children have slightly higher needs for essential amino acids, protein combining may be helpful in meeting the protein needs of infants and children. Examples of protein combining include a grain with a nut (bread with almond butter), a grain with beans (refried beans in a flour tortilla), and soy food with grain (tofu and pasta).[4]

Zinc-Rich Foods		
The RDA for children ages one to ten is 10 milligrams.		
Food	**Amount**	**Zinc (in milligrams)**
Bran flakes	1 cup	5.0
Wheat germ	2 tablespoons	2.3
Textured vegetable protein (TVP)	½ cup	1.4
Garbanzo beans	½ cup	1.3
Lentils	½ cup	1.2
Lima beans	½ cup	1.0
Tofu or soybeans	½ cup	1.0
Corn	½ cup	0.9

Source: Position of the American Dietetic Association: Vegetarian Diets

Here is a sample list of vegetarian foods that contain five grams—or about one-third—of the daily protein needed by a three-year-old:

- ⅓ cup (heaping) beans or other legumes
- 1 cup brown rice
- 1¼ tablespoons peanut butter
- ½ cup quinoa (a grain)
- 1 ounce firm tofu
- ⅔ ounce cheese
- ½ cup soy yogurt
- 2 slices bread
- ⅔ cup milk

Fat

During childhood, fat is needed for growth—especially in infancy, when fat intake should be 40–50 percent of calories. After the age of two years, the Pediatric Panel of the National Cholesterol Education Program recommends 30 percent or less of calories from fat.[5]

Diets that do not include fish or eggs lack an omega-3 fatty acid called DHA. Linolenic acid from vegetable sources can be converted to DHA, but the process may not be efficient. Sources of linolenic acid include flaxseed, walnuts, walnut oil, canola oil, linseed oil, peas, milk, cheese, and yogurt.[6]

Vegetarian children have an edge over their meat-eating counterparts, because vegetarians eat less fat and cholesterol. However, because toddlers and preschoolers sometimes have trouble meeting calorie needs—especially on a vegetarian diet high in bulk—fats may need to be added to the diet in the form of vegetable oil or nut butters.

Helpful Tips for Vegetarian Toddlers

- Nuts and seeds can provide trace minerals as well as fat and calories. Vegan children over three should eat them daily. Make sure to finely chop or blend nuts and seeds into food to avoid choking. A variety of nut butters are found in health-food stores.
- Blackstrap molasses is high in calcium and iron. It can be added to cake, pancake, and cookie batter; mixed into milkshakes; and cooked into baked beans.
- Nutritional yeast—Red Star T6635—is a reliable source of vitamin B_{12} and can be mixed into a white sauce for vegetables or pasta, added to beans, and included in scrambled tofu or other recipes.
- Regular healthy snacks are important for all children, including vegetarian children.
- Preschoolers like finger food. Try sandwich fillings like hummus or refried beans with mashed avocado, peanut butter blended with banana or crushed pineapple, egg or tofu egg salad, or cheese.

❓ Questions You May Have

Q: My son Sean is six and refuses to eat meat! He will not eat beans (except refried), tofu, or vegetables either. Help!

A: Many kids simply don't like the texture of meat. However, he may enjoy fish or chicken the way many kids like them—as nuggets or sticks. Eggs also provide high-quality protein. Or try a tuna or peanut butter sandwich. Nothing is wrong with refried beans if they are low-fat; a bean burrito makes a great dinner. Also try the many vegetarian frozen foods like corn dogs, chick pieces (Morningstar Farms), and veggie burgers. Try to make sure he is eating plenty of fruits and milk; if not, give him a daily multivitamin supplement.

Q: Are vegetarian diets always healthy?

A: The healthiness of any diet depends on the food choices. When vegetarian diets started to be popular in the '60s and '70s, they contained a lot of full-fat dairy products that made the diet high in saturated fat. Now we are more savvy about how to eat low-fat and vegetarian. If the diet is very restricted for some reason, it can be unbalanced and not meet nutrient needs.

Q: My nine-year-old won't eat any meat or chicken. How can I prepare food for him without cooking two meals a night?

A: It would not be a bad idea for the whole family to have some meatless meals. If there are some definite carnivores in your family, remember to avoid calling these meals "meatless." Here are some examples:

- Modern beanie wienies: Baked beans with sliced soy dogs
- "The works" pizza without the meat (or just put meat on one side)
- Spaghetti with "meat" sauce: Replace the meat with Harvest Crumbles (frozen soy protein) or textured vegetable protein (found in bulk at health-food stores).
- Bean burritos
- Vegetarian chili (canned)
- Pasta primavera: pasta with vegetables, with or without sauce

For nights when the rest of the family would be eating meat, have some vegetarian convenience foods on hand that your child can make herself or help prepare and serve:

- Veggie burgers
- Chicken "filets" (frozen)
- Corn dogs
- Canned refried beans
- Other beans and bean soups, including lentil and black bean

▼

Diet Plans for Vegan Children

On the next page are some meal plans that might be helpful in planning a healthy vegan diet.

Toddlers and Preschoolers (ages 1–4)

Food Group	Number of Servings
Grains	6 or more (A serving is ½ to 1 slice of bread, or ¼ to ½ cup cooked grain or pasta, or ½ to 1 cup ready-to-eat cereal.)
Legumes, nuts, and seeds	2 or more (A serving is ¼ to ½ cup cooked beans, tofu, tempeh, or TVP; 1½ to 3 ounces of meat analog; or 1 to 2 tablespoons nuts, seeds, or nut or seed butter.)
Fortified soymilk	3 (A serving is 1 cup fortified soymilk, infant formula, or breast milk.)
Vegetables	2 or more (A serving is ¼ to ½ cup cooked or ½ to 1 cup raw vegetables.)
Fruits	3 or more (A serving is ¼ to ½ cup canned fruit, ½ cup juice, or 1 medium fruit.)
Fats	3 (A serving is 1 teaspoon margarine or oil.)

School-Aged Children

Food Group	Number of Servings
Grains	6 or more for 4- to 6-year-olds; 7 or more for 7- to 12-year-olds (A serving is 1 slice of bread; ½ cup cooked cereal, grain, or pasta; or ¾ to 1 cup ready-to-eat cereal.)
Legumes, nuts, and seeds	1½ to 3 for 4- to 6-year-olds; 3 or more for 7- to 12-year-olds (A serving is ½ cup cooked beans, tofu, tempeh, or TVP; 3 ounces of meat analog; or 2 tablespoons of nuts, seeds, or nut or seed butter.)
Fortified soymilk	3 (A serving is 1 cup fortified soymilk.)
Vegetables	1 to 1½ for 4- to 6-year-olds; 4 or more for 7- to 12-year-olds (A serving is ½ cup cooked or 1 cup raw vegetables.)
Fruits	2 to 4 for 4- to 6-year-olds; 3 or more for 7- to 12-year-olds (A serving is ½ cup canned fruit, ¾ cup fruit juice, or 1 medium fruit.)
Fats	4 for 4- to 6-year-olds; 5 for 7- to 12-year-olds (A serving is 1 teaspoon margarine or oil.)

Note: Serving sizes vary depending on the child's age.

Source: By Reed Mangels, reprinted with permission Vegetarian Resource Group (VRG), P.O. Box 1463, Dept. IN, Baltimore, MD 21203. (410) 366-VEGE website:www.vrg.org

Dental Health

This chapter answers such questions as:

- *What starts the process of tooth decay?*
- *How soon does my child need fluoride?*
- *Which source of fluoride is most important—our water supply or our toothpaste?*
- *My child's teeth seem to be turning dark. What might be happening?*
- *What is "baby-bottle tooth decay"?*
- *What can I do when my child is unable to brush after a meal or snack?*
- *How can I help my child to not be afraid of going to the dentist?*

When a child's first tooth makes its arrival, it's usually a "Kodak moment," and the important milestone is recorded in a baby book. Even more attention should be given to the second, tenth, and twentieth tooth once each comes in, because your careful efforts now may affect your child's teeth for a long time. Good oral hygiene (daily tooth brushing and cleaning) should begin with that first tooth—and getting enough fluoride, of course, is also important.

Cavities

The occurrence of dental caries, or cavities, tends to increase as a child grows older. A recent study found that 74 percent of children were cavity free at the age of five years, but only 33 percent were cavity free by the time they were teenagers.[1]

Cavity formation = a fermentable carbohydrate* + a susceptible tooth + bacteria + time

* A fermentable carbohydrate is a sugar or starch that can be broken down by bacteria in the mouth.

For a cavity to occur, several things are necessary. When bacteria and a fermentable carbohydrate interact on the surface of a tooth, the bacteria produces acids. When the acidity level (pH) reaches 5.5 or less, the tooth's enamel starts to break down. During this breakdown, minerals are lost and a small hole, or cavity, forms in the tooth.

Cavity prevention = good oral hygiene + adequate fluoride + a proper diet

Good oral hygiene (discussed in depth in the last section of this chapter) is a major factor in preventing cavities. The discovery that fluoride is vital for healthy teeth has led to the most significant improvement in dental health in the last thirty years. Fluoride, when present in the body's circulation while teeth are being formed, makes teeth harder and more resistant to decay.

▼

Getting Adequate Fluoride

Make sure adequate fluoride is present in your water supply by inquiring with your local water department. In some areas, fluoride is naturally present in the public water supply; in other areas, fluoride must be added to the water supply. You can also have the fluoride level of your water checked for a small fee. People who drink well water, bottled water, or water from a filtration system need to know the fluoride level of their supply as well.

Topical fluoride, found in toothpaste, also offers protection to teeth. However, since the toothpaste marketed to children (in flavors such as bubble gum and tutti-frutti) tastes good enough to eat, supervise your child's brushings to see that he doesn't eat any of it. Excess fluoride can be toxic! If your child cannot spit out the paste without swallowing (before four to five years), use a toothpaste without fluoride. Don't worry—systemic fluoride found in the water supply is much more important to teeth than topical fluoride found in toothpaste!

What If Your Water Does Not Contain Adequate Fluoride?

If there is not enough fluoride in your drinking water, your baby will need a prescription for fluoride from your physician or dentist.

Supplemental Fluoride Dosage Schedule			
Concentration of Fluoride in Drinking Water (in ppm*)	6 Months to 3 Years (milligrams/day)	3 to 6 Years (milligrams/day)	6 to 16 Years (milligrams/day)
<0.30	0.25	0.50	1.00
0.30–0.60	0	0.25	0.50
>0.60	0	0	0

Source: Journal of the American Dental Association, 1994.

*ppm = parts per million

Other babies who need a supplement are:
- breast-fed infants;
- infants receiving ready-to-feed formula; and
- infants receiving formula mixed with water that doesn't contain fluoride (such as bottled water).

See the chart on the previous page for the American Dental Association and the American Academy of Pediatric Dentistry's recommended supplemental fluoride dosage schedule.

Keep in mind that too much fluoride (in amounts over 2 ppm), can change the color and shape of teeth. If you find that your water has too much fluoride, discuss this with your dentist.

▼

The Food Factor

Which is better for teeth—potato chips or raisins? Neither, really. Potato chips are starchy, which can promote tooth decay as much as or more than some sticky, sugary foods that stay on teeth longer. Remember, fermentable carbohydrates are foods that can be broken down by bacteria in the mouth. Both simple sugars (such as sucrose, glucose, and fructose) and cooked starches (found in baked goods, breads, and pastas) are fermentable. The fermenting of carbohydrates starts the process of tooth decay. Other factors contributing to tooth decay are:

Beware of Baby-Bottle Tooth Decay

Such decay is caused by a baby going to sleep with a bottle filled with any carbohydrate-containing liquids, including breast milk, formula, milk, juice, and soda. Avoid putting your baby in bed with a bottle or letting your baby fall asleep with a bottle in his mouth!

- how often teeth are exposed to fermentable carbohydrates;
- how long these foods stay in the mouth;
- how much food sticks to teeth;
- the amount of time between eating and brushing (within a half hour of eating is best);
- eating sugary foods alone (such as between meals) or with a meal; and
- eating a food at night, when saliva that would wash away the sugar is in short supply.

▼

Protective Foods

Some foods show promise of actually protecting teeth from decay. Cheese, both natural and processed, and milk appear to protect teeth.[2] In fact, in a recent study, milk seemed most protective in children who ate the most sugar.[3] It is thought that milk and cheese help prevent cavities in two ways: by affecting the decaying process and by helping to add minerals to the enamel of softened teeth.

▼

Healthy Teeth in a Nutshell

Use these tips to decrease your child's risk of cavities:

- Make sure your children have a source of fluoride, either through drinking water or supplements.
- Have your children brush their teeth, preferably after every meal but especially at night.
- Schedule dental checkups and cleaning for your children twice a year, beginning by age two years. (Some dentists like to wait until age three.)
- Include tooth-friendly snacks when kids cannot brush afterward. (See list at right.)
- When eating out or unable to brush for other reasons, follow a meal or snack with milk, cheese, or sugar-free chewing gum to help prevent cavities. The sugar-free gums that seem to prevent plaque formation are those containing zylitol, sorbitol, saccharin, aspartame (sugar replacers), or Chlorhexidine.[4]
- Limit the amount and frequency of sweetened beverages and other plaque- and cavity-promoting foods.
- Make sure to provide a healthy, balanced diet to ensure strong teeth and gums.

▼

Tooth-Friendly Snacks

The list below is modified from *Nutrition in Infancy and Childhood,* 6th edition, by Cristine M. Trahms and Peggy L. Pipes.

Protective Foods:
- Carrots
- Cheese, both natural and processed
- Hard-boiled eggs
- Milk
- Nuts and seeds
- Peanut butter
- Plain or sugar-free yogurt
- Tuna
- Turkey and other protein foods

Other Tooth-Friendly Snacks:
- Avocado
- Bell peppers
- Broccoli
- Cabbage
- Cauliflower
- Celery
- Cucumber
- Jicama
- Radishes
- Tomatoes
- Tomato or vegetable juices

Snacks That Contain the Most Fermentable Carbohydrate:

Remember, such carbohydrates can lead to cavities!
• Bagel
• English muffin
• Fruits (fresh, unsweetened and sweetened)
• Popcorn
• Unsweetened fruit juices
• Whole-grain and white breads and crackers

The Most Unfriendly Snacks:

Make sure to brush shortly after eating.
• Bread
• Candy bars, hard candies
• Cookies
• Crackers
• Doughnuts
• Jelly beans, raisins, gummy bears, and other sticky sweets
• Potato chips
• Sugar-rich foods (brownies, bars, frosted cupcakes, and so on)
• Sweet drinks

The Best Snacks:

These are snacks that include a protective food.
• Peanut butter on graham crackers
• Natural or processed cheese and whole-grain crackers
• Yogurt with fruit
• Milk with popcorn
• Turkey sandwich

Chatting with Clark Gregor, D.D.S.

Q: What do you see as the main problem with children's dental health?

A: **At 1–2 years:** I still see baby-bottle cavities. These cavities are caused by allowing a baby to go to sleep with a bottle that contains formula, juice, or milk. It is best to not let your child sleep with a bottle; if a parent does allow a bottle when falling asleep, the bottle should be filled with water only.

At 3–5 years: During these years, I see cavities on the chewing surfaces of teeth. While food selection and systemic fluoride are helpful here, the most important cavity prevention is good hygiene. Cavities in baby teeth must be addressed early. If not treated, these cavities can lead to toothaches, abscesses, and premature tooth loss. Should baby teeth be lost prematurely, it is important to see a dentist right away. The dentist's treatment will help maintain proper spacing in the child's developing mouth. This will limit serious malocclusions (misalignments of top and bottom teeth) and help decrease the need for additional procedures, such as braces, in the future.

At 6–10 years: Around age six, a child's first permanent molars will erupt into the mouth. These teeth are more likely to develop cavities than any other teeth. For this reason, a sealant should be placed on these teeth soon after they erupt. A sealant is a plastic-like material that covers the grooves on the chewing surface of a tooth. When a sealant is in place, cavities cannot form on that part of the tooth. Sealants can last for years. Many dentists also place sealants on baby teeth. This practice is a good idea if the baby teeth have deep grooves or if the child is cavity prone.

Q: When should you take your child for his first dental visit?

A: At about age two. Some dentists do not want to see children for their first visit until age three. This varies among practitioners. The most important factor is to make the child feel good about going to a dentist. This is best accomplished by taking the child in before any problems develop.

The first time I see a child, I make sure it is a positive experience—one that could be called a "get-to-know-the-dentist" visit. I limit this visit to a quick and easy exam. I never perform any procedures unless an emergency situation exists. I chart the patient's mouth and look for any developmental deformities. I then reschedule the patient for a cleaning and X-rays. This way, the first visit is very short and very positive. By using this approach, we are helping to eliminate fear of the dentist.

If problems are encountered, you will have to take the child to see a dentist sooner. For example, a visit is needed if a parent notices red or bleeding gums or bumps on the child's gums. Another example is if the child has a fall or otherwise experiences trauma to the mouth or chin.

Almost all children fall when they first pull themselves up to attempt to walk or stand. It is common for a child to fall forward and bump his chin, lip, or teeth on a coffee table or the floor. If this happens and the parent feels that the child may have damaged soft or hard tissues, it's time to take the child for an emergency visit to the dentist. Most general dentists will see children for such an emergency. If your child has a traumatic injury, call your family dentist. He or she will either see the child or refer you to a pediatric dentist.

Q: When should parents start brushing their children's teeth?

A: Since tooth decay knows no age limits, oral hygiene has to start when the first tooth erupts into the mouth. For most children this is around six months of age. While it's possible to brush a baby's first teeth, I recommend cleaning these teeth by wiping the teeth with a piece of clean, moist gauze. This needs to be done twice a day. Start using a toothbrush as soon as a child can hold his mouth open for a parent.

Q: How about flossing?

A: A child's teeth need to be flossed as soon as he has two or more teeth that touch. Flossing is done to prevent cavities and gum disease where a toothbrush cannot reach. Since a toothbrush can't fit between teeth that touch or under gums, these areas must be cleaned with floss. The parent has to be the one to floss the child's teeth until the child is old enough to do this for himself (usually not until age nine or ten).

Floss a child's teeth after brushing just before bed. Wrap the floss around the middle fingers of each hand and use your index fingers to gently work it between the touching teeth. The parent must be extra gentle with dental floss so as not to cause pain to a child's sensitive gums. Keep the floss from touching the child's gums until you have been flossing for a few weeks. When both child and parent are comfortable with flossing, begin gliding the floss down so that it just slides under the child's gums.

Q: When do you think children are old enough to brush on their own?

A: At first only the parent brushes. Then, as the child matures, he usually wants to start brushing on his own. At this point it is important to allow the child to have an active role in his health care. It's time to let the child start to brush; then the parent will finish by quickly going over each tooth surface once.

Later, when the child reaches the age of five or six, the parent can allow him one brushing session alone per day while the parent continues to help with the other brushing session. At this point I recommend that after breakfast the parent place the toothpaste on the child's brush and watch as the child brushes, making sure that he takes adequate time to brush each tooth surface. Then, before bed, the parent can allow the child to start brushing, but continue to help the child finish, thus making sure that all of the plaque is off the child's teeth before bed.

By the time a child reaches age eight or nine

years, he should be brushing on his own. The parent should still watch him from time to time, making sure the child is taking enough time to clean each individual tooth surface.

Q: Should a child start using fluoride-containing toothpaste as soon as he starts brushing? If not, when?

A: While it is important for a child to have enough systemic fluoride from the time he is six months old, it is just as important to make sure he is not ingesting too much. To avoid getting too much fluoride, a child should use non-fluoridated toothpaste until he is old enough to swish and spit without swallowing. There are many non-fluoridated children's toothpastes on the market. If none of these are available, the parent may use fluoridated toothpaste, but only use a very small amount and never allow the young child to dispense the toothpaste.

A parent can clean a young child's teeth equally well by brushing with water alone. However, to make the brushing experience more fun for your child, you may want to add a trace of toothpaste or dip the toothbrush in a mild, good-tasting mouthwash.

Once the child is old enough to swish and spit without swallowing, you should start using fluoridated toothpaste to expose the child to a topical fluoride source. The child should brush at least twice a day, after breakfast and before bed. The child should brush for a longer period than an adult: about two minutes. Immediately after brushing, the child should swish and spit twice without swallowing any toothpaste.

Q: What if a child consumes too much fluoride?

A: It is important for all children to get an adequate amount of fluoride in their diet so that they develop cavity-resistant teeth. But that fluoride should come from their drinking water or from fluoride supplements, so that just the right amount of fluoride is ingested. If a child ingests too much fluoride, he can develop very dark and malformed teeth. This is why no child should ever swallow fluoridated toothpaste.

Have your water analyzed for fluoride and take these findings to your dentist to determine if your child needs supplements. Also, it's important to let your dentist know if your child is drinking bottled water, soda, and juices that were made using another water source. If your child drinks beverages that were prepared at another location, contact the bottler to obtain the level of fluoride.

Q: Do you see any dietary trends in the U.S. that are harmful to our children's teeth?

A: One distressing trend is that soda and other sweet drinks are replacing water and milk as the drinks of choice. First, these new beverages bathe teeth in fermentable sugar. Second, they are replacing water (a source of fluoride) and milk (a source of calcium necessary for strong bones and teeth). Sodas and sweetened drinks should not have a regular place in a child's diet.

Q: Should kids avoid sweets?

A: Sweets between meals can often have a negative effect in the mouth. Remember

---

Tips for Weaning from a Pacifier

- First, avoid depending on the pacifier too much. While it may comfort your child the first few months, try to help him find a way to comfort himself without it.

- If your child is hooked on the pacifier, try to reduce the times you allow him to have it—for example, only at sleep times.

---

that many foods contain fermentable carbohydrate in the form of sugar or starch. Children usually do not brush after eating snacks, and this can lead to plaque formation. While it is not necessary to avoid sweets altogether, it is best to limit sugar intake between meals. If your child does sometimes eat sweets between meals, make sure he brushes after eating, or at least have him swish with water for thirty seconds. While this is not as effective as brushing and flossing, it will help remove some of the sugar deposits from teeth.

Q: I've heard that sugar-free gums may help prevent cavities if chewed between meals. What do you think?

A: Sugarless gum is a fine idea between meals. It helps stimulate increased saliva production, which can serve to clean the teeth and buffer acids caused by plaque. The best sugarless gum for fighting plaque contains xylitol as a sweetener. Xylitol gum can help reduce caries rates more than any other sugar-free gum.

Q: Dr. Gregor, what else should parents know about their child's dental development?

A: Pacifiers and thumb sucking can cause developmental problems for a child's bones. I recommend throwing away all pacifiers at age eighteen months. You will most likely have one or two nights of crying, but this is a small price to pay to improve the way your child's jaws develop.

Almost all children are thumb suckers at some time. This is usually self-limiting when children realize that other children their age do not suck their thumbs. Most children stop around age four when preschool starts—again due to peer pressure. If it continues past age five, consult your dentist. If this is not an area he or she is comfortable dealing with, you may be referred to a pediatric dentist.

Another important consideration is that many diseases can appear in the mouth and jaws in childhood. While it is true that most of these conditions are rare, it is also true that some can have devastating consequences. The best way to catch any problems is to see your dentist regularly.

Food Safety

Though the food supply in the United States is one of the safest in the world, it's not perfect. As consumers, we must take responsibility to help ensure safe food for our families. And when you have children, it is especially important to consider the particular food safety risks for children:

- The younger the child, the less developed is her immune system and the more she may react to food-borne bacteria and viruses.
- Children eat more calories of food per pound of body weight than do adults. Children also eat fewer types of food in greater volume; thus, the risk of dietary exposure to pesticides is greater.
- Because of their low body weight and periods of rapid growth, children are more sensitive to chemicals in the environment, such as lead and endocrine disruptors.

Food Safety in a Nutshell:

- Follow the food safety tips in this chapter. Especially important are cooking perishable foods like meat to the proper internal temperature and storing food at the proper temperature.
- Check to see if your home is likely to have lead. Lead is often found in the pipes and soldering of older homes, lead-based paint, and imported ceramic ware.
- Make sure your child eats a variety of foods with plenty of fruits and vegetables. This is vital.
- These foods appear to contribute the highest insecticide exposure for children: apples, pears, peaches,

grapes, oranges, peas, green beans, potatoes, tomatoes. Buy organic, if possible.[1]

• Be careful with the use of plastics when cooking and storing; some chemicals in plastics can seep into food. Make sure containers you use for the microwave are microwave safe. Use wax paper or paper towels to cover food in the microwave. Unless labeled "polyethylene," avoid using Styrofoam or plastic wrap (especially wrap containing PVC, or polyvinyl chloride) to store or cover high-fat foods.

▼

Pesticides

The very thought of pesticides in your children's food may make you shudder. In 1997, several brands of baby foods were found to have detectable pesticides, though the levels were below government standards. Until recently, government standards were the problem; the standards were the same for infants and adults. Now, however, these standards are in the process of being changed. In addition, The Gerber Company has taken the initiative to protect babies from pesticides. It has banned most organophosphates and other pesticides from nearly all of its products.

A few years earlier, in 1993, the National Academy of Sciences released an important report called "Pesticides in the Diets of Infants and Children." The report concluded that the federal government should change some of its scientific and regulatory procedures to give infants and children greater

protection from possible adverse health effects of pesticides in their diets.

Children may be more or less sensitive to pesticides than adults, depending on the pesticide to which they are exposed. Children consume more calories of food per unit of body weight and much more of certain foods, especially processed foods, than do adults. Unfortunately, information on pesticide residues and the effects of processing on residue concentrations is inadequate for foods eaten by infants and children.

Based on the recommendations from the National Academy of Sciences, a new bill, called the Food Quality Protection Act, was signed into law in 1996. This bill changed how pesticides in food are regulated. Based on the new law, all exposures to pesticides must be shown to be safe for infants and children, with a clear consideration of the sensitivity of young children to these chemicals. In addition, when determining a safe level for pesticide in food, the Environmental Protection Agency (EPA) must explicitly account for all infant and child exposures to other pesticides and toxic chemicals that share a common toxic mechanism (are toxic in the same way). The law allows for only very narrow exceptions.

Pesticides are an unfortunate reality in our society. The good news is that under the new law, the EPA will be examining tolerances for all pesticides within ten years. The bad news is by the time they are finished, our children will probably be adolescents or adults. Until the new law makes its impact on pesticides in our food, here are some things your family can do:

1. *Buy a wide variety of fruits and vegetables.* This will help limit exposure to residues on specific types of produce. DO NOT reduce your family's fruit and vegetable intake for fear of pesticides! The risk of chronic disease from not eating enough produce is much greater than the risk of substantial pesticide residues on your food.

2. *Wash or peel produce before eating it.* Peeling apples, peaches, and pears in particular can drastically reduce pesticide residues. Wash produce well under running water, scrubbing well when the skin will be eaten. Discard the outer leaves of lettuce and cabbage. Several products available on the market are designed to better clean the dirt and pesticides from foods. (One such product is FIT, from Proctor and Gamble.)

3. *Grow your own fruits and vegetables.* This will not only shield your family from pesticides (that is, if you don't use any), it will give your family the freshest food and probably the most nutrient-rich food available. Gardening is also a great family activity and offers an opportunity to discuss nutrition with your kids.

4. *Buy organic produce and processed foods made from organic ingredients.* It is hoped the National Organic Program will go into effect soon, making it possible to buy foods that you can know for sure are organic.

5. *Buy foods in season.* Buying cantaloupe in the middle of January, for example, means that the cantaloupe must have been shipped from somewhere warmer, usually Mexico or South America. The long trip to northern markets usually means more pesticides will be applied to keep the product bug-free until it makes it to local groceries. You can also cut down on pesticides by buying locally grown foods from a farmer's market.

6. *Buy organic baby food.* At least two national brands of organic baby food are available: Earth's Best and Gerber Tender Harvest. Or make your own using organic and/or home-grown produce.

7. *Keep in mind that produce is not the only food that contains pesticide residues.* The fat of meat, fish, and poultry can also contain pesticide residues and other chemicals . . . one more reason not to eat the fat!

8. *Know which foods contain more pesticides.* (See the chart on the next page.)

High-Risk Foods for Kids

As we've seen, kids tend to eat the same small number of foods. In practice, this can cause a larger amount of pesticides in the diet, even if the food eaten is not the most contaminated. For example, children under the age of one eat apples, apple juice, peaches, and pears in amounts that are five to fifteen times the national average intake per pound of body weight. Non-citrus juices account for 6 percent of total calorie intake of three-to-five-year-olds, which is about three times the average intake.[2]

Nine Most-Contaminated Foods Having High Intake by Children

The items below are listed in descending order from food with most contamination to food with least contamination.

Food:	Alternatives with fewer pesticides, similar nutrients:
Apples	Apple juice or almost any other fruit (except those listed at left). Note: New Zealand apples have fewer pesticides than U.S.-grown apples.
Pears	Bananas, kiwi, or almost any other fruit (except those listed at left)
Peaches	Canned peaches or nectarines, tangerines, oranges, watermelon, U.S.-grown cantaloupe
Grapes	Blueberries, bananas, melon, or almost any other fruit (except those listed at left). Note: Grapes from Chile have highest pesticide concentration; those from Mexico and South Africa have less.
Oranges	U.S. cantaloupe, watermelon, blueberries, raspberries
Peas	Dried beans, broccoli, lettuce
Green beans	Dried beans, sugar snap peas, asparagus. *Note:* Canned and frozen have more pesticide than fresh.
Potatoes	Corn, broccoli, cabbage
Tomatoes	Melon, cabbage, kiwi, mango

Consumers Union, the nonprofit organization that publishes *Consumer Reports Magazine,* has recently done an extensive study of government pesticide residue data. It has looked specifically at children's eating patterns (the amount and types of foods kids usually eat) to determine which foods contribute the most pesticides to an average kid's diet.

Consumers Union has identified nine high-intake foods of kids that are most likely to contribute to pesticide exposure in children. They are listed above (in descending order of amount of pesticide) along with food alternatives with fewer pesticides and similar nutrients. Remember, you don't necessarily need to eliminate the nine offenders from your child's menu; just reduce the pesticide residues by peeling or washing with a very diluted soap solution.[3]

Not All Bad News

There are some healthy foods that also have low amounts of pesticide residues. (See chart at right.) Consumers Union found that carrots, corn, bananas, milk, and meats—all favorites with children—are less likely to contain residues from pesticides. Other foods rated low on the pesticide scale were frozen canned U.S. orange juice and U.S. broccoli and canned peaches. Not quite as low, but still relatively "clean," were frozen and canned sweet peas, U.S. and imported apple juice, frozen winter squash from Mexico, tomatoes from Canada, Brazilian orange juice, and U.S. wheat.

❓ Questions You May Have

Q: What about foods that adults eat?

A: When Consumers Union looked simply at amount and types of pesticides used, these were the worst: fresh peaches (both domestic and imported); frozen and fresh winter squash grown in the U.S.; domestic and imported apples, grapes, spinach, and pears; and U.S.-grown green beans. Just because a food is grown in the U.S. doesn't make it necessarily better. Eleven out of twelve foods were U.S.-grown.

Q: Do processed foods have less pesticide than fresh?

A: Generally, yes. Toxicity scores for apple juice, orange juice, and canned peaches are far lower than for the fresh fruits. Canned spinach and canned or frozen corn and canned or frozen peas also have low toxicity scores. But frozen green beans and frozen winter squash each had toxicity scores higher than those for the corresponding fresh crops.[4]

Q: Organic foods are expensive; is buying them the only way I can lower our exposure to pesticides?

A: No. Washing, peeling, and removing outer leaves greatly reduces pesticide residues. Often, so does buying locally grown foods. Another sometimes more cost-effective option is produce labeled "No Detectable Residue," or NDR. These foods

---

Twelve Least-Contaminated Foods

Listed in ascending order from food with least contamination.

Avocado

Corn

Onions

Sweet potatoes

Cauliflower

Brussels sprouts

U.S. grapes

Bananas

Plums

Green onions

Watermelon

Broccoli

Source: Reprinted with Permission, Environmental Working Group.

---

are not organic, but are grown in such a way that no residues are left.

▼

Food-Borne Illness

According to government estimates, as many as 9,000 Americans—mostly the very young and the elderly—die each year due to a food-related illness and millions more are sickened. Is your kitchen safe from bacteria and viruses? What you can't see can hurt you, so prevention is the key to keeping away food-borne illnesses, such as salmonella, E. coli, and others. Answer the Food Safety Quiz on the next page to find out how your kitchen rates.

Food Safety Quiz

Answer yes or no to the following questions. Give yourself one point for each yes.

Do You . . .

1. Buy refrigerated and frozen food last at the grocery store, proceed home immediately, and put them away first?

2. Thaw frozen meats in the refrigerator or microwave, not on the counter?

3. Make sure dairy or protein foods are not out of the refrigerator for more than thirty minutes?

4. Keep the refrigerator set at 40°F and keep hot foods above 140°F?

5. Use a separate cutting board for raw meat, seafood, and poultry?

6. Wash children's hands with soap and warm water before eating?

7. Wash your own hands after every visit to the bathroom, after helping a child in the bathroom, after changing a diaper, and after blowing a child's or your nose?

8. Feed baby food out of a bowl, not directly out of the jar?

9. Discard formula after forty-eight hours?

10. Use a food thermometer to make sure meat, fish, and poultry are cooked to the correct temperature?

11. Use paper towels to wipe up the juice from raw seafood, poultry, and meat?

12. Regularly wash the sponges or cloths you use to clean counters?

How Did You Do?

10–12   Excellent: very clean kitchen

6–9   Good: could be a bit cleaner

<6   Fair: could be a lot cleaner

Many food-borne illnesses are due to human influences. When you have children, good food-safety habits become even more critical because children's immune systems are weaker and more likely to be strongly affected by food poisoning. While adults may just get a little sick with food poisoning, children can get fatally ill. The U.S. Department of Agriculture estimates that anywhere from 350 thousand to 2.5 million Americans are taken ill (and 350 to 2,500 die) every year after eating salmonella-contaminated poultry and meat (about 1 percent of all cattle is also infected).

The estimates are so broad because most food-poisoning cases are never reported to health authorities. "For every one we hear about, twenty to one hundred go unreported," says Tom Gomez, a USDA epidemiologist at the Centers for Disease Control (CDC) in Atlanta. Follow the advice below to keep your family safe.

Buying and Storing Food

Hot or Cold Is How to Hold

- Take control of your food's safety the moment you pick it up at the grocery store. Pick up the perishable cold and frozen foods right before you check out to decrease the time those foods are kept at room temperature.
- If seafood, meat, or poultry will be used within two days, store it in the coldest part of the refrigerator (usually under the freezer compartment or in a meat keeper). Otherwise, freeze it.
- Keep your refrigerator at 40°F or below and your freezer at 0°F. Buy a refrigerator/freezer thermometer and monitor the temperatures regularly.
- Clean the inside of your refrigerator regularly with a weak bleach solution. (See sidebar on page 93.)
- Don't get sick; cool it quick! Refrigerate cooked food within two hours (one hour in hot weather). When refrigerating large batches of leftovers, divide them into small, flat containers so they will cool quickly. For thick foods, such as stews and hot puddings, limit depth of the container to two inches.
- Keep leftovers only about three days.
- If you buy live shellfish, such as lobster, crab, oysters, clams, and mussels, discard any that die in storage or that have cracked or broken shells.
- Remember: When in doubt, throw it out!

When in Doubt, Throw It Out!

Safe refrigerator and freezer storage time limits are given for many common foods in the table on pages 88–89. But what about something you totally forgot about and may have kept for too long?

- Danger! Never taste food that looks or smells strange to see if you can still use it. Just discard it.
- Is it moldy? The mold you see is only the tip of the iceberg. The poisons that molds can form are found under the surface of the food. You can sometimes save hard cheese, salamis, and firm fruits and vegetables by cutting the mold out; make sure to remove a large area around the moldy part. However, most moldy food should be discarded.

Preparing Food

- Wash hands thoroughly with hot, soapy water before and after handling any raw food.
- Thaw frozen seafood, meat, and poultry in the refrigerator. Beware of special thawing trays; their advertising material may imply it is safe to keep food at room temperature for extended periods of time, but it isn't! In fact, the USDA, FDA, and Federal Trade Commission have issued a Consumer Alert in regard to using thawing trays.[5]
- Make it a law: use the fridge to thaw! To maintain food quality, thaw food

How Long Does It Keep?		
Product	**Refrigerator (40°F)**	**Freezer (0°F)**
Eggs		
Fresh, in shell	3 weeks	Don't freeze
Hard-cooked	1 week	Don't freeze well
Raw yolks, whites	2–4 days	1 year
Cooked Food (general)		
Commercial brand vacuum-packed dinners with USDA seal	2 weeks, unopened	Don't freeze well
Ham, canned (label says "keep refrigerated")	6–9 months	Don't freeze
Ham, fully cooked		
whole	7 days	1–2 months
half	3–5 days	1–2 months
slices	3–4 days	1–2 months
Lunch meats		
opened	3–5 days	In freezer wrap,
unopened	2 weeks	1–2 months
Pre-stuffed pork and lamb chops, chicken breasts	1 day	Don't freeze well
Soups and stews, vegetable or meat	3–4 days	2–3 months
Store-cooked convenience meals	1–2 days	Don't freeze well
Store-prepared (or homemade) egg, chicken, tuna, ham, macaroni salads	3–5 days	Don't freeze well
TV dinners, frozen casseroles	Keep frozen until ready to serve	3–4 months
Bacon and Sausage		
Bacon	7 days	1 month
Hard sausage, pepperoni, jerky sticks	2–3 weeks	1–2 months
Sausage, raw, from pork, beef, turkey	1–2 days	1–2 months
Smoked breakfast links, patties	7 days	1–2 months

How Long Does It Keep?

Product	Refrigerator (40°F)	Freezer (0°F)
Fresh Meats		
Chops, lamb	3–5 days	6–9 months
Chops, pork	3–5 days	4–6 months
Ground turkey, veal, pork, lamb (and mixtures)	1–2 days	3–4 months
Hamburger and stew meats	1–2 days	3–4 months
Hot dogs		
opened package	1 week	
unopened package	2 weeks	
Roasts, beef	3–5 days	6–12 months
Roasts, lamb	3–5 days	6–9 months
Roasts, pork and veal	3–5 days	4–6 months
Steaks, beef	3–5 days	6–12 months
Variety meats (tongue, brain, kidneys, liver, heart, chitterlings)	1-2 days	3–4 months
Fresh Poultry		
Chicken or turkey		
whole	1–2 days	1 year
pieces	1–2 days	9 months
Cooked Meat/Poultry Leftovers		
Chicken nuggets, patties	1–2 days	1–3 months
Cooked meat and meat dishes	3–4 days	2–3 months
Cooked poultry dishes	3–4 days	4–6 months
Fried chicken	3–4 days	4 months
Gravy and meat broth	1–2 days	2–3 months
Pieces covered with broth, gravy	1–2 days	6 months
Pieces, plain	3–4 days	4 months
Other		
Mayonnaise, commercial (refrigerate after opening)	2 months	Don't freeze

Source: Partnership for Food Safety Education.

overnight in the refrigerator. To thaw food more quickly, remove from original container, place in a zip-lock bag, and immerse in cold water, changing the water every half-hour. Frozen food thaws at the rate of about one pound per half-hour.
- Defrost food in the microwave only if it will be cooked immediately.
- Follow these tips for safe microwave defrosting:
  - Turn and rotate food or stir to ensure even defrosting.
  - Separate pieces of meat and poultry as soon as they are soft enough.
  - Cover foods with wax paper while defrosting to promote even heat distribution.
- Marinate food in the refrigerator, not on the counter. Discard the marinade after use because it contains raw juices, which may harbor bacteria. If you want to use the marinade as a dip or sauce, reserve a portion before adding raw food, or bring the marinade to a boil.
- Watch that plate—don't cross-contaminate! Do not allow cooked food to come in contact with raw products. Use separate cutting boards and utensils or wash items in the dishwasher or in hot soapy water between use. (See Cutting Board Safety, page 94.)

Cooking Temperatures

Warning: If meat and poultry are mishandled when raw, they may not be safe to eat even after proper cooking.

Ground beef must be cooked to an internal temperature of 160°F. The U.S. Department of Agriculture says that using a meat thermometer is crucial; research results indicate that some ground meat may prematurely brown before a safe internal temperature has been reached. On the other hand, research findings also show that some ground meat patties cooked to 160°F or above may remain pink inside for a number of reasons; thus the color of meat alone is not considered a reliable indicator of ground beef safety. If eating out, order your ground beef to be cooked well-done.

Microwave Cooking

Where would we be without our microwaves for thawing and cooking food? If you use a microwave, you should know some of its quirks:
- Never partially cook food in the microwave unless you plan to cook it fully immediately. Partial cooking can allow harmful bacteria to grow. Be careful when thawing meat, because it is easy for it to start cooking in places.

- When microwaving meats of unequal sizes, place thick pieces around outside of dish and thin pieces in the center.
- To make sure food cooks or thaws evenly, cover food with a glass or plastic cover or wax paper, stir or turn over food midway through cooking, and rotate dish manually if your microwave does not have a rotating plate. When defrosting separate pieces of food, such as chicken or steak, stop as soon as they are soft enough.
- When reheating leftovers, cook until steaming hot.
- Recipes for the microwave usually recommend "standing" times. It is important to follow these recommendations, because the food continues to cook during the standing time. After the standing time is completed, check the food in several spots with a meat thermometer to be sure the product has reached the proper temperature.

Cooking Seafood

Some fish and shellfish are small, and it may be difficult to test their temperature. Use the following tips to make sure seafood is done:

- For fish, slip the point of a sharp knife into the flesh and pull aside. The fish should be white and starting to flake. Let fish stand three to four minutes to finish cooking after microwaving.
- For shrimp, lobster, and scallops, check color. Shrimp and lobster turn red, and

---

Safe Internal Temperatures

- Whole poultry and thighs: 180°F (82°C)
- Poultry breasts: 170°F (77°C)
- Ground chicken or turkey: 165°F (74°C)
- Reheated ground beef patties and ground beef casseroles: 165°F (74°C)
- Pork: 160°F (71°C)
- Most seafood: 145°F (74°C) for fifteen seconds

---

their flesh becomes pearly opaque. Scallops turn milky white or opaque and firm.
- For clams, mussels, and oysters, watch for the point at which their shells open. That means they're done. Throw out those that stay closed, because they were dead before cooking.

Eggs

- Cook eggs thoroughly until both the yolk and white are firm, not runny; scramble until no liquid egg is visible.
- Thoroughly cook pasta dishes and stuffings that contain eggs.
- Use cooking-based recipes for hollandaise and similar sauces.
- Do not eat raw eggs or serve food with raw eggs in it. (Gone are the days of eating cookie dough!)
- Cook egg dishes or casseroles to an internal temperature of 160°F.

Safe Cooking with Slow Cookers

- Keep everything clean. Wash hands before and throughout food preparation. Begin with a clean cooker, clean utensils, clean cutting boards, and a clean work area.
- Keep perishable foods refrigerated until preparation time. The slow cooker may take several hours to reach a safe, bacteria-killing temperature. Constant refrigeration assures that bacteria, which multiply rapidly at room temperature, won't get a head start during the first few hours of cooking. Animal foods should be in the 40°–140°F danger zone for no more than two hours.
- Completely thaw meat and poultry and cut into small pieces to ensure thorough cooking. Do not use the slow cooker for large pieces, like a roast or whole chicken, because the food will cook so slowly it could remain in the bacterial danger zone too long.
- Fill the slow cooker no more than two-thirds full. If it's filled beyond this point, the heat may not penetrate all parts of the food.
- Preheat the cooker and add hot liquids if possible. Set the cooker on the highest setting for the first hour of cooking time; then choose the setting required by the recipe.

- Do not warm cooked foods or reheat leftovers in the slow cooker. Repeated handling can introduce bacteria to cooked foods, and the slow cooker cannot get hot fast enough to keep these bacteria from multiplying. If serving cooked food for a party or buffet, bring the food to a boil on the stove, then use the slow cooker to keep it piping hot.
- Cover the meat or poultry pieces with liquid. Liquids, in addition to keeping meats and poultry moist and tender, are good conductors of heat.
- Keep the lid in place. Remove the lid only as often as is necessary to stir the food or check for doneness. Significant amounts of heat are lost each time the cooker is uncovered.

Source: Modified from Slow Cooker Safety Fact Sheet, developed by Susan Brewer, Extension Specialist, Food and Nutrition, with the University of Illinois Cooperative Extension Service.

Serving Temperatures

- Don't keep cooked food out of the refrigerator for more than two hours.
- If you have to keep food out for an extended period, make sure to keep hot foods hot at 140°F (60°C) or higher, and cold foods cold at 41°F (5°C) or lower.

▼

Cleaning

Use disposable paper towels or napkins to wipe off the juice from raw poultry, seafood, beef, and pork. Then clean the surface with an antibacterial cleaner or a weak bleach solution (see sidebar).

Make sure that whatever you use to clean with is clean. What is the dirtiest object in your house? Probably the sponge or dishcloth you use to clean your kitchen. A study at the University of Phoenix at Tuscon showed that two-thirds of the 1,000 kitchen sponges tested across America contained bacteria, such as *Salmonella, E. coli, Campylobacter, Clostridium perfringens,* and *Staphylococcus,* that are major causes of food-borne illness. People who like their kitchens spick-and-span may actually be making the problem worse by spreading the bacteria present in a used sponge all over their kitchen!

Another study at the University of Phoenix found the sink and sponge to be the spots with the largest amount of bacteria. Chuck Gerba found that in some cases a flushed toilet had less bacteria than a kitchen sink.[6]

? Questions You May Have

Q: What about antibacterial sponges?

A: Research has shown that the antibacterial product contained in these sponges reduced bacteria *in the sponge* by 99.9 percent. Dr.

The Best Cleaning Solutions

If you want to do a good job cleaning your house, you need a cleaning solution that is antibacterial, right? Well, it's not that clear anymore that a germ-killing soap is what we need for hands, dishes, and counter-tops. Stuart Levy, M.D., of Tufts University Center for Adaptation Genetics and Drug Resistance suggests that antimicrobial products can contribute to antibiotic resistance. In other words, instead of killing the germs on your countertop, that new antibacterial spray may just do enough damage to the germ for it to mutate to become resistant to antibacterial products. It may be better to save the antimicrobial products for a time when you really need them—for example, when someone who is vulnerable to disease is coming to visit.[a]

The best solution for disinfecting may be the simplest and cheapest of all—that is, one made from bleach. Keep bleach solution in a clearly marked, child-proof spray bottle. The Centers for Disease Control recommend the following recipes for disinfecting solutions:

- Bleach disinfecting solution: 1 tablespoon bleach per 1 quart cool water (for use in bathrooms, diapering areas, and so on)

- Weaker bleach disinfecting solution: 1 tablespoon bleach per 1 gallon cool water (1 teaspoon per quart of cool water) (for use on toys, cutting boards, eating utensils, and so on)

Source: The ABC's of Safe and Healthy Child Care, CDC.

[a]Levy, S.B. Antimicrobial resistance:bacteria on the defense, British Medical Journal, 1998; 317: 612-613 (5 September) (Tufts University Health and Nutrition Letter, October 98, 16:8(1-5).

Michael Doyle, who served on the EPA committee that reviewed the sponge, says, "People may have a false sense of security that if they use the antibacterial sponge, it will kill microorganisms it comes in contact with. It doesn't."

Q: *What about regular sponges? Are there effective ways to clean them?*

A: Microwaving sponges and putting them in the dishwasher have been recommended in the past. According to Michael Doyle, Ph.D., "If you heat a wet sponge in the microwave for sixty seconds, that should kill most bacteria present. But over time, your sponge deteriorates. The dishwasher has to get to 160 degrees to adequately sanitize a sponge, and I wouldn't bet on it. If you want to be safe, just don't use a sponge to wipe up the juices from raw meat and poultry—use paper towels."[7] If you use sponges for other kitchen cleaning, replace them often (about once a week). Sanitize sponges that must be kept longer by soaking them overnight in a bleach-and-water solution (one teaspoon chlorine bleach to one quart water).

▼

Cutting Board Safety

The Meat and Poultry Hotline recommends that consumers use plastic or glass surfaces for cutting raw meat and poultry. However, wooden cutting boards used exclusively for raw meat and poultry are acceptable. Whichever you use, be sure to use a different board for cutting other foods, such as produce and bread, and practice the following safety measures:

Food Safety Resources

If you want to keep up with hot topics in food safety or if you have questions, the following resources can help:

- U.S. Department of Agriculture Food Safety and Inspection Service (FSIS) http://www.usda.gov/agency/fsis/home page.htm

- Hot Topics in Food Safety from the North Carolina Extension Service http://www.ces.ncsu.edu/depts/food-sci/agentinfo/hot/index.html#top

- Meat and Poultry Hot Line: 800-535-4555

- Wash cutting boards with hot water, soap, and a scrub brush to remove food particles.
- Sanitize both wooden and plastic cutting boards by either running them through an automatic dishwasher or cleaning them with a solution of one teaspoon liquid chlorine bleach per quart of water. Flood the surface of the board with the bleach solution and allow it to stand for several minutes, then rinse and air dry or pat dry with fresh paper towels. You may want to keep a spray bottle filled with the mixture on hand to sanitize counters and toys that kids put in their mouth. (Make sure to label it!)
- Replace battered cutting boards. Even plastic boards wear out over time. Once cutting boards become excessively worn or develop hard-to-clean grooves, they should be discarded.[8]

▼
Safe Grilling

Ah, summer. Picnics at the beach, the smell of burgers on the barbecue. However, just when you think life couldn't get any better, it could get a lot worse for you and your family. Follow these tips to ensure that your summer fun won't be ruined by a food-borne illness:

- Completely thaw meat or poultry before grilling to ensure even and thorough cooking.
- Marinate meat, fish, or poultry in the refrigerator. Do not use the leftover marinade unless it is boiled first to destroy any bacteria.
- Do not precook meat unless you plan to grill immediately. For some foods, such as chicken parts, precooking in the microwave cuts down on cooking time. However, if meat is precooked and refrigerated, any bacteria still present can grow to an unsafe level.
- Don't judge doneness by looks alone. Cooking time depends on many factors: type of meat, size and shape, heat, temperature of coals or grill, and the weather. Since grilled meats often brown fast on the outside, it is important to check the internal temperature with a meat thermometer to make sure they reach a safe temperature, as listed here:
  - Whole poultry: 180°F
  - Poultry breasts: 170°F
  - Hamburger: 160°F
  - All pork: 160°F
  - Beef or veal steaks, roasts, chops: 145°F

- When reheating take-out foods and hot dogs, grill the food to 165°F or until steaming hot.
- To keep grilled meat hot, put it to the side of the grill rack, not directly over the coals. At home, you can keep meat hot in a 200°F oven, a chafing dish, a slow cooker, or on a warming tray. Cooked food should be kept at 140°F or warmer to prevent bacteria growth.
- If you buy take-out foods (such as fried chicken or barbecued beef) that you plan to reheat on the grill, but the food won't be eaten within two hours of pick-up, buy the food ahead of time and chill it thoroughly before reheating.
- When taking food off the grill, don't put the grilled items on the same platter that held the raw meat.
- If grilling away from home, pack clean, soapy sponges, cloths, and wet tow-elettes to clean all the surfaces you will use. Make sure to have plenty of clean utensils and platters to separately handle raw and cooked foods.
- In hot weather (90°F and above), never leave food outside for more than one hour.
- At home, store leftovers in the refrigerator or freezer within two hours of taking food off the grill.
- If leftovers have been off the grill for less than one hour, you can safely transport them home in a cooler filled with ice. Discard any food left out more than two hours (or one hour in hot weather 90°F or above).

Approximate Grilling Times

Cooking times vary depending on temperature of coals, distance of food from coals, and so on. Since food often browns quickly, use a thermometer to make sure food has reached a safe internal temperature.

Item	Size	Grilling Time	Internal Temperature (in degrees F)
Beef:			
Steaks	¾ inch thick	3–4 minutes/side	Medium-rare 145 Medium 160
Hamburger patties	½ inch thick	3 minutes/side	Medium 160
Kebabs	1-inch cubes	3–4 minutes/side	145–160
Ribs	1-rib portions	10 minutes/side	Medium 160
Lamb:			
Chops	1 inch thick	5 minutes/side	145–160
Ground lamb	4 ounces, ½ inch thick	3 minutes/side	Medium 160
Pork:			
Chops	¾ inch thick 1½ inches thick	3–4 minutes/side 7–8 minutes/side	Medium 160 Medium 160
Tenderloin	½–1½ pounds	15–25 minutes total	Medium 160
Veal:			
Chops	1 inch thick	5–7 minutes/side	145–160
Chicken:			
Breast with bone	6–8 ounces	10–15 minutes/side	170
Boneless breast	4 ounces	6–8 minutes/side	170
Legs or thighs	4–8 ounces	10–15 minutes/side	180 or until tender and juices run clear
Drumsticks	4 ounces		180 or until tender and juices run clear

Source: Food Safety and Inspection Service, USDA, Consumer Education and Information, May 1997, "Grilling and Smoking Food Safety."

Does Grilling Pose a Cancer Risk?

Some studies have suggested cancer risk may be related to eating food cooked by such high-heat cooking techniques as grilling, frying, and broiling. Based on present research findings, eating moderate amounts of grilled fish, meat, and poultry cooked without charring to a safe, yet medium temperature does not pose a problem. To avoid charring, microwave meat until partly done immediately before placing it on the grill, and remove visible fat than can drip on the coals and cause a flame-up.

Picnics and Eating on the Road

Plan Ahead:
- If you travel longer than thirty minutes, place perishable food in a cooler with ice or freezer packs. You can make your own ice packs: place ice cubes in a freezer bag and wrap the bag with foil. Frozen juice boxes, cans of fruit, and applesauce also make good ice packs.
- When carrying drinks, consider putting them in a separate cooler, so the cooler with perishables is not opened frequently.
- Make sandwiches ahead of time, wrap each individually, then put each in a separate bag and freeze. Simple sandwiches like cheese, meat, and ham freeze best. Do not freeze mayonnaise,

lettuce, or tomatoes–bring them in separate containers and add them to sandwiches when ready to eat.
- Keep raw meat and poultry separate from cooked foods and foods that will be eaten raw, such as fruits and vegetables. Try double-bagging meats or putting in spill-proof containers.
- Bring picnic-safe foods, such as fresh, canned, or dried fruit; raw vegetables; crackers; and cookies.
- Bring along plenty of drinking water. Always assume that water from streams and rivers is not safe for drinking.
- Keep the cooler in the car, rather than in the trunk where it may be hotter.

At the Picnic Site:
- Keep the cooler in a shady spot.
- Keep the cooler covered with a blanket, towel, or tarp–preferably a light-colored one.
- At the beach, partially bury the cooler in the sand, cover with blankets, and shade with an umbrella.
- Use disposable towelettes for cleaning hands.

What You Should Know about Lead

Although you may not consume lead consciously, you may receive a regular dose of lead from your drinking water, lead crystal, or pottery with lead-containing glaze.

According to the EPA, as many as forty million people may have too much lead in their drinking water. Pregnant women and children run the highest risk of problems from lead exposure because of increased absorption. Lead exposure can cause increased rates of miscarriage and still births and such long-term effects as learning disability, brain damage, hyperactivity, high blood pressure, and kidney disease.[9] You may be exposed to too much lead if:

- *Your home was built between 1978 and 1988.* Lead solder was used in home plumbing during those years. In older homes with lead solder, minerals usually coat the pipes and keep the lead from leaching out.
- *Your home was built before 1930.* These homes often used lead pipes instead of copper ones. Also, water companies installed lead pipes underground to bring water to homes built during the first part of the century.
- *You have "soft" or acidic water.* Soft or acidic water can strip away the coating or the solder on the inside of water pipes. If no lead was used either in your pipes or in the service pipes carrying water to your home, you are safe even if you do have soft water.

To be safe, you should have your water tested for lead. This service costs from fifteen to twenty-five dollars. (Avoid do-it-yourself tests; they are often inaccurate.) Beware of scam artists who provide free lead testing and then sell you a treatment system you don't really need. The EPA action level for lead is fifteen parts per billion. It is suggested that you take action to decrease the lead in your water if it has fifteen parts of lead per billion in "first draw" (or five parts per billion after you have let the water run for a minute or more).[10]

A reverse-osmosis or distillation system can remove lead, but can be expensive and waste resources. Some systems can also remove many other potentially harmful substances in your water. Watkins has a system that is also supposed to remove the dangerous cryptosperideum bacteria. Less-expensive treatments are also available, such as filter systems and even a drip carafe (like Brita Water Filter System); make sure that the equipment is certified by the Water Quality Association or the National Sanitation Foundation (NSF).

To decrease the lead in your water until you can do further testing or treatment, run the cold water for several minutes before using. (Instead of wasting the water, consider saving it to water plants, wash windows, and so on.) If you usually use hot water for cooking or to make coffee or tea, use cold water instead. For the first time, new faucets are available that don't leach unsafe levels of lead. Make sure your faucet is certified by the NSF.

Other possible sources of lead exposure include leaded crystal decanters, ceramic pottery (especially imported), and lead-based paint that is chipping or partially removed. (Paint applied before 1978 contains lead.) Stripping lead paint from your home should only be done by a professional certified or licensed in lead safety. If not removed properly, the fine lead particles can circulate in the air and cause even more problems. Hot, acidic drinks like coffee can cause lead to leach from lead-glazed mugs. Don't store acidic beverages in or drink them from leaded crystal because lead can leach into food or drink. If you eat canned imported foods regularly, the cans may contain lead solder.[11]

For more information, contact:
- National Lead Information Center
  1-800-LEAD-FYI

This association can inform you which types of water filters handle lead removal:
- Water Quality Association
  4151 Naperville Road, Lisle, IL 60532

This organization sets the standards for water treatment systems:
- National Sanitation Foundation
  P.O. Box 1468, Ann Arbor, MI 48106

This agency can give you a list of state-certified testing labs and can answer questions about the water supply:
- Environmental Protection Agency
  Safe Drinking Water Hotline
  800-426-4791 (202-382-5533 in Washington, D.C.)

This company makes two inexpensive lead-testing kits, one for water and one for ceramic ware, crystal, and even children's toys:
- Frandon Enterprises
  800-359-9000

If you think your job is exposing you to dangerous amounts of lead, contact the nearest office of the Occupational Safety and Health Administration (OSHA—listed under U.S. Department of Labor in the phone book) or call OSHA's Office of Information and Consumer Affairs at 202-523-8151.

▼

Other Chemicals in Food

Are You Adding a Pinch of Plastic to Your Food?

Think twice before you wrap your cheese with plastic wrap. Ditto for defrosting plastic-wrapped chicken in the microwave or for using margarine tubs to heat up leftovers in the microwave. The reason? Researchers are discovering that some plastics contain chemical additives that can pass into food during storage and cooking.

These chemicals can act as "endocrine disruptors," or EDs. Endocrine disruptors can make their way into your food when it comes in contact with certain plastics, plastic wraps, Styrofoam, and polystyrene containers. Because the additives can generally dissolve in fat, they tend to move more freely into high-fat foods.

Researchers aren't yet certain of the effects of EDs in humans, but they suspect they could affect reproductive system development; thyroid functions like hearing, immune function, and cognition; and the risk of breast and testicular cancer. Scientists also fear that endocrine disruptors could do the most damage during times of rapid growth: the prenatal period, infancy, early childhood, and puberty.

"Endocrine disruptors may have a wide variety of effects on growth and development," says Deborah Wallace, Ph.D., staff ecologist at Consumers Union, which recently tested plastic wraps for the presence of endocrine disruptors. Young children are more vulnerable than adults to effects of endocrine disrupters, because children are still growing and developing. Their tissues are receptive to hormonal signals during developmental changes. "Some EDs mimic hormones, giving false physiological signs, while others can keep natural hormones from acting. Even very low doses of endocrine disruptors at particularly vulnerable times in development can lead to abnormalities. Children exposed to environmental EDs have shown problems such as lowered IQs, short attention spans, and abnormal immune systems," explains Wallace, who is also a researcher at Columbia University Center for Children's Environmental Health.

Animal evidence has shown that environmental endocrine disruptors may be the culprit for male gulls and fish with feminized reproductive tracts, alligators with shrunken genitals, and frogs with extra or missing legs. The EPA and health agencies from around the world are currently evaluating the effects of endocrine disruptors to determine what steps should be taken. In the United Kingdom, plastic wrap is manufactured so that the plastic by-products don't migrate into food. Though research in this area is still in its infancy, there are some things you can do to limit your family's exposure to potential EDs in food:

- *Buying:* Individually wrapped sliced cheese is a good choice. Other cheeses should be purchased from the deli and freshly wrapped. If packaged in plastic wrap or shrink wrap, repackage when you get home. Deli or take-out food in foam cups or plates should be transferred to a different container when you get home.
- *Storage:* Don't wrap high-fat foods, such as cheeses, cold cuts, cake, pies, and meat, in plastic wrap. It's better to store them in baggies, microwave-safe plastic bowls, or glass containers. Plastic containers with a "2" or "5" inside the recycling symbol on the bottom are made of polyethylene and polypropylene and are considered to be free of potential endocrine disruptors.
- *Cooking:* Use wax paper or plastic wrap labeled "polyethylene" to cover food in the microwave and leave an inch between food and the wrap. Avoid those wraps labeled "PVC." Use microwave-safe plastic, glass, or ceramic to cook or reheat in the microwave.

Other Environmental Chemicals in Food

As mentioned before, children are more sensitive to the effects of chemicals because of their small size and rapid growth. Besides the advice already mentioned, just a few more tips will complete the discussion:

- Avoid fish from polluted waters. If you are recreational fishers, make sure to check local advisories. Each state has advisories for local rivers, lakes, and streams that are polluted.

• Have your water checked to make sure it has no chemical residues. Water filtration systems are mentioned above under lead.

• Avoid eating the fat from meats, since that is where chemicals tend to accumulate.

• Encourage a variety of foods. (Sometimes this is tough with kids!)

Section II

Feeding Your Child

Breastfeeding and Bottlefeeding

Note: This chapter applies to the normal-weight infant in good health. If your baby was born prematurely or has any medical problems, your physician may have different feeding guidelines for you.

Congratulations! You are the parent of a new baby. During the first few weeks, you may wish that your baby had come with feeding instructions. This chapter will help you understand the finer points of feeding your baby.

In the first week or so, your baby may cry—sometimes a lot. Remember that crying is the only way your baby can communicate his needs. Generally a baby's cry will mean one or more of the following:

- He wants to be cuddled.
- He is tired.
- He is bored.
- He needs his diaper changed.
- He is overstimulated.
- He is in pain or is sick.
- He is hungry—and has probably been hungry awhile!

As time goes on, you will become better at translating his cries. Don't assume that when your baby cries, he is always hungry. This assumption can lead to overfeeding, and you will not be doing your baby a favor. Crying is a late sign of hunger; you should try to feed him before he cries. Following are the early hunger signs:

- eye movements
- lip smacking and opening and closing mouth
- hand-to-mouth action
- rooting

▼

Rooting and Suckling

Babies are born with a rooting reflex. When a baby's cheek or lip is stroked, he will turn toward what touched him, so that his mouth comes in contact with it. If the stimulus is a source of food—either a breast or a bottle—and he is hungry, he will latch on and begin sucking. If your baby is not hungry, he will neither root nor suck.

▼

Signs That Your Baby Is Full

Babies have different ways of telling you that they are no longer hungry. They may spit out the nipple or begin to play with it or bite it. They may gradually drink less or may fall asleep. It is up to you to tune into your baby to discover when he is full. This brings me to our next important point—a schedule.

Whether you breast-feed or bottle-feed, you will hear about putting your baby on a feeding schedule. Let me introduce a concept that may be new to you: Your baby is the boss of his eating habits. As hard is this

is to accept, it will make life much easier for you and your child in the long run. Your baby should be in charge of his eating because he is the only one who knows if he is hungry. And since babies are all different, they will need to eat at different intervals, which may change from day to day.

For example, take the case of the active or "fussy" baby. He may need to be fed as often as every one and a half hours, while the quiet, complacent baby may consistently eat every three and a half hours. Neither feeding schedule is right or wrong. When-ever your baby needs to eat is the right time!

Generally, breast-fed babies eat more often than bottle-fed babies since breast milk is lower in fat. During a period of several weeks, my son Robert would finish breastfeeding and twenty minutes later, would want to eat again. I must admit that it was frustrating at times to spend most of my day feeding him, but I went along with his needs, and the eating marathon didn't last very long. That told me that he must have been going through a growth spurt. To this day, Robert, now four, is definitely the boss of his eating. He may ask for four helpings of beans, but when he is full, he stops.

It is important that you go with the flow and feed your baby when he "asks" for it—and stop feeding him when he is full. If you are trying to get your baby to eat a certain number of ounces or for a certain number of minutes, don't! Forcing food on babies when they are no longer hungry can interfere with their own appetite regulation. Babies are born with the ability to eat when they are hungry and stop when they are full. Many adults, however, no longer eat to their appetite; somewhere along the way they learned to ignore their own feelings of hunger and fullness. This may have been due to well-meaning parents intent on getting them on a feeding schedule as babies, or to parents or caregivers who encouraged them to clean their plate. Lifelong eating habits really do start in early childhood.

Note: If your baby is following his own appetite, but does not seem to be eating well, he should be evaluated by a physician.

Other Details of Infant Feeding

Burping

Regardless whether you breast-feed or bottle-feed, you will want to burp your baby during the feeding. How often you burp your baby depends on the amount of air he swallows and whether he tends to be gassy. In general, breast-fed babies are burped after they finish feeding from one breast and after they stop feeding. Babies fed formula or breast milk in a bottle should at first be burped after every ounce to ounce-and-a-half. As the baby gets older and his gastrointestinal system matures, the burping can gradually decrease.

To burp your baby, hold him with his head on your shoulder and rub or gently pat his back until the air is brought up. You can also hold him on your lap, while supporting his head, and pat or rub his back.

Weaning

Most health professionals recommend that infants be weaned from a bottle to a cup at one year of age. This advice, like most advice regarding babies, may not work for every baby. Sometime between nine months and eighteen months is a good time to make the switch. If your baby stops breast-feeding before nine months, switching to a bottle is best. If you discontinue breastfeeding after nine months, you can try giving him a cup first. If your baby refuses or can't seem to master drinking from a cup, his intake of formula may decrease too much; then it is best to go back to the bottle.

Spitting Up

All babies spit up from time to time. Sometimes babies spit up what seems like their whole meal. Spitting up has a couple of possible causes: Maybe your baby swallowed a large air bubble, and when it came up, so did his milk. Or perhaps he was encouraged to drink more than he could handle. Keep in mind, however, that if your baby spits up often, projectile-vomits, or has continuous colic, it may be a sign of a medical problem or allergy, and you should contact your baby's health-care provider.

Infant Growth

Chapter Four offers a general discussion of growth. However, certain things apply to an infant that don't apply to an older child.

- The first few days after birth, a newborn loses up to 10 percent of his birth weight, but he should regain it by his two-week checkup.
- After two weeks, normal weight gain is considered four to seven ounces per week.
- Babies grow very fast the first year, and they deposit a lot of baby fat. Your baby will also develop a big belly. I remember a photo opportunity I had when my son Nicolas was about three months old and was in the tub lying on one of those giant sponges. He looked like a giant tadpole! With his big round belly and his skinny arms and legs sticking out, the only thing missing was a tail! A big stomach is normal for a baby and is no cause for alarm or for any cutting down of his food intake.
- Growth charts have their uses, but they are sometimes abused. A growth chart helps your baby's health-care provider look for any negative trends or patterns in his growth. For example, if your baby has been growing at the fiftieth percentile for months and then drops to the tenth percentile, he should be evaluated. A growth chart should not be used as some sort of goal sheet to make your child fit into a random growth curve, such as the fiftieth percentile.
- Breast-fed babies are leaner than bottle-fed babies. Breast-fed babies appear to grow less rapidly than bottle-fed babies up to the age of eighteen months. This is no cause for concern or for supplemental feeding of formula or early introduction of foods. This difference in body composition may prove to be a long-term benefit, perhaps resulting in a smaller chance of adult obesity.
- Early introduction of solids (before four months) will not make your baby sleep all night and may cause long-term food allergies or respiratory problems such as asthma.

The rest of this chapter will focus on the two ways of feeding your baby—breastfeeding and bottlefeeding—as well as factors that apply to both methods.

Breastfeeding

Breast milk is the best source of nutrition for your baby. It is the model from which formula is manufactured. Breast milk is a "living fluid," containing active compounds important to your baby's current and future health. Unlike the pasteurized milk that adults drink and that is used in manufactured formula, breast milk is always changing to meet your baby's needs. Even during one breastfeeding session, milk changes from "foremilk" (a low-fat milk) to "hindmilk" (breast milk that is higher in fat). Of course, breastfeeding also provides a wonderful bonding experience between mother and baby.

In the short term, breast-fed infants are healthier than those nourished with formula. For example, breast-fed babies have fewer occurrences of ear infections, respiratory infections, urinary tract infections, and gastroenteritis. Developmentally, evidence shows that breast-fed infants have higher IQs than bottle-fed babies. This is thought to be due to fats found in breast milk that are not added to formulas in the United States. These fats are essential to the developing brain. Since brain tissue continues to grow through the first two years of life, this nutrient may play an important role. The long-term health benefits of breastfeeding continue to follow your baby as he grows into a child and adult. Breastfeeding may be related to a decreased risk of Crohn's disease, insulin-dependent diabetes, and lymph cancer.[1]

Breastfeeding also provides health benefits to the mother: a reduced risk of osteoporosis, premenopausal breast cancer, and cancer of other reproductive organs.[2] Economic benefits include no formula to buy, less time missed from work due to a sick child, and fewer health-care expenses such as doctor visits and prescriptions.

Breastfeeding Success

Breastfeeding success depends on you and the support you have around you. Breastfeeding is most successful if you start within the first hour after your baby is born, if he is alert. You may need help getting started. Ask for advice from a lactation consultant or a nurse at the hospital. Once you are home, a visit with a nurse from your HMO or health department is also helpful.

Although breastfeeding is natural, it may not come naturally to everyone. Therefore, it's helpful to know a few basics before you get started.

Surround Yourself with Support

No matter how prepared you feel to begin nursing your baby, you will find that you will want to talk to someone who has been there. The first week or two after Nicolas was born, I often called my friend Candi, who had nursed her daughter. Find a friend or acquaintance or La Leche League leader whom you can call with questions. A strong support system can make a big difference in your success. If possible, seek out some of the following resources while you are pregnant:

- Husband, partner, or close friend who supports breastfeeding
- La Leche League leader or lactation consultant
- Pediatrician and staff who are supportive and knowledgeable about breastfeeding (Interview them while you are pregnant.)
- A baby-friendly hospital—with a lactation consultant available every day, a rooming-in option for baby, and a policy of not giving bottles to breast-feeding infants
- Reading material on breastfeeding (Read it while you are pregnant.)

In the hospital, let the nurses know that you plan to breast-feed and that you don't want any bottles given to your baby so that nursing can become established. If supplements are requested by your doctor, seek the advice of a lactation consultant to develop a plan for feeding without the use of a bottle.

Positioning: Don't Hesitate to Get Help!

Positioning your baby correctly so that he can latch on to your breast is probably the most important factor for successful breast-feeding. If the nerves in the nipple (located under the areola) do not get enough stimulation, and the milk sinuses are not adequately compressed, you might not produce enough milk. Also, just a slight difference in your baby's position can make a huge difference in nipple pain. I know—I've been there! After having several problems getting my first baby to nurse the first two weeks, I called a lactation consultant. After she observed Nicolas for just a few minutes, she pinpointed the problem: he was not positioned correctly. The pain I had experienced was not due to breastfeeding; it was due to poor positioning. Within a week, we were well on our way to success!

Once nursing is well established, you may prefer to change feeding positions throughout the day; for example, giving the first feeding while in bed, the next feeding in a rocking chair, and the next one on the couch, using pillows.

The positioning information that follows is modified from *Breastfeeding: A Mother's Gift* by Pamela Wiggins, IBCLC. (Used with permission.)

Positioning Your Baby

To make any position work best, bring baby's head and mouth to the nipple (as opposed to moving breast and nipple to the baby). Make sure to get most of the areola (the dark skin around the nipple) into the baby's mouth. Baby's body should be facing mom's, and as much as possible, baby's arms should be around mom's breast, not between baby and breast. Feeding your baby skin-to-skin with the baby unclothed except for a diaper helps the baby stay alert and also helps you to see his position. You can position your baby several ways:

The Cradle or Madonna Hold

This is the most common breastfeeding position.

- First, make yourself comfortable. Sit in a comfortable chair (use a footstool if you are short) or prop yourself in bed with several pillows.
- Rest the baby's head on your forearm, directly facing your breast. His body should be facing you. Never have the baby's head turned and his body facing upward. This makes it hard for him to swallow. His back should be supported by your arm and his bottom held up with your hand. Hold the baby level with your breast and don't lean forward.
- Move your baby, not your breast, to get a good alignment. You might have to use a pillow on your lap to help support him.
- Tickle his lip with your nipple, and wait for him to open his mouth wide. (Hint: If you open your mouth wide, he may mimic you and open his.)
- When his mouth is wide open, quickly pull him to your breast so that the chin touches the breast first. He should now latch on to the breast just right.

- The lower lip should be as far from the base of the nipple as possible, and you should be able to see some of the areola above the top lip. If he is not positioned just right, take him off and start over.
- If you have had a Cesarean section, you can still nurse in the cradle hold position. Have the nurse help you prop up in bed, and use lots of pillows. To protect your incision, use a pillow in your lap for the baby to lie on.

Across-the-Lap Hold or Transverse Cradle Hold

In this position the baby is held across the lap, like in the cradle hold, but in the opposite arm to the breast being used.

- Position your baby's body along your forearm, still turned toward you; his head and neck should be supported by your hand rather than the bend in your elbow. (For example, when baby's head is in front of your right breast, your left arm and hand are supporting his head.)
- Use your other hand to support the breast and help positioning and latch-on. Some moms may find it a little harder to keep the baby close enough to the breast in this position.
- Always remember, no matter what position you use, a baby must be latched on correctly. His chin must be tucked in close, and some of the areola must be showing above his top lip. His top and bottom lips should both be flanged out. His tongue should be well over his bottom gum.

Clutch (Football) Hold

Some mothers who have had Cesareans prefer the clutch (football) hold. This is a good position for preemies, for moms dealing with overactive letdowns, for helping sleepy babies become more alert, and for encouraging babies to open jaws wider. The clutch hold is also a good way to nurse twins simultaneously.

- Supporting your baby's neck and head, tuck the baby's body under your arm at your side. His feet should be close to your back.
- Tickle his lips, and as soon as he opens wide, pull him to the breast, making sure the chin touches the breast first.

Lying Down to Nurse

- Many mothers who have had Cesareans are more comfortable, or find it easier, to use a side-lying position. However, to avoid choking, this position is often reserved for the baby who has good latch-on and better head and neck control.
- Have a nurse help you turn over on your side and lay the baby facing your breast.
- Follow the same steps as outlined for the cradle hold, but place your baby on his side and facing you. You might put a pillow behind him to help keep him in place. The baby's head may either be on your arm or on the bed, whichever is more comfortable.
- Arrange pillows behind your back to support your weight and to make you more comfortable.

Frequency of Feedings

Whether at the doctor's office or with mothers at the mall, this question will come up: "How many times a day do you feed your baby?" There is no one right answer to this question. The answer should be "Whenever he wants."

During the first few weeks, your baby will feed often. This establishes your milk supply. The more he sucks, the more milk you make. When your baby is seven to ten days old, you may notice that he drinks more often but your breasts are soft. This is normal and not a sign that your milk is drying up. As long as your infant is showing signs of adequate intake (see below) and is gaining weight, you can rest assured that he is drinking enough.

Signs That Your Newborn Is Drinking Enough:

- He drinks at least eight to twelve times in a twenty-four hour period.
- He has six or more wet diapers per day.
- He has four or more generous bowel movements daily.
- He gains twenty to thirty grams (close to an ounce) per day after day five.
- He has not lost more than 7 percent of his birth weight.

If your baby does not show one or more of the signs listed above, contact your physician.[3]

Listening to Your Baby Drink

Turn off the radio and the TV and listen to the melodic suck-and-swallow of your baby nursing. If you can hear your baby swallowing milk, that is one sign that he is drinking enough. Before your milk comes in, you should be able to hear an audible swallow—a *cah-cah* sound—about every five to seven times that he sucks. After your milk comes in, you should hear him swallow about every one to three sucks.

Colostrum: "Magical" First Milk

The first few days after your baby is born, your breasts make a special kind of milk called colostrum. It is thin and yellowish. In fact, you may think there is something wrong with your milk. There isn't. Colostrum is made specifically for the first few days of life; it changes in character until day ten to fourteen, when it is called "mature milk." Colostrum contains important antibodies that help your infant fight disease.

Troubleshooting

The list of challenges below may or may not happen to you. However, even if you do experience any of these challenges, they in no way reflect your ability to successfully nurse your baby! As mentioned earlier, breastfeeding does not necessarily come naturally to all mothers or all babies, so get help early; then just relax, go with the flow, and be flexible.

Sore Nipples

Although breastfeeding may take a little getting used to, and your nipples may be tender, they should not be painful, cracked, or bleeding. If they are, reevaluate the positioning of your baby or how your baby is latching on. Make sure:

- The baby is facing you and his mouth is wide open when he puts his mouth to your breast. His tongue should be covering the lower gum line to protect the mother's breast from abrasion.
- Most of the areola should be in his mouth; his mouth should be centered on your nipple. Tongue and lips must be high enough on the areola to compress the milk reservoirs to stimulate letdown.
- His lips should be turned out. If his bottom lip is tucked in, use your finger to pull down on the bottom of his chin.

Give Your Breasts Some TLC:

- Nurse more often but for shorter periods of time to keep your baby from getting too hungry and sucking more vigorously.
- If one nipple is more sore than the other, start with the less-sore nipple. When your baby gets to the second breast, he will drink less vigorously.
- Change positions at every feeding.
- Rub breast milk on your nipple after feeding and let air dry. Using a 100-percent pure lanolin like Lansinoh can also help prevent nipple drying, soreness, and minor abrasions. (Lansinoh can be bought over the counter but may need to be ordered.) Prescription creams are available for soreness.

Breastfeeding Diet

You need to eat more while breast-feeding than you did while pregnant. Make every bite count! Most breast-feeding women need 2,000–2,400 calories per day, depending on how active they are. Eat a variety of foods and pick foods from all food groups. The following list adds up to 2,400 calories. (Remember that you may need less than that.)

12 servings of starches or grains

4 servings of fruits

4 servings of vegetables

7 ounces of protein

4–5 servings of dairy products or high-calcium foods

5 servings of fat

Source: Swinney, Bridget, M.S., R.D. *Eating Expectantly.* Minnetonka: Meadowbrook Press, 1996.

- Do not use soap or alcohol on your breasts; they cause drying and irritation. Don't scrub nipple-areola area.
- Wear breast shells to keep bra or clothes from rubbing against nipples.

Plugged Ducts

Your breasts have a network of tubes called ducts, similar to the ductwork in an air conditioner that carries cool air to all the rooms in the house. If one duct is closed off, more air goes to the other ducts and the closed room gets very hot. If, for some reason, your breast is not emptied of milk, the milk can harden into small, tender lumps and plug up a duct. If caught early, this condition can be easily remedied. Apply warm, moist heat and massage before nursing and make sure to nurse often in different positions, emptying the breasts.

Breast Infection

When a plugged duct gets infected, it can cause an infection called mastitis. Mastitis produces flulike symptoms with aches and fever of 100.5°F or greater. You may experience breast pain and redness and a lump that you can feel. Warm compresses and frequent feeding in different positions can help. Your physician may prescribe an antibiotic (usually Keflex, because it doesn't pass into the milk). Continue nursing your baby often, get plenty of rest, and drink plenty of fluids. Your breast infection will soon be a thing of the past.

Cramps

Some cramping is normal as the products of pregnancy are expelled. Also, because of the hormones released during breastfeeding, cramping can happen the first few days of nursing. The more children you have had, the more intense the cramping can be. Although you may not think of this cramping as a "benefit," it is. It helps the uterus return to its pre-pregnant state.

Engorgement

When your milk comes in, your breasts may swell, or become engorged. If your baby has been feeding often, you probably won't have engorgement. If you do, nurse your baby frequently and have the following items ready if needed: a breast pump for between feedings and warm compresses. Taking a warm shower before nursing may help, as will using cold compresses after the feeding.

Peggy Connor, R.N., a maternal-child health nurse in Virginia, also recommends cabbage leaves for the relief of pain and stinging that sometimes comes with engorgement. You will need the green outer leaves of the cabbage, which are usually taken off prior to putting the cabbage on the shelf in the grocery store. Tell the produce department you need them for medicinal purposes. Wash the leaves well, soak them in ice water, then beat them with a clean meat mallet to get juices to the surface. Surround your breast with the leaves for several minutes.

Nipple Confusion

A nipple or pacifier made out of rubber is very different from a human nipple, and babies suck on them differently. Babies can get confused if they use a rubber nipple or pacifier too early in breastfeeding, which may make it difficult to get back to nursing. When Nicolas was born, he was given a bottle of sugar water because he was having trouble nursing. The two weeks after we went home were tough, as I had to retrain him to a human nipple and teach him to nurse at the same time. A lactation consultant helped us immensely.

Avoid giving your baby pacifiers and rubber nipples, and make it clear in the hospital that you don't want your baby to receive any bottles or pacifiers. Besides possibly interfering with breastfeeding, pacifier use has been liked to reduced IQ in one study.[4]

If you must give your baby supplemental formula or water in the early weeks, give it with an eyedropper, sippy cup, or supplemental nursing system. (This system is an aid that consists of a small bottle with a small tube worn around the mother's neck. The bottle is filled with formula, water, or breast milk (if available). The tubing carries the liquid down the mother's breast to the nipple area, where the baby can be fed. This helps to continue training the baby, held in mother's arms in a breast-feeding position, while stimulating the breast to produce milk.)

Returning to Work

For many women, their decision to return to work after having a baby is the biggest factor in choosing whether to nurse. Be aware that work environments are becoming more supportive of breastfeeding. Studies have shown that breastfeeding not only makes for happier, more productive employees, it also improves the bottom line:

- Breastfeeding moms take fewer sick days to be home with sick babies, because breast-fed babies don't get sick nearly as often as bottle-fed babies.
- A working mother may have an easier time making the transition back to work, knowing that while she works, her body is making breast milk that is healthy for her baby.

To make breastfeeding fit into your work schedule, you must plan ahead, even before your baby is born. Here are some tips:

During Pregnancy
Talk to your boss about your maternity leave and return date. If possible, work out an extended maternity leave, part-time work schedule, or flexible hours. Explain that your baby, your health, and your job all benefit

from breastfeeding. Breastfeeding moms miss fewer days at work due to sick babies. Assure your boss that breastfeeding won't take much time from work, either. In fact, if you use a double-pumping kit, you can empty the milk from both breasts in ten to fifteen minutes. If you pump three times a day, you can do it forty-five minutes or less. Some women find that they don't really take any time off to pump. They simply close their office door, put up a "do not disturb" sign, and pump while they are working.

Find a suitable place for expressing milk while at work. Some large companies have a room reserved for this, but you may have to improvise with an unused storage room or office. The human resources department may be able to help you. If you have an electric pump, make sure there is an outlet in the room you plan to use for pumping.

This is also a good time to find a day-care provider who is supportive of breastfeeding. The perfect provider is one who can bring your baby to work at lunchtime. You should explain to the caregiver that you don't want your baby fed within the two hours before you pick him up, if possible. If the baby is too hungry, the caregiver should try to give him an ounce of water or breast milk. You should give your caregiver very specific instructions on how to store and heat breast milk. (See page 119.)

Before Returning to Work
A week or two before you return to work, you should start pumping at home. Pumping after you feed your baby will help maintain your milk supply and will get you used

to pumping. When your baby is four to five weeks of age, you should also try giving him a bottle. Because your baby associates Mommy with breastfeeding, try to arrange someone else to give him the bottle, preferably when you are not there.

You may even want do a "dry run" of a day or half-day at work. Take your baby to your baby-sitter; return home and pump when you would normally feed him (or pump) at work. Then you can fine-tune your schedule.

Back to Work

Going back to work in the middle of the week makes the transition easier. Nurse your baby once before you leave in the morning, right when you get home from work, and again before bedtime.

For pumping at work, bring a picture of your baby, a glass of water, and a small snack with you. Try to relax and think of your baby, and the pumping should go fine.

On the weekend, exclusively breast-feed your baby to keep up your milk supply. Also set priorities and catch up on rest.

Colic

Mention the word colic, and listen to the horror stories. Colic, or the persistent, unexplained crying of infants, places tremendous stress on a family and occurs in about 10–30 percent of babies. Colic generally starts between three days to three weeks after birth. As a general guideline, crying lasts more than three hours and occurs more than three days in any one week.[5]

Colic often occurs in the evening and usually disappears by four months of age.

Causes of colic may include intolerance or allergy to cow's-milk protein, lactose intolerance, intestinal hyperperistalsis, neuro-hormonal immaturity, maternal anxiety, and family stress. Since the last two causes also happen because of colic, a vicious cycle can occur.

Helping the Colicky Baby

Since the exact cause of colic isn't known, many remedies may or may not work for you. Rocking, dancing, and walking with baby; continuous background "white" noise (a fuzzy TV screen, the bathroom fan, the sound of a shower running); and a hot water bottle on the stomach help some babies. Mylicon drops–an over-the-counter medication that contains simethicone–can be used with your doctor's permission. Womb-sounds recorded on tape, infant massage, mechanical swings, crib sound/motion devices, and swaddling have also been known to comfort some infants.[6] Parents have also been known to drive their baby around in the car at night, put them in the car seat on top of a clothes dryer in action (make sure to hold the car seat so it doesn't vibrate off the dryer), and other unconventional methods. Desperate times call for desperate measures!

If nothing seems to work, your baby may have a food allergy. The infant of parents who both have allergies and related illnesses (food allergies, hay fever, eczema, asthma), is at higher risk for food allergies. The most likely culprit is milk and milk products in the mother's diet. Try avoiding all milk products, including milk, cream, cheese, sour cream, yogurt, margarine, and butter. Also look on the label of prepared foods to make sure they don't contain any of these products, as well as casein, caseinate, whey, lactalbumin, sodium caseinate, lactose, nonfat milk solids, cream, and calcium caseinate.

Milk protein in breast milk peaks at four to six hours after mom eats a dairy product. If you and your health-care provider determine that your baby is allergic to cow's-milk protein, you will need to avoid dairy products. Once your baby is a few months old, he may be able to tolerate a challenge of some type of cow milk protein in your diet. Work with your health-care provider or lactation consultant to help with this situation.

If it is necessary to supplement your breast milk at this time, try either a soy formula or a hypoallergenic formula such as Nutramigen, Alimentum, or Neocate. Though soy formulas are much more economical than hypoallergenic formulas, as many as 25 percent of babies with cow's-milk protein allergies are also allergic to soy protein.

If milk is not the colic culprit, you can look at other dietary factors. Other foods mom eats that are associated with colic are cruciferous vegetables (such as cabbage, broccoli, and cauliflower), onions, and chocolate.[7]

Let's face it: Exchanging your favorite foods for a very basic diet while trying to figure out what is bothering your baby is no fun. You may even hear a little voice telling you, "Just give him a bottle!" You may also hear some loud voices—from husband, family, friends—telling you the same thing. However, if you take the trouble to find out what food your baby doesn't tolerate, you might save him from lifelong problems with allergy-related diseases, such as asthma, eczema, and hay fever, especially if your family is prone to allergies. By delaying exposure to cow's-milk protein through your breast milk, you can prevent those diseases as well as provide all the other benefits of breast milk.[8] Don't give up!

After lots of rocking, diet changing, and mylicon drops, many families find they can blame the colic on nothing more than the immaturity of the baby's gastrointestinal system. Your baby will probably outgrow his colic on his own in a few months.

? Questions You May Have

Q: My daughter's bowel movements look very strange. What should they be like?

A: Breast-fed babies tend to have loose, yellow stools resembling the color of mustard. I admit, they do look a bit strange until you get used to them.

Q: My breasts are very small; can I make enough milk?

A: Breast size has nothing to do with milk production. You should have no problem nursing your child. And don't forget the perk of experiencing a bigger bust size while breast-feeding!

Q: I have to go back to work in six weeks. Is it worth it to nurse so short a time?

A: Absolutely. Women who breast-feed their infants, even for six weeks, give them disease-fighting antibodies. Because breast-fed babies get sick less often, you will miss less work and make fewer trips to the pediatrician.[9]

Many women also continue to nurse while at work. Some women can pump at work, while others ease into a schedule that involves nursing several times after work and feeding with formula the rest of the time. Of course, the more breast milk your child gets, the better! Look into such options as a reduced or flexible work schedule, renting an electric pump for easy pumping during breaks, finding day care close to your work so that you can nurse at lunchtime, or having a caregiver or friend bring your baby to you several times a day. Where there's a will, there's a way!

Q: My diet is awful. Should I still nurse my baby?

A: Yes. But be sure to take a vitamin supplement to fill in the nutritional gaps and try to improve your diet as much as you possibly can.

Q: Do I need to give my baby water?

A: No. The only reason you would need to is if it is very hot and/or humid.

Vitamin Supplements for Baby

Other than the nutrients mentioned below, your breast milk provides everything your baby needs.[10]

Vitamin D

We get most of our vitamin D from sunshine. If your baby gets less than thirty minutes of sunshine per week when clad in only a diaper, or less than two hours of sunshine per week when dressed but with a bare head, or if you live in a climate with little sunshine in the winter months, your baby probably needs a vitamin D supplement of 400 IU per day. Your physician will have to give you a prescription.

Vitamin B_{12}

If you are a strict vegetarian and do not take a vitamin B_{12} supplement, your baby will need 0.3–0.5 micrograms per day.

Fluoride

If your water is not fluoridated, your baby will need a fluoride supplement of 0.25 milligrams daily after six months of age. You can call your local water department to find out how much fluoride is in your water.

Iron

As your baby starts eating solids at about six months, you should feed him high-iron cereals and teething biscuits.

Vitamin Supplements for Mom

Nursing moms continue to make high-quality milk even on days when their diet isn't up to par. Do keep in mind, though, that if your diet isn't very good most of the time, your own nutrient stores could be used up in keeping your milk nutrient-rich for your baby. Many women choose to take a multivitamin-mineral supplement.

Expressing Milk

If you are going back to work, or if you simply want to have some time away from your baby, you will want to express some breast milk and store it for later use. Milk can be expressed in several ways: by hand, with a plastic pump, or with an electric or battery-operated pump. If you express on a regular basis, you may want to rent or buy an electric double pump. This allows you to pump both breasts simultaneously—all in about twenty minutes.

Storing Breast Milk

Store breast milk in a clean plastic bottle or bottle bag. Breast milk can be kept in the refrigerator for twenty-four hours and in the freezer for up to three months. (Do not store breast milk in the doors of the refrigerator or the freezer, but in the back, where it is coldest.) If you have a freestanding freezer, you may store milk for up to six months. A word of caution, though: Try to give milk to your baby fairly close to the time you express it. Since the composition of breast milk changes over the course of breastfeeding, milk from the first month might not satisfy a six-month-old baby as well as the milk you are currently making. Make sure to label your milk with the date you pumped (or a

"use by" date) and with a name if the breast milk will be fed in a day-care setting.

Thawing Breast Milk

Breast milk should be thawed in the refrigerator or in a container with warm water running over it. It should not be thawed at room temperature or in a microwave.

▼

Bottlefeeding

What brand of formula should you give your baby? All in all, formulas are alike in that they try to imitate the composition of breast milk. From time to time, a new discovery is made about breast milk, and the formula companies race to be the first to use it in their formula. The list below will help you navigate the different formulas. Your physician or health-care provider can help you decide which brand and type is the best for you.

Types of Formula

- *Formula with iron:* If your baby is full term and is not at high risk for allergies, this is the formula to use.
- *Soy formula:* For babies with milk-protein intolerance and for families who choose to raise their children vegetarian.
- *Lactose free:* For babies who can tolerate milk protein but cannot digest lactose or milk sugar.
- *Follow-up formulas:* Intended for babies four months and older who eat some

solid food. These formulas offer no real advantage over regular formula.

- *Formula with low iron:* Not recommended except for certain rare conditions.
- *Special formulas:* These formulas should only be used upon the advice of your physician.
- *Formula for premature babies:* Neocare by Ross Laboratories and Enfamil 22 by Mead Johnson are both formulas with higher calorie content.
- *Hydrolyzed formulas:* These formulas have protein broken down so it is easier to digest. Examples are Nutramigen and Pregestimil by Mead Johnson and Alimentum by Ross Laboratories. These formulas are sometimes recommended for babies who are at high risk of developing allergies and those who have severe colic.

Three Stages of Convenience

Formula comes in three forms: ready-to-feed, concentrate, and powder. Powder is the least expensive; the price goes up significantly with every jump in convenience. The option you choose depends on your budget and preference.

- Ready-to-feed can be very convenient when you don't have access to water or if the water is unsuitable for drinking. It is, of course, the most expensive.
- Concentrate is cheaper and requires some mixing. However, you need a safe, clean source of water. Unused formula (both concentrate and ready-to-feed) should be discarded within forty-eight hours.

- My personal favorite is the powder. You can mix what you need—one bottle at a time if needed. It is perfect for the mom who is nursing and supplementing with formula. It also has a nice "milk" look and smell, instead of the darker color that canned formula sometimes has.

Mixing and Sterilizing

The only requirements for mixing formula are clean bottles (use a dishwasher or wash with hot water and soap) and a safe, clean water supply. Try to use boiled, cooled tap water when preparing formula for the first four to six months of life, when your baby is more vulnerable to bacteria and viruses. (Or use bottled water, but then your baby may need a fluoride supplement.)

Tips
- Following directions on package, sterilize bottles and nipples before using for the first time.
- After bottles and nipples have been washed, allow them to air-dry on a clean towel and store in a covered, clean container or zippered bag.
- Wash the outside of the formula can. Always wash your hands before preparing formula.
- Prepare formula according to package directions. Some parents like to prepare all the bottles for the day, while others prefer to make one bottle at a time.
- Once you have opened a can of either concentrated or ready-to-feed formula, cover it and refrigerate. If you will not

have access to a refrigerator, prepare only what you need for each feeding.

- Discard unused formula forty-eight hours after opening (or whenever specified on label).
- Do not save formula left over in bottle for the next feeding; bacteria from baby's saliva can grow in the milk and make him sick later—or cause thrush, a fungal infection in the mouth.
- Do not leave baby's formula at room temperature for more than one hour.
- If you do not have a dishwasher, wash the bottles and nipples with hot soapy water; you may also want to sterilize them once a week by boiling them. If you have well water or your water is not chlorinated, the American Academy of Pediatrics recommends boiling bottles, nipples, and utensils.
- Start with four-ounce bottles, so your baby has less risk of swallowing air. When your baby starts drinking more, you can buy eight-ounce bottles.
- If you are traveling, bring along bottled water, empty bottles, and a can of powdered formula. Mix only as much as you need.

Errors in Formula Preparation

Not following the package directions for preparing the formula can be bad news. Here are two common mistakes:

Overdiluting

If you make orange juice from concentrate for your family, you may occasionally add an extra can of water to stretch the concentrate or to cut the sweetness. Never try the same thing with your baby's formula. Overdiluting formula and overfeeding an infant with water has led to "water intoxication," failure-to-thrive, and even seizures.[11] Make sure to follow the directions exactly for diluting formula. Your baby should not need extra water except during hot or humid weather, or when he has diarrhea or vomiting. In either case, consult your health-care provider first.

Underdiluting

Not adding enough water to concentrated or powdered formula can be just as dangerous as adding too much. It increases the work of the immature kidneys and can lead to dehydration.

Special Formulas

It may be clear from the beginning that your baby cannot tolerate his formula. Constant crying, colic, bloody diarrhea, or throwing up a feeding are signs that need medical evaluation. Your health-care provider will most likely have you switch your baby to soy formula. Soy formula is lactose-free and has the same nutrient combination as formula made from cow's milk. If your baby also has a problem with soymilk, this means he is probably allergic to the protein in the soy and cow based formulas. Hydrolyzed formulas are formulas that have been altered to be easily digestible. Examples of these are Nutramigen, Pregestimil, and Alimentum. They are expensive and have

Signs of Cow-Milk Allergy
Cramping, recurrent severe and often bloody diarrhea, frequent vomiting, persistent colic, eczema, hives, persistent runny nose, recurrent bronchitis, asthma.

an unpleasant odor and taste. However, they are just the thing for the highly allergic infant. In fact, some research has shown that in families where parents have many allergy-related problems (asthma, eczema, food allergies), giving the baby either breast milk from mom who is following a hypoallergenic diet or an extensively hydrolyzed formula, such as Nutramigen, can prevent the onset of allergies.

What about Follow-Up Formulas?

Follow-up formulas are not really needed, since your baby's nutrient needs can be met with his regular formula and, starting at six months, with the addition of cereals and other foods.

Other Liquids

Goat's Milk
In some circles, goat's milk is recommended for infants. However, it is low in iron, folic acid, and vitamins C and D, and is hard for an infant's kidneys to tolerate during the first months of life. It should be avoided unless recommended by your physician.

Juices, Teas, and Other Liquids
Besides water, do not give your child any other fluid before the age of six months.

Even when you do introduce your six-month-old to juice, limit it to four ounces. Because juice tends to be filling and may take the place of more nutrient-dense foods, you may want to dilute two ounces of juice with two ounces of water.

Six months is a good time to begin using a sippy cup. By drinking juice from a cup, your baby is much less likely to gulp it down quickly, as he might do with a bottle. Learning how to drink from a cup may take a while, so be patient. And remember, it may take three to four years to drink from a cup without spilling.

Avoid teas. A few isolated cases of liver and neurologic injury occurred in infants who were given home-brewed mint teas. Certain types of mint plants contain pennyroyal oil, which is very dangerous to infants.[12]

Colas and other sweet drinks should not be part of your child's diet; they contain empty calories, caffeine, and other additives your baby doesn't need. Humans have a natural preference for sweets, so hold off on them as long as you can.

How Much Should Your Baby Drink?

Your baby should drink about twenty-four to thirty-two ounces of formula every day. However, remember that babies are excellent at regulating their own intake. They will eat more when they are hungry and less when they are not. Your baby is the boss! (Of his eating, that is.) The amount of formula he drinks at each feeding will only be two to four ounces the first few months. Gradually, he will drink more at each feeding and reduce the number of times he eats. By six to nine months, when he is also eating some solids, your baby will drink six to eight ounces at a feeding and may have only four bottle feedings a day.

Your Baby's Growth and Development As It Relates to Eating

During the first year of life, some very amazing things happen. See the chart below to see what you have to look forward to.

Sleeping through the Night

Babies usually sleep through the night when they are about two months old. If your baby sleeps through the night before then, make sure his intake is adequate. (See page 112.) If you are nursing, it is important that you feed your baby during the night for the first six to eight weeks to build up your milk supply. If your baby sleeps more than four hours, you should wake him up to nurse him.

If your baby does not sleep through the night, he could be going through a growth

Age	Development	Result
1–3 months	• Rooting reflex causes baby to turn head toward stimulus so that the mouth finds food. • Immature suckling	• Baby finds nourishment even though he cannot see it at first. • Baby can drink milk but automatically spits out solids.
4–6 months	• Mature sucking, side-to-side movement of tongue • Maturing head, neck, and shoulder muscles • Can grasp an object and put in mouth	• Can take food from a spoon • Can hold bottle himself • Allows easier positioning for feeding
7–9 months	• Can move jaws up and down to chew • Can sit up • Can grasp objects with fingers and transfer from one hand to another	• Ready for soft, mashed table foods • Ready to finger-feed
9–12 months	• Has more precise pincer grasp and can consciously move things from hand to mouth.	• Ready to learn to self-feed, which will be refined during the second year

Source: Nutrition in Infancy and Childhood, 6th edition, by Pipes, P. and Trahms, C. (McGraw Hill, 1997)

spurt, or he may just like your company in the middle of the night! Babies often get used to nighttime feeding, even if they are not hungry. To find out if he is really hungry, try just holding him without feeding him. If he is bottle-fed, you could try giving him a bottle with a few ounces of water. Sleep experts have various theories about getting your baby to sleep through the night. Generally, they encourage you to teach your baby to get himself back to sleep. This is done by waiting longer and longer before going to console him if he is crying. Following are some good resources on sleep:

- Ferber, Dr. Richard. *Solve Your Child's Sleep Problems*. New York: Simon & Schuster, 1985. The "sleep doctor" in many parents' opinions, Dr. Ferber is most well known for his "progressive-waiting method" meant to help babies five months and older fall asleep.

- Mindell, Jodi. *Sleeping through the Night: How Infants, Toddlers, and Their Parents Can Get a Good Night's Sleep*. New York: Harper Collins, 1997. A new book that uses a varied Ferber method good for newborns to three-year-olds.

- Sears, William. *Nighttime Parenting*. New York: Plume, 1985. On the other end of the spectrum from the authors of the books above, Dr. Sears is a long-time advocate of the family bed, in which babies get their needs met without child or mom becoming completely awake. While not for every family, Dr. Sears offers a method of sleeping harmony that he asserts is good for a child's self-esteem.

Warning! Do not feed your baby cereal in his bottle or with a spoon before four months of age. Not only is this practice not effective in getting him to sleep through the night, it can cause food and respiratory allergies.

Feeding Your Baby

Introducing Solids

The phrase "introducing solids" is a bit misleading. Your baby's first solids aren't really solid at all, but just liquids thickened with a bit of cereal. In any case, this is your baby's introduction to the world of adult food. Somewhere between four and six months, you will introduce your baby to solids in the form of infant cereal. According to the American Academy of Pediatrics, breast-fed infants generally do not need solids until six months of age.[1]

When Is Your Baby Ready for Supplemental Food?

Your baby's growth and development don't follow an exact time line—and you shouldn't either. Supplemental foods should be started when your baby is developmentally ready and seems to need them. Your baby may be ready for supplemental foods when she:

- is at least four to six months old;
- can move her tongue back and forth and can draw in her lower lip as a spoon is removed;
- can take a soft or mashed food from a spoon (if she spits it out after a few tries, she is probably not ready yet);
- can hold her head up; and
- seems hungry even after eight to ten feedings of breast milk or forty ounces of formula in twenty-four hours.

Giving babies foods high in nitrate, such as beets, carrots, and spinach, before four months can cause methemoglobinemia, a condition that alters hemoglobin in the blood.

▼

The First Food: Cereal

Rice cereal is recommended as the first food because it is the least allergenic. Some tips for your baby's big step into the world of adult food follow:

- Start with a teaspoon of rice cereal mixed with enough breast milk or formula to have the consistency of a thin soup. As your baby develops more tongue control, you can make the cereal thicker. Experiment to find the right consistency. If, after several days of giving your baby cereal, the cereal still comes right out of her mouth, consider these possible causes: (1) The consistency is not right. (2) She is not developmentally ready for cereal. If so, stop for now and try in a few weeks or a month.
- Feed your baby with a plastic or rubber-coated spoon to prevent gum injury.
- Feed cereal to your baby twice a day—morning and night.
- Don't put cereal in your baby's bottle. Using a spoon helps her develop her tongue muscle, which helps promote clear speech later.
- Your baby will start with a tablespoon or less of cereal mixed with liquid at each feeding. She will gradually eat four to

No Honey for Your Honey

Because of the risk of botulism, don't give your baby honey until her first birthday.

six tablespoons of dry cereal mixed with breast milk or formula.
- Do not add sugar or salt to your baby's cereal.
- After at least a week, when it is clear that your baby tolerates rice cereal, you can try other single-grain cereals, such as oats or barley.
- Wait until your baby is seven to nine months old before you feed her wheat, Cream of Wheat, mixed cereals, and high-protein cereals.
- Once your child eats cereal regularly, you may consider jarred cereal as an option. However, dry cereal is more economical and less wasteful.

▼

Adding Other Foods to Your Baby's Menu

Have you ever seen those adorable baby pictures in which a baby wears her carrots from head to toe? Soon you will know firsthand that those pictures are not posed; they are real life! Take a deep breath and relax. Stock up on Shout liquid cleaner and make sure your mop is working. You are entering the baby-food zone.

Vegetables are generally introduced first (after cereal). Babies have an automatic

Allergy Alert

To detect food allergies, give your baby only a small amount of a new food the first day and look for signs of allergy, such as diarrhea and skin rashes. Wait three days before you introduce another new food, and try no more than two new foods per week. This helps you make sure your baby tolerates a food before you move on to the next one. If your family has a history of allergies, don't introduce your baby to citrus fruits or their juices until one year of age.

preference for sweets; by offering vegetables first, you help them develop their taste for veggies before fruits. Yellow vegetables like squash, sweet potato, and carrots are usually well accepted. Next try green vegetables, such as green peas, spinach, and green beans. To screen for allergies, introduce the vegetables one at a time, with three-day intervals in-between.

After your baby has tried a variety of vegetables, you can go on to fruits. Your baby will more than likely love fruits. Introduce them the same way you introduced vegetables: one at a time, with three-day intervals in-between. Stifle the urge to buy those yummy-sounding desserts with names like Peach Cobbler and Dutch Apple Dessert. They have about the same number of calories as the same amount fruit, but some of the calories come from added starches and sugars—empty calories that your baby doesn't need.

More Baby-Food Basics

- Don't feed your baby food out of a jar and save the rest for the next feeding; this practice can cause bacteria to grow in leftover food. Instead, transfer a small amount of food to a bowl, cover and store the jar, then feed from the bowl.
- Don't give your baby any mixed food that contains two or more foods new to her. If your child shows an allergic reaction, you will not know which food caused it. Signs of allergy include rash, diarrhea, severe colic, and vomiting.
- Let your child decide when she is finished eating. When your child is full, you will probably notice that she moves her head away from you, closes her mouth or covers it with her hands, shakes her head, and/or throws spoon, plate, or cup overboard.
- Feed your infant cereals and baby foods in addition to—not instead of—breast milk or formula. Offer the breast milk or formula first, then the foods.
- Cook, purée, and strain fruits—with the exception of mangoes, banana, and very ripe pears and peaches, which can all simply be mashed with a fork.
- Avoid giving your baby fruit with small seeds, such as raspberries, strawberries, and grapes—unless, however, you are willing to peel, seed, and chop the grapes once your baby can chew. (Yes, I have done this!)

▼

Summary of Addition of Solids to Your Baby's Diet

You may find that the recommendations that follow are a bit vague. A range of ages given is because babies progress differently. While some babies are ready for infant cereal at four months, others should wait until five or six months. Some babies can skip the puréed-baby-food stage at six months and jump to mashed table foods. Some babies will take much longer before progressing to table foods. It all depends on when they are developmentally ready and accepting of new foods and textures. Observing your baby is important. Follow her lead.

Four to Six Months: Cereal

- Introduce rice cereal first.
- Start with 1 teaspoon cereal mixed thin with 2–3 tablespoons breast milk or formula. Gradually increase the amount of cereal to 1 tablespoon mixed with breast milk or formula.
- Give cereal twice a day, generally at breakfast and dinner or bedtime.
- Give breast milk or formula five or more times per day, 5–7 ounces per feeding, for a total of 23–32 ounces a day.

Five to Seven Months: Veggies and Fruits

- Add strained or puréed vegetables. Good starter vegetables: avocado, carrots, squash, sweet potato.
- Next, add strained or puréed fruit. Good starter fruits: banana, pears, applesauce, peaches.
- Start with 1 teaspoon and increase to 1 tablespoon, twice a day.
- Gradually increase to 4 tablespoons a day.
- Give breast milk or formula four to five times a day, 5–7 ounces per feeding, for a total of 24–32 ounces a day.

Seven to Ten Months: Protein

- Add protein foods: 4 tablespoons a day. Good starter protein foods: egg yolk, tofu, mashed beans (without skin), puréed meats (lamb, veal, poultry), small amounts of cheese and yogurt (unless allergy prone).
- Add juice: 3–4 ounces in a cup. Avoid citrus until one year.
- Add finger foods: teething crackers, Cheerios, and other foods that don't need much chewing.
- Offer table foods: mashed or cut into small pieces, like mashed potatoes, vegetables, cut-up pasta, or macaroni.
- Give breast milk or formula three to five feedings a day, 5–8 ounces per feeding, for a total of 24–32 ounces a day.
- At this age, your baby's meals start to resemble those of adults–balanced meals with snacks between.

Ten to Twelve Months: Mostly Table Foods

- Add finger foods and cut-up food from the table: bite-sized pieces of soft meat (except hot dogs), soft cooked vegetables, and fruits cut into cubes or strips.
- Introduce soft foods like macaroni and cheese, casseroles, cheese, and yogurt.
- You may now add wheat cereals. If your child is allergy-prone, wait until one year or later to introduce wheat.
- Give breast milk or formula three feedings a day, some from a cup, for a total of 24 ounces a day.

Twelve to Eighteen Months: What the Family Eats

- Add fish, honey, and most other foods your family eats; avoid those foods that can cause choking. (See chart at right.)
- You may now switch to whole milk and start citrus fruit and juice.
- Begin weaning from the bottle. Your child is getting more skilled with a spoon.

▼

Sample Menu

Following is an example of what your six- to seven-month-old baby's diet might look like. Remember, there is no set formula for when you should offer fruits, vegetables, and cereal, as long as your baby eats them several times a day.

Choking Alert

Choking on food (as well as other small objects) is a problem for kids until they reach the age of five years. You will need to be careful about foods that can cause choking. Most choking deaths occur in kids under three years. Peanuts are the food that causes most choking injuries. Below are some tips:

The First Year:

- Avoid fruits or vegetables with seeds.
- Avoid food with a peel on it.
- Avoid peanut butter, unless mixed with a generous amount of mashed banana or applesauce.
- Cut foods into small bites to avoid choking.

Avoid Until at Least Age Four:

- Grapes (unless cut in half or smaller)
- Hot dogs (unless quartered; NOT in round pieces)
- Nuts (unless finely chopped)
- Popcorn
- Other hard, round foods, such as raw carrots
- Hard candies

Always:

- Be present when your child is eating.
- Don't let her run around while eating. Keep her seated.
- Keep mealtime quiet. Laughing, screaming, and even talking with food in the mouth can result in choking.

Early Morning

Some babies like to wake up before the birds, have a pre-breakfast snack of breast milk or formula, and then go back to sleep.

Breakfast

• Breast milk or 6–8 ounces formula
• 1–2 tablespoons rice cereal, mixed with breast milk or formula

Mid-Morning

• Breast milk or 4 ounces formula
• 1–2 tablespoons strained fruit

Lunch

• Breast milk or 6–8 ounces formula
• 2–4 tablespoons strained vegetable
• 1–2 tablespoons strained fruit

Mid-Afternoon

• 3 ounces fruit juice in a cup

Dinner

• Breast milk or 6–8 ounces of formula
• 1–2 tablespoons cereal mixed with breast milk or formula
• 2–4 tablespoons strained vegetable

Bedtime

• Breast milk or 6–8 ounces formula

▼

Protein Power

Between seven and ten months, as your baby starts eating more solids and reducing the amount of formula or breast milk she drinks, she will need more protein and iron from other sources. This is when you should start introducing your baby to protein foods. If you have ever seen, smelled, or tasted baby-food strained meats, you won't have any problem understanding if your baby refuses them. You may opt for making your own meats by using a blender or mini-chopper. Finely ground, cooked beef or poultry and mashed canned tuna mixed with a little broth also works. And soon, you can chop poultry very finely or mix with mashed vegetables. (See tips for making baby food later in this chapter.)

Don't worry if your baby is not a good meat eater at the beginning. My son Robert was a vegetarian by choice until the age of eighteen months. He ate vegetables and loved mashed pinto and baked beans, but he refused meat, chicken, and fish. These are good sources of protein:

• Mashed beans, canned refried beans
• Mashed tofu or tofu mixed with vegetables
• High-protein cereals
• Yogurt and small pieces of cheese (if your child is not allergy-prone)

▼

Making Your Own Baby Food

You don't have to rely on jarred baby food for your baby—making it yourself is a snap. You will need:

• Food grinder or mill, food chopper, food processor, or blender (As your baby gets older, you can just use a fork to mash the food.)

- Ice cube trays if you want to make enough to freeze

What's the Right Texture for Your Baby's Food?

Your baby's first food should be puréed and fairly thin (similar to a thick soup). As she gets used to eating from a spoon, you can make the texture of her food a little thicker. There are no specific rules about when to feed your baby thicker foods; it all depends on your baby's individual development. Pay attention to the signs your baby is giving you: If she is having trouble, you may need to go back to a finer texture. Keep experimenting to get the right consistency.

As your baby's development progresses, so should the texture of her food. Begin making food a little thicker and then a little lumpier. Next, you can move on to simply mashing the food with a fork or potato masher. Finely chopping and then coarsely chopping are next (except for meats, which should be chopped finely until your baby can chew very well).

Tips:

- Make sure your hands and all utensils used in making baby food are clean; babies are more susceptible than adults to bacteria carried in food.
- Don't add any salt or sweetener to food. Babies don't have the same tastes as adults.

- Use fresh or frozen fruits and vegetables. If fresh, use within a day or two of buying so that they contain as many vitamins as possible. Make sure to wash produce well immediately before using. See Chapter Eight for a discussion of pesticides.
- To help retain nutrients, cook fruits and vegetables in a minimum of water or steam until just tender. If possible, use the nutrient-rich leftover cooking water to purée the baby food. (You can also add this water to soups or sauces for the rest of the family.)
- Store homemade baby food in an airtight container, refrigerate, and use within three days.
- If making more than a serving or two, you may want to freeze the rest in ice cube trays. After the food freezes, remove the cubes from the tray and place in zip-lock bags. Frozen fruits and vegetables can be kept in the freezer for up to six months; meat, fish, and poultry should be used within ten weeks. To defrost, place a cube in a small dish in the refrigerator or place in a zip-lock bag in cool water. Don't defrost in a microwave unless you plan to serve immediately—and make sure to stir well to ensure the heat is well distributed.

General Instructions for Making Puréed Baby Food

1. Steam or cook vegetable or meat in small amount of water until soft. Cut meats into small pieces first.

2. Place the cooked food in a food processor with enough cooking juice, breast milk, or formula to make a thin purée. Experiment with the texture that works for your baby, gradually making the food thicker as she is ready.

Easy Meats:
- Chicken and turkey breast
- Canned tuna
- Veal
- Lean ground beef
- Pork loin

Fruits That Can Be Puréed without Cooking First:
- Apricot (ripe or canned)
- Avocado
- Banana
- Blueberries
- Cantaloupe, honeydew, watermelon
- Mango
- Peach
- Pear
- Plum

Note: Strawberries, raspberries, and blackberries can be puréed raw, but they must also be strained to remove their seeds. Grapes and cherries must be pitted and peeled before puréeing. They are better saved until later, when you can simply pit and chop them and your baby can finger-feed herself.

Foods That Should Be Cooked First:
- All vegetables
- Apples, prunes, and fruits that are not very ripe

Vegetables That Purée Easily:
- Asparagus (remove fibrous ends first)
- Beets
- Broccoli
- Carrots
- Cauliflower
- Chard
- Garbanzo, pinto, or black beans
- Peas
- Potatoes
- Spinach and other greens
- Sweet peppers
- Sweet potatoes
- Turnips
- Winter squash

Mixing Foods

Feed your baby new fruits and vegetables one at a time with three days between to check for allergies. Once you are certain she has no reactions to food, you can begin mixing them. This is also a way to try vegetables that your baby might not like alone. For example, she may not like cauliflower, but likes it mixed with a little mashed potatoes. Here are some good flavor combinations:

Vegetables:
- Mediterranean Mix: garbanzo beans and spinach
- Veggie Stew: carrots, potatoes, peas
- Winter Veggie Blend: turnips and carrots
- Go Green: peas and green beans

- Only Orange: sweet potatoes and carrots
- Really Red: beets and potatoes
- Green Spuds: potato, broccoli, spinach

Fruits:
- Apple-pear
- Apricot-banana
- Banana-pineapple
- Blueberry-pear
- Mango-pineapple
- Peach-raspberry (strained)
- Plum-apple
- Raspberry-apple (strained)
- Fruit cobbler (cooked small fruit pieces—try blueberries, apples, or peaches—with infant oat cereal)

As your baby gets older, experiment with different textures by mixing fruits or vegetables with:
- Cooked bulgur or brown rice
- Infant cereal
- Mashed potatoes
- Tiny pasta
- Wheat germ

Tone down strong flavors by mixing in yogurt and/or cereal.

Mixed Dinners

Once your baby has gone through the gamut of vegetables and meats, you may want to try jarred dinners. Dinners contain about half as much protein as strained meats alone, but your baby may like them better. You may also want to make your own dinners—they will taste better and cost less.

Start with the flavor combinations below or just use food from your table (before adding any seasoning).

Mixed Dinner Recipe

¼ cup puréed or finely chopped meat or poultry, tofu, cottage or grated cheese

¼ cup mashed or chopped cooked vegetables

½ cup starchy food, such as potato, rice, bulgur, macaroni or other pasta (Tiny pasta called acini de pepe is smaller than rice.)

1. Place your choice of the above ingredients in a small mixing bowl.

2. Mix together, adding just enough liquid (vegetable or chicken broth, formula or milk) to hold together.

3. Mash to the consistency that your baby needs.

Makes: 1 cup (enough for several servings)

Good Flavor Combinations:
- Chicken ABCs: chicken, alphabet pasta, peas
- Turkey 'n' Dressing: turkey, ½ cup crumbled cornbread, green beans
- Creamy Beef: ground beef, rice, broccoli, yogurt
- Something Fishy: tuna, rice, avocado
- Veal Français: veal, white beans, yogurt
- Chicken Delight: chicken, asparagus, potato

Vegetarian Mixed Dinners

If your baby turns her head away from meat, or if you are raising your child vegetarian, try these combinations:

- Cheesy Broccoli: broccoli, tofu, potato
- Olé: refried pinto or black beans (without spices), rice, avocado
- Mac 'n' Cheese: macaroni, colby cheese, cauliflower
- Asian: tofu, cabbage, rice
- Winter White: cottage cheese, cauliflower, tiny pasta
- Stew: white beans, carrots, green beans, potatoes
- Fall Harvest: sweet potatoes, winter squash, tofu
- Spring Feast: asparagus, soy cheese, rice

▼

Finger Foods and Self-Feeding

Your baby will probably make it evident that she is ready to try to step into the big world of self-feeding. Grabbing food with her hands or taking the spoon from you are good signs. A normal step in development, your child will have to do some playing with her food to learn how to handle it and eat it. She will probably be so giddy with the fact that she can pick up her food and put it in her mouth that it will be delightful for the family to watch.

Good Finger Foods:

- Small pieces of well-cooked vegetables (naturally small or cut into small pieces): peas, carrots, zucchini, green beans without strings, sweet potato, potato. When you don't have the time or the food on hand to make your own, some convenience foods can come to the rescue: Gerber has a "Graduates" line of food that includes Diced Carrots, Diced Green Beans, and Mixed Vegetable Dices; also available are diced dinners and diced fruit, all perfect for self-feeding.
- Small or cut-in-half blueberries and small pieces of raw pear, peach, banana, apricot, mango, plum, cantaloupe, and watermelon (without seeds). Make sure that fruit is very ripe and is peeled.
- Small pieces of cooked fruit, such as apple, not-quite-ripe pear, and peach
- Stewed dried prunes, apricots, and raisins, cut into pieces
- Zwieback crackers, Cheerios, oven-dried toast cut into small pieces, teething crackers, and cooked macaroni cut in pieces

Buying a lot of expensive toddler food is not really necessary. You will soon find yourself cutting some of your own meals into small pieces for your baby!

▼

Gearing Up for Self-Feeding

A few things will make your life easier when your baby starts feeding herself:

- *Spill protection:* You will either want to cover the floor under the highchair with a clean plastic shower curtain, big plastic mat, or towel. Or, you may want to have a canine cleanup crew come in after the feeding!

- *The right utensils:* Short-handled baby spoons with soft tips are perfect for first feeders. Utensils with curved ends prevent babies from putting the utensil too far into their mouth (or throat). They are also bigger than straight-handled baby utensils, and so are easier to hold and maneuver.

- *The right outerwear:* Your baby will need to graduate from the small baby bibs to large bibs that cover most of her front. Plastic bibs with pockets that catch food are also available. My son loved watermelon at this age and after several post-watermelon baths, I invested in a bib that had long sleeves. This offers super protection from messy foods.

▼

Saying Bye-Bye to the Bottle

While saying good-bye to the bottle is, in a sense, closing the first chapter of your baby's life, it must be done—usually in the second year. Most health professionals recommend babies be drinking from a cup by the age of one year, but in many cases, it takes longer than that. My own children were off the bottle between fifteen and eighteen months. Switching to a cup is important for several reasons:

- Using the bottle too long can adversely affect tooth and jaw development.
- Drinking from a bottle is so easy that it might compete with eating "real" foods.
- Some babies use a bottle more or less as a pacifier. It is important that young children learn new ways to comfort themselves.

Here are some tips for making the transition from bottle to cup:

- When you introduce juice, serve it in a sippy cup.
- Make a big deal about graduating to a cup and let your child pick out a special one. As a transition to the cup, we used a refillable plastic bottle (like a sports water bottle) with a closeable spout to take in the car and on the go.
- If your baby is having trouble letting go of the bottle, do it gradually, one meal at a time.

- If the bedtime bottle is a special, comforting time, you may want to hang on to it for a while. Or simply provide a cup, but don't give up the cuddle!

▼

Eating Together

Babies tend to eat on their own schedules. However, as your baby gets older, you will want her to sit at the table with you for part of your dinnertime, even if she is only eating a snack. You are a model for your child, and by watching you, she can learn many things at the dinner table. She can learn, for example, how to eat with utensils, that we usually don't eat with our hands, that we drink when we are thirsty, and that mealtime is a pleasant event where we talk together. Your baby is a sponge, soaking up everything she observes with her senses. Listening to conversations at the dinner table can be very important for her speech development. Your child will also learn manners while sitting with you at the table. As your child gets older, she will learn not only by watching but also by doing. Do keep in mind, however, that as children first get more mobile, they won't want to sit very long.

Feeding Your Toddler and Preschooler

The last year has flown by, and now your baby is toddling around and exerting his independence in almost every situation. As he gains more control over his physical world, he will also want more control of other things—including eating. The next few years will be important ones for your child as he begins to develop his own eating habits, as well as food likes and dislikes. This is also the time that your child will start noticing what you are doing! So set a good example, and don't eat anything that you don't want him to eat!

Once your child enters the preschool years (ages three to five), he will be full of fun. This a great time to get your child involved in cooking. Not only can he help pick foods at the grocery store and help in the kitchen, he also wants to—grab the opportunity while you can! If you make cooking fun now, you will be patting your child on the back in six or seven years when he is making dinner for the family! An Easy Bake Oven—the toy of choice for baby-boom girls of the sixties (and one of my favorite toys)—is still available and is a great way to get your son or daughter interested in cooking.

For moms and dads who are not sure about getting their son involved in cooking—it's easier for him to start now than to learn when he is eighteen and on his own!

Cooking together also sets up some great family traditions. In our family, Robert helps Dad make the crepe batter on Saturday mornings. Even if Robert is watching his favorite movie, he comes running when he hears "time to make crepes!" He breaks the eggs, adds the milk and vanilla, and helps with the mixer. In a few years, he may be the one in charge of making the crepes!

Setting Up Boundaries

Toddlers and preschoolers want to exert some control over what they eat. This is an important time to set some boundaries. Clarify roles and responsibilities around eating and set rules for mealtimes, snacks, and where your family eats.

Who's in Charge of What?

Remember these rules: Parents are in charge of what food they offer and when they offer it. Children are in charge of deciding how much, if any, they will eat. If these rules aren't followed during the toddler years, power struggles can happen. Your child has learned how to twist you around his little finger if, when he says "eggs," you start scrambling!

Changes in Appetite

At about one year or older, you will notice a drop in your child's food intake as his growth slows after a year of tremendous progress. You may find yourself saying, "My child has started eating like a bird." As hard as it may be at times, trust your child's appetite: When he gives a signal he's done, he is—don't push!

Toddler Tangles: Pick Your Battles

Since this is the time when a toddler wants to be independent, he will be showing off his new-found ability to say "NO!" or "Do myself." Let him, unless what he is doing could cause him harm. Being too controlling when it comes to food can harm his natural ability to eat for his own appetite. This could lead to disordered eating. Your job is to find a healthy compromise—somewhere between being too controlling and too permissive.

Preschool Pressures

You may find that once your child starts preschool, he is affected by peer pressure. It's amazing that the influence of friends can start this early, but it does. Sometimes you have to explain why people eat differently. For example, "Johnny's mom may let him eat candy every day with lunch, but our family has different rules. For us, candy is a food for special times." Sometimes explanations don't help, and you may not want to bother with long explanations or logic for the young preschooler. Just say that every family has different rules.

Preschoolers often get stubborn about food choices. Again, it's better not to lock horns over it. Stick to your guns when you feel it's important, but be flexible when you can.

The following situations are typical for toddlers and preschoolers, but the solutions may not be what first comes to mind. . . .

Food Jags

Those two four-letter words usually bring back memories for parents. A food jag is normal, no matter how bizarre it seems while your child is in the middle of one. Just like adults, children find a food they like, and they stick with it. However, kids tend to want their favorite food at every meal.

Jack wants grilled cheese for the third time in two days. Should Mom get out the pan? No! Giving in to food jags is okay occasionally–but only if it doesn't turn Mom or Dad into a short-order cook! I once had a friend who would end up making two or three different things for her son, trying to find the food that he would eat that night. Even young children can learn to manipulate the situation–they know what your hot buttons are.

Go along with your child for a while. If you give too much attention to the subject, the food jag may hang around a little longer.

For example, if he wants an apple for snack every day, fine. But at some point you run out of apples and you need to give him pears. He'll get through it. You can also give more variety to food jags by making a similar food. You might say, "I'm sorry, honey, we are out of macaroni–but we do have spaghetti!" Or make the macaroni in a new way–with ground beef and tomato sauce, perhaps.

Do you feel as if you need to try something altogether different when your child keeps asking for the same thing? The suggestions below may help your child make the switch to other foods.

More Tips for Dealing with Food Jags
- After a while, conveniently run out of the food in question.
- Give him the food after he has eaten something else.

Food Jag Variations	
If Your Child Likes:	**Try Making:**
Macaroni and cheese	Chili Mac with a cheesy tomato sauce (recipe page 298) Spaghetti à la Carbonara (recipe page 317)
Chicken nuggets	Fish Nuggets (recipe page 305) Oven-Fried Zucchini Sticks (recipe page 180) Baked chicken
Peanut-butter-and-jelly sandwiches	Peanut-butter-and-honey sandwiches (recipe page 312) Pabble, a spread for sandwiches (recipe page 310) Peanut-butter-and-banana roll-ups (in tortillas)
Grilled cheese sandwiches	Grilled ham and cheese Tuna melt with cheese Cheese quesadillas made with corn tortillas
Potato chips and other snack foods	Pretzels, wheat crackers, baked corn tortillas, carrot sticks, sugar snap peas

l food a different way,
n expand his diet. For
macaroni and cheese is the
food of choice, add pieces of chopped
chicken or tuna to it. Or make plain
macaroni as a side dish with something
else. If your child is a peanut-butter
lover, try stuffing celery with peanut
butter or make a peanut butter sauce to
go with a stir fry.

- Try to fill in the missing pieces of his
diet with healthy snacks.
- Set rules for when the food is allowed.
For example, he can have peanut butter
and jelly for snacks, but not for lunch
and dinner.
- Make sure your child takes a multivitamin-mineral supplement daily if his
food choices don't have variety.
- Keep trying to introduce your child to
other foods, but hide your frustration if
he doesn't like them or won't taste them.
- Offer food choices to help your child
feel in control. Do you want peas or
corn tonight? Would you like milk or
chocolate milk? Do you want your
burger with or without cheese?
- Offer your child an opportunity to help
you prepare some foods. He might be
more willing to get off his food jag.
- If the food jag goes on for more than a
month or two, you might want to consult your health-care provider.

The Short-Order Line

Sarah sees what's on the table for dinner,
and she doesn't like it. She whines that she
wants a peanut-butter-and-jelly sandwich.
You think, "Well, that's easy to make; perhaps I should." Don't! Children need to
learn that what's served is dinner for the
evening. Just make sure to have bread, fruit,
and milk on the table so that she has something else to eat. You can also try to make at
least one thing she likes at a meal. This is
also a good time to get your child involved
in meal planning. "Well, you don't like what
we have tonight. But perhaps you can help
me plan what's for dinner tomorrow!"

Johnny Jump-Up

Johnny just can't sit at the table for more than
a few minutes. Then you've got to chase him
around the house with a fork full of food.
This is not a pretty picture. First of all, it reinforces the negative behavior (because Johnny
is getting attention). Second, a child can
easily choke when running and eating. Make
the rule that you must sit at the table to eat.
Even if a child is not hungry, he should be
encouraged to sit with the family while they
eat. As soon as a child figures out that getting
to play instead of eat is not that easy, he will
get into the habit of eating with the family if
he is hungry. As children get older and have
longer attention spans, they should be able to
sit at the table even if they are not hungry.

The Meal Skipper

Don't fret when your child sometimes
totally skips a meal or eats very little. There
are several reasons. Kids eat according to
their appetite, and they may not be hungry.
Some kids eat very well at one or two meals

and aren't interested in eating the last meal. That was our Robert. When he was between two and three years, he would eat a big dinner or big lunch but not both. In fact, sometimes he didn't eat dinner at all. Although we were a bit worried at first, we finally realized that this was just him and since he was growing fine, that was all right. However, there may be other reasons for a poor appetite.

Too much snacking between meals, snacking too close to a meal, and having too much juice, sweet drinks, or milk between meals can also be the problem. Limit juices to one cup a day and avoid sweetened drinks. Milk should not be limited unless your child is drinking it excessively between meals and it is affecting his appetite for meals. Although between-meal snacks are important for toddlers and preschoolers, they need to be scheduled midway between meals so as to not interfere.

My son Nicolas was often not hungry after kindergarten. Finally, we realized that he was given a snack right before school was out at 11:00 A.M.! A later lunch was the solution. A child who consistently has a poor appetite, however, may have a medical problem, such as anemia.

Bribing and Begging

"I made a nice chocolate cake for those who eat their green beans." "No TV tonight if you don't eat that casserole!" "I made that just for you!" "Just three more bites and you're done!" It's so easy to fall into this trap of bribing, threatening, and piling on the guilt. After all, our kids' eating habits seem to reflect on our success as parents (not to

mention our cooking). And, of course, we are all concerned about our children's health and nutrition. But wait. Remember that it's for your child to decide whether he is going to eat and how much. Your job is preparing the food and serving it. Try to separate yourself emotionally from the issue. If you try to force your child to eat, you may win the battle, but you will lose the war! Studies show that when a kid is forced, bribed, and coaxed to eat, he will actually eat less than when he is left to eat at his own pace.

Kids Behaving Badly

"Yuck!" "Do I have to eat this stuff?" "Why can't we have something good for dinner?" It is often these types of comments that turn the dinner hour into an emotional battleground. These words do come out of the mouths of babes, especially when they start preschool or have older siblings.

Try not to give it too much attention, but do let your child know how to express himself more respectfully. For example, rephrase it. "I hear that you don't care for green beans, but there are also apples on the table for you to eat." Let your child know what the expected behavior is at the table, including how to turn down food politely. Let him also know that if he cannot behave properly, he will have to leave the table (or whatever your family decides) until he can. When he refuses food, however, treat it matter-of-factly. "That's fine; you can still eat the bread, fruit, and chicken." (Of course, adults at the table also have to use their best manners if they want their children to imitate them!)

I Don't Like It! (Never mind that I've never tasted it!)

Some kids are more reluctant than others to try new foods. It may take ten times of offering a new food before it is tried. Don't make a big deal of it, or your child may learn that it's a good attention-getter. Be sure to compliment him when he does try something new. The tips below will help in setting the stage for healthy eating behaviors.

▼

Making Mealtime Go Smoothly

Imagine this: You have been working all day and you're tired. You've just sat down to watch your favorite TV show, and *boom!* Your husband drags you to the kitchen, sits you down at the table, and says, "Dinner-time! I've been working all day to make you this new dish: Chicken Fried Unidentified! I hope you like it!" Chances are, you'd feel frustrated and maybe even throw a few unkind words at your doting spouse.

While keeping that picture in your mind, think of this. Your child has had a long day at day care. He is now back at "home sweet home" and has just started watching his favorite video or playing with his favorite toy. Then a faraway voice calls, "Jason, time to come to the table for dinner! I've made you a surprise!" He may be hungry, but he is also tired and now frustrated—not in the best mood for eating the new dish you have prepared just for him. He may say a few unkind words, too.

How can we make the dinner hour go a bit more smoothly?

Get Ready . . .

1. Have a schedule and let your child know what to expect day to day. (Since kids don't eat well when they are tired, try to have dinner rather early.) After he comes home from day care or from being out, let him know that he has half an hour to play. (Since time is a tough concept, find a way to explain this that he understands.) Or, if you are going out to eat, you can let him know that and set the stage for a positive experience.

2. Give your child a five-minute warning. This helps him prepare himself to separate from his current activity.

3. If your child is excited before dinner, try to take a few minutes with a calming activity such as reading.

4. The predinner hour is often when your toddler or preschooler wants all of your attention. This makes it tough to get dinner on the table. Try having meals that can be prepared quickly, or put your child to work in the kitchen with you. He can put the napkins on the table, help stir, or watch and ask questions as you explain how you're making a dish.

Get Set . . .

1. Make mealtime pleasant. Try to avoid nagging, arguing, and other unpleasant conversation at the table.

2. Don't mind messes. Toddlers still need to play with their food somewhat to explore it. And they will continue to spill their milk and other food as they learn to handle utensils. Just learn to live with it; it will be many years before mealtimes are a squeaky-clean event. (Our clean-up crew, our two dogs, loved sitting under the high chair waiting for the next accident!)

3. Make it easy for your child to eat. He should sit in a high chair or appropriately sized booster chair. Give him utensils that are easy to hold and a plate that has sides that he can push against to help with feeding himself.

4. Set a good example. Model good behavior and good eating habits at the table, and you will be surprised at what your child picks up!

Go!

1. Arrange food nicely on the plate. Try to respect your child's idiosyncrasies about his food. ("The peas can't touch the potatoes!" or "Can I have sandwich triangles?") If you know that your child likes his pasta without spaghetti sauce, leave some plain for him.

2. Make sure the food is in small enough pieces for your child to feed himself.

3. Try to plan meals that look good, using different shapes, colors, and textures.

4. Serve small portions. Kids are sometimes overwhelmed when portions are too big.

5. Serve age-appropriate foods. At two or three years, a child cannot chew steak well, even if it is cut into small pieces. Have a softer substitute on hand.

6. Give your child choices so that he feels he has more control—for example, "Do you think we should have peas or carrots tonight?" or "Do you want the orange or the green cup?"

7. Serve new foods with a positive attitude and persistence: Serve them first, when your child is hungriest. Serve a tiny portion. Serve a new food with a food that is your child's favorite. Serve the new food again, perhaps in a different way, even if he didn't like it the first time.

8. Turn off the TV during dinner and get rid of other distractions (for kids and parents) such as toys, books, the mail, and the newspaper. That way everyone can focus on eating and enjoying the company.

▼

Preschool Appetites

Preschoolers will continue to have appetites that wax and wane, depending on:
- their growth status;
- their activity level;
- what they eat when they are not with you; and
- their mood.

Continue to trust your preschooler's appetite. Preschoolers would often rather play than eat. Establish guidelines for your family so that your child has ample opportunity to eat before he is excused to go play. Don't, however, chase your child around the house with a plate and a fork trying to get him to eat. And don't try to force or bribe. If he doesn't eat well at this meal because he's not hungry or is distracted, save the meal for snacktime. He will eventually eat. Just make sure you do your responsibility well: set a good example and offer healthy meals and snacks. Refer to the Food Guide Pyramid for Young Children for nutrition guidelines for children ages two to six years.

▼

Preschool Fitness

Between the ages of three and five, kids also establish their "activity identity." Now is the time to integrate regular, fun exercise into your child's life. Regular walks, trike or bike riding, playing ball, and playing in the park all count toward having fun and staying fit! At the appropriate age, encourage your child to take part in sports such as swimming, T-ball, and soccer. Recreation centers often have team sports for kids as young as three, but to ensure a positive first experience, make sure your child is ready for this.

The reason activity is so important now is that kids can easily establish the habit of being sedentary. Watching TV and movies and playing video or computer games are easy to do hour after hour. Make sure to limit sedentary activities such as TV or video games to two hours a day or less. Such "couch potato" habits are associated with childhood obesity. Watching TV and playing video games also take your child away from important educational activities such as building with blocks, working puzzles, socializing with friends, reading, and drawing.

If your child is not with you during the day, make sure your day-care provider allows plenty of time for physical play (outdoors if weather permits) and doesn't use the TV as a baby-sitter. Be sure to ask questions about what TV movies and programs your child is allowed to watch; sometimes when older and younger children are mixed in a day-care situation, the younger children may be watching shows that are not age-appropriate.

For more information on fitness, please see Chapter Two.

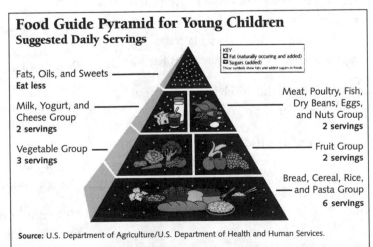

Food Guide Pyramid for Young Children
Suggested Daily Servings

KEY
☐ Fat (naturally occuring and added)
☐ Sugars (added)
These symbols show fats and added sugars in foods.

Fats, Oils, and Sweets — **Eat less**

Milk, Yogurt, and Cheese Group **2 servings**

Vegetable Group — **3 servings**

Meat, Poultry, Fish, Dry Beans, Eggs, and Nuts Group **2 servings**

Fruit Group **2 servings**

Bread, Cereal, Rice, and Pasta Group **6 servings**

Source: U.S. Department of Agriculture/U.S. Department of Health and Human Services.

Low-Fat Alternatives	
Instead of:	**Serve:**
Milk (whole)	2%, 1%, or skim milk
Cheese (regular)	Reduced-fat cheese
Burgers, hot dogs	Veggie burgers, turkey burgers, soy dogs
Chicken nuggets, fried chicken	Baked coated chicken
Fish sticks	Baked or grilled fish
Chocolate-chip cookies, cake, pie	Fresh fruit, ginger snaps, oatmeal cookies, Katie and Nicolas's Fruit Crisp (recipe page 217), low-fat cakes
Ice cream	Frozen yogurt
Milkshakes	Smoothies (recipe page 285)

Trimming the Fat

Once your child turns two, he doesn't need as much fat as he did the first two years. In fact, now the percentage of fat in his diet should be equal to that in yours—about 30 percent. In Chapter Two, we discussed how eating right and forming good habits in childhood can help prevent heart disease, cancer, and other conditions that are affected by the amount of fat in the diet. Well, now is the time to begin—when your toddler is eating mostly adult food and forming his own food preferences. Above are some ways to trim the fat from your toddler's diet.

Remember, healthy food habits started now are likely to stick with kids as they grow older.

Ground Rules for Eating at Home

Now is the time to decide with your partner on rules for eating in your home. Having ground rules for eating helps your child accept rules for other behaviors as he gets older. Some of the rules our family has established for eating include:

- Eating only at the table, in designated eating areas, or outside, and always eating Popsicles and other messy foods outside. (Families that skip this rule generally have spotted carpet and furniture!)
- Everyone stays at the table until everyone else is finished. (We started this rule when our youngest was between three and four.)

- If you're hungry enough for dessert, you're hungry enough for fruit. (Most families have some rule regarding dessert.)
- Everyone takes his own plate and cup or glass to the sink area. (This rule can also be started at around three years.)
- Everyone eats a "polite bite." We especially encourage this rule for new foods.

▼

Day-Care Meal Plans and Procedures

At some point, you will probably need someone else to care for your child, whether a licensed day-care center or home provider, a grandparent, a friend, or drop-in-care at a mother's-day-out program. Because food provided outside the home can account for a significant amount of your child's calories and nutrients for the day, be sure to observe the nutrition and feeding program offered. These elements should be present:

- Children in day care for eight hours or less should receive at least one meal and two snacks or two meals and one snack.
- Children in day care for more than eight hours should receive two meals and two snacks or one meal and three snacks.
- Children should not be given sweet, sticky snacks, such as raisins, jelly beans, or fruit rolls.
- The Food Guide Pyramid for Young Children should be followed as a guideline for the types of food offered. Whole grains, fruits, and vegetables should be emphasized.
- Furniture and eating utensils should be age-appropriate and developmentally suitable. Children should be able to touch the floor with their feet when seated. Eating utensils should be appropriate in size and weight to match the children's motor skills and to protect children from choking.[1]
- Children under the age of three should not be given food that is the size or shape of a marble because that presents a choking hazard. Examples are hot dog pieces, whole grapes, marshmallows, and melon balls. Chips, pretzels, nuts, hard candy, and popcorn also pose a choking hazard.
- Children should be offered small portions and second helpings, not one large portion.
- Children should not be forced to eat, nor should food be offered as a reward or punishment.
- Meals should be presented in a family-style eating arrangement to promote good table manners. Children should receive assistance with eating as they need it; child-care providers should always be nearby when children are eating.

Special Handling for Infants

- Bottles should not be allowed to warm to room temperature for long periods; this promotes bacterial growth.
- Formula or milk left in a bottle after a feeding should be discarded.

- Bottles, nipples, and bottle caps should be disinfected by washing in a dishwasher or by boiling for five minutes prior to filling.
- Bottles should be heated in a bowl of hot water for five minutes. Bottles should never be heated in the microwave.
- Before feeding, the temperature of the milk should be tested.
- Frozen breast milk should be thawed in the refrigerator or under cold running water–not on the counter.
- Young infants should always be held during bottlefeeding; a bottle should NEVER be propped. Older infants should be in a sitting position.

Hand Washing

There is no better place for the spread of disease than–you guessed it–day care! Because of constant contact with body fluids (diapers) and kids' hand-to-mouth habits, hand washing for children and day-care providers is of the utmost importance. Here is when hands should be washed:

Children:
- Immediately before and after eating
- After using the toilet or having their diapers changed
- Before using water tables
- After playing on the playground
- After handling pets, pet cages, or other pet objects
- Whenever hands are visibly dirty
- Before going home

Note: Because dirt and germs often accumulate under the nails, children should be taught how to use a nail brush.

Day-Care Providers:
- Upon arrival at work
- Immediately before handling food, preparing bottles, or feeding children
- After using the toilet, assisting a child using the toilet, or changing diapers
- After contacting a child's body fluids, including wet or soiled diapers, runny noses, spit, or vomit
- After handling pets, pet cages, or other objects
- Whenever hands are visibly dirty or after cleaning up a child, the room, bathroom items, or toys
- After removing gloves used for any purpose (gloves should not be a substitute for hand washing)
- Before giving or applying medication or ointment to a child or self
- Before going home

Good Hand-Washing Technique
Judging by the guidelines from the Centers for Disease Control, most of us only do a fair job of washing our hands. You may be surprised by these guidelines; a modified version of which appears below. You and your day-care provider should follow them.
- Always use warm running water and liquid soap (use a dime- to quarter-size amount).
- Continue washing hands for fifteen seconds after lather appears.

• Rinse hands, then dry them with a disposable towel while water is still running. Use a paper towel to turn off the faucet to avoid re-contaminating hands by touching a dirty faucet.

• Consider using lotion that can be squirted out without the hand having direct contact with the spout. Dry, chapped hands are more susceptible to germs.

CHAPTER TWELVE

Feeding Your School-Age Child

What you will find in this chapter:

- *Snack Food at School*
- *Packed Lunches*
- *Game Plan for Eating at School*
- *Junk Food*
- *Advice for This Age*
- *School Lunch Regulations*
- *Nutrition Teaching Tips*
- *Eating for Sports*

This chapter answers such questions as:

- *We never seem to have time for breakfast—any suggestions?*
- *What extra nutritional needs do athletic children have?*
- *How can I teach my eight-year-old about nutrition?*
- *How can I help my child avoid unhealthy food choices at school?*
- *My child has behavioral problems at school. Can this be food-related?*
- *What are the latest regulations on school meals?*

At age six, your child will spend more time at school and with friends, and you will start having less control over what she eats. Soon, in the "I'll-have-what-she's-having" stage, peer pressure will exert even more influence on her food habits. The following overall suggestions can help you balance the changing situation:

- Continue offering a very healthy diet to your child when she is with you.
- Have as much of an influence as you can over times when she is away from you. For example, if you and your child decide that she will sometimes buy her lunch at school, look at the school lunch menu together and choose with her the best days to buy and the best entrées to choose. (More about school lunch later.)

Snack Food at School

Foods that compete with nutritious foods are often available in snack and cola machines at school. These may be turned off during certain hours, and some states even have laws that prevent competitive foods from being sold on school premises. Although an occasional snack or drink out of the machine isn't going to be detrimental to your child's health, a daily habit could be, since the purchased food will probably take the place of an after-school snack of fruit or milk. Discuss this with your child and agree to make such purchases an occasional thing. You might also discuss alternatives to the snack machines with your principal. (Keep in mind that these machines are often a source of revenue for the school.)

Packed Lunches

If you pack a lunch for your child, you probably know that if her lunch box is empty when she comes home, she has eaten, traded, or tossed some or all of it. You may never really know what happens to your child's lunch–just as you may never find out what your child did in school–because many times she simply doesn't remember.

You can be sure that sooner or later your child will ask for Lunchables and other prepackaged lunches. See Chapter Twenty-One for the facts on convenience foods. As a rule, it is best to give your child some choices about her lunch, because then she will be more likely to eat it! (See Chapter Thirteen for packed-lunch ideas.)

Game Plan for Eating at School

Get Ready . . .

Obtain a monthly school menu and discuss it with your child. Decide how many times a week and which days your child will buy her lunch. Then discuss the choices for each of those days, letting her know your nutritional concerns, if any. Have your child circle the choices you agree to. This activity offers a natural way to teach and discuss nutrition. And over the months you may be surprised: Your child may begin telling you which entrées are the unhealthy choices–and why!

Get Set . . .

Have your child add to the grocery list foods that she would like in her lunch. Have her help you think of creative ways to make her lunch, enlisting her help whenever appropriate. Give in to some of her quirks and special requests if you can. For example, your child may never eat canned pine-apple at home, but she wants you to buy her the individual serving cans of pineapple to take to school. Let her–at least she may be eating fruit! If your child is buying her lunch on certain days, remind her of the healthy food choices you agreed on.

Go!

Many school cafeterias let kids take what they want from the line. Remind your child to select the fruits and veggies. Occasionally, eat with your child at school. This is the best way to know what the foods are like and to show your child you care about what she eats! A lunchtime visit also provides an opportunity to get to know kitchen staff and ask questions.

Junk Food

As your child spends more time with other children, she will pick up both good and bad habits from them. The combined

Breakfast Makes the Grade— Make It a Daily Priority!

Many children do not eat breakfast. A morning meal, however, gives children a jump start on learning. Kids who do eat breakfast have been reported to concentrate better; have better overall test scores; solve problems more easily; and have reduced hyperactivity, decreased absences and tardy rates, and improved psychosocial behaviors. No time for breakfast?

- Have your child eat breakfast at school.

- Keep on hand these grab-and-go foods: yogurt, bananas, apples, bagels, granola bars or cereal bars, boxed juices, small boxes or baggies of dried fruit, string cheese and crackers, cereal in individual boxes or zip-lock bags.

- Set the table and put the cereal on the table the night before—all you'll have to do is pour the cereal and milk!

influences of other kids, TV, and other outside factors can lead your child to crave junk food, candy, and anything fried. The commercials on TV have a huge influence on kids. Kids who see commercials for sugary food will choose more sugary food. Even children who can't read or talk can recognize a logo or box design at the store. For example, at the age of three, my son noticed the little *m* at the bottom of commercials during the Olympics. Of course the *m* stood for McDonald's.

What kids see on TV often influences what they ask their parents for at the grocery store—especially cereal and candy, the foods most advertised to kids. Unfortunately, but not surprisingly, a majority of parents give in and buy what their children want.

Advice for This Age

- Explain that food and other commercials are trying to talk people into buying something, even though it may not be a nutritious or wise choice for them. Also explain that commercials can be tricky—for example, they may not tell the whole story about whatever they are trying to sell.
- Limit commercial TV watching. PBS has wonderful educational shows and does not have paid advertisements.
- Give in occasionally to the food your child asks for, but try to stick to your family's nutritional philosophy as much as possible.
- To satisfy your child's cravings for junk food, buy baked, breaded chicken nuggets and fish pieces and try to incorporate healthy sweets, such as fruits, into her diet.

School Lunch Regulations

In 1993, the School Nutrition Dietary Assessment study found that an average school lunch contained 38 percent fat, 15 percent saturated fat, and almost 1,500 milligrams of sodium! "Clearly, these numbers are much different from those recommended by the Dietary Guidelines for Americans and National Research Councils' Diet and Health

Recommendations, which include 30 percent fat, 10 percent saturated fat, and 800 mg of sodium in a lunch meal," says Connie Evers, M.S., R.D., and author of *How to Teach Nutrition to Kids*.

And there's more bad news. The United States Department of Agriculture (USDA) reports that:

- On any given day, 35 percent of elementary-school children eat no fruit, and 20 percent eat no vegetables.
- Of children ages six to eleven, 27 percent are considered obese.
- Ninety percent of children consume fat above the recommended level.

Such studies and reports led many concerned groups to request changes in the requirements for school meals—meals that provide a significant portion of a child's daily nutrition.

In 1995, new regulations were passed that require schools to meet the Dietary Guidelines for Americans. These guidelines recommend that no more than 30 percent of an individual's calories come from fat, and less than 10 percent from saturated fat. Regulations also established a standard for school meals to provide one-third of the Recommended Dietary Allowances of protein, vitamin A, vitamin C, iron, calcium, and calories.

The USDA launched Team Nutrition, an initiative designed to help make implementation of the new regulations in schools easier and more successful. For instance, the program encourages schools to prepare food that meets dietary guidelines while tasting good, to provide positive messages about food, and to foster an understanding that good nutrition and physical activity are keys to educational success.

While it's easy to criticize those who plan school meals, would you want their job? They walk a fine line between the picky eating habits of kids and the regulations that require healthy foods. And selecting and serving the food is one thing, but getting kids to eat it is quite another.

A survey done by Consumers Union of fifth to eighth graders found that of the 28 percent of kids who chose a vegetable at school, only one-third ate all or most of it. Students who took fruit on their tray ate it just over 50 percent of the time. By contrast, kids who brought their lunch ate it better overall: Their fruit was all eaten 75 percent of the time; sandwiches were eaten 78 percent of the time; chips, 82 percent; cookies, 85 percent; juice, 90 percent.[1]

Clearly, putting theory into practice needs some work. How can we help get kids to eat better lunches? Teaching your children about nutrition, beginning when they are small, may give them the understanding and extra motivation to follow through on healthy choices.

▼

Nutrition Teaching Tips

- Keep it positive; make it fun.
- Focus on your child's life today. Use sports or improved grades as a motivational tool for eating well. "You might

run faster in the race if you eat a great breakfast that morning."

- Real-life experience is better than thousands of words. Once I let my son Nicolas have a big piece of birthday cake for breakfast on a school morning. (Even dietitians have to let a kid be a kid sometimes!) At the end of the day, he told me that he really felt awful later that morning and that he didn't have much energy for running. I explained that when a lot of sugar is eaten on an empty stomach, it may give you quick energy, but soon after you usually feel a big letdown. Never again has he asked for anything that sweet for breakfast!

- Integrate nutrition into other subjects. There are some great science experiments that teach the value of good nutrition. Also, there's plenty of math involved in cooking.

- Take advantage of the many opportunities for edible art!

- Minimize outside food influences. Saturday morning cartoons are notorious for advertising less-than-healthy food. However, watching the commercials with your child gives an opportunity to discuss and analyze them together. Food advertising is also creeping into the school system as schools look for other revenue sources. For example, our district school lunch menu now has ads printed on it for foods as well as TV shows.

- Don't forget the power of letting your child help plan and prepare meals—it's hands-on food and nutrition education!

Nutrition Education: A Great Resource

How to Teach Nutrition to Kids by Connie Evers M.S., R.D. (24 Carrot Press, 800-291-6098) gives practical tips on integrating nutrition education into your child's life—while having fun. It's also the perfect gift for teachers and principals; an accompanying Leader's Guide is also available.

Eating for Sports

At about age seven or older, your child might get somewhat serious about sports. There seems to be pressure to start kids earlier in sports, and it's getting more competitive, too. Can nutrition make a difference in your little athlete's performance? Yes. Below are some tips to give your child a nutritional edge.

- Eating regular meals and snacks is important, especially on the day of a game or event.

- Small, frequent meals are best on days with several games or competitions.

- A high-carbohydrate meal with moderate protein and fat (for example, pasta with tuna and milk) an hour before a game may make a difference.

- If your child is sensitive to gas-causing foods such as cabbage, onions, and dried beans, avoid these the day of a game.

- Adequate hydration is vital. Make sure your child drinks before, during, and after physical activity. A good indication of hydration is the color of urine. If you notice that the color of your child's urine is dark, she is not drinking enough. Pay even more attention to fluids when she is exercising in very hot or humid weather.

- The need for extra calories varies with each sport. A baseball game is unlikely to require a lot of additional calories, whereas a game of soccer might. Unless your child is losing weight, following her hunger cues should give her enough calories for whatever sports she is doing. If she cannot eat enough to supply the energy she needs with regular meals and snacks, you may need to supplement her diet with high-calorie or high-fat foods like nuts, peanut butter, extra oil, or milkshakes.

? Questions You May Have

Q: What about sports drinks—are they a good idea?

A: Sports drinks are not really needed—except when your child is participating in an endurance sport that lasts longer than an hour, or if she simply runs out of steam and could use an extra carbohydrate boost during the activity. Endurance sports are cycling, swimming, running, and any other

---

Keeping Active: It's Important for Everyone!

Even if your child is not interested in organized sports, there is no reason she should not enjoy other physical activities such as cycling, swimming, and walking. In fact, it may be more important to get your child involved in these types of activities, which she can do all her life. Keeping active is so important during the school years—again, the habits formed now may last a lifetime! Tell your child to get moving—and go with her!

---

sport that has continuous action. A bowling game or tennis match where there is a lot of standing doesn't count!

For a different type of pick-me-up, try orange slices. They're a great snack that provides both quick energy and fluid during breaks in the action. Just watch the youngsters gobble them up!

Q: Do kids who participate in sports need extra protein?

A: No. A common myth is that protein builds muscles. While it has been shown that some athletes, such as weight lifters, may need a small amount of extra protein, most people already eat twice as much protein as they really need. If your child eats a balanced diet, she should have all the protein she needs for strong muscles.

Complete Menus for All Occasions

About *Healthy Food for Healthy Kids* Recipes

Disclaimer

The recipes in this book are recipes that many kids like. There is no guarantee that your child will like all of them. The recipes have been tested with kids of all ages. In testing the recipes I found that the only recipes that just about all kids like are dessert recipes.

Recipes that list milk do not usually specify the type of milk. If your child is still drinking whole milk, you will probably use whole milk in the recipe. If your child is over two, however, you can use any type of milk in the recipe, even skim milk.

Usually, there is no specific oil listed in recipes. But in general, I recommend cooking with canola or olive oil, since they have the highest amount of monounsaturated fat.

Yields and Serving Sizes

For your convenience, the yields listed for the recipes are for adult serving sizes, whereas the nutrition analysis is usually based on a smaller, kid-sized serving size.

Nutrition Analysis

The recipes were analyzed using a computer program. The Key Nutrients listed are the nutrients found in large amounts in a recipe. They are listed as percentages of the

Dietary Reference Intakes and Recommended Dietary Allowances for children ages one to three. I chose this age range because it is during this time that most parents worry that their children may not be getting enough vitamins and minerals. Each recipe was analyzed for a typical serving size for this age group. But of course that does not mean that your child should not eat more than this amount!

About *Healthy Food for Healthy Kids* Menus

The following menus are meant to help you put recipes together in a healthy, inviting way. Keep in mind these tips when planning menus:

- Choose foods with a variety of colors and textures.
- Choose flavors that complement each other.
- Choose foods from different food groups.

The menus only include a beverage if it is a recipe from this book. If no beverage is listed, serve milk or juice. The recipes marked with an asterisk are especially fast to prepare. Page numbers are noted next to the recipes found in this book. Recipes are not included in this book for well-known or self-explanatory foods.

Happy eating!

▼

Breakfast Menus

Apricot Bread, 324
Grinchmeal, 247

Poached eggs
Bran Muffins, 248
Sip of Sunshine, 223

---

*Waffle Sundae Clouds, 263

---

*Cranapple Sauce, 208
Cinnamon toast
Cocoa Mocha, 274

Trail-Ride Zucchini Muffins, 262
Honeyed cream cheese
Pear slices

Yummy-but-Healthy Cake, 265
Banana Smoothie, 285

---

*Scrambled eggs in a tortilla with cheese and salsa
Sparkling apple juice

Nutrigrain waffles topped with Bananas NeeNee, 202

---

*Flying Saucers, 243, with cooked apples

Spiced Heart Scones, 259, with jam
½ grapefruit
Yogurt

Savory Corn Griddle Cakes, 256,
  with maple syrup
Peach Smoothie, 285

Blueberry Coffee Cake, 235
Fresh orange

CooCoo Crunchies, 238, with banana
  and milk

Cranberry Bran Muffins
Eggs over easy
Orange juice

Tired of the Same Old Breakfast?

Bread Pudding, 236, with peaches
Cocoa Mocha, 274

Queso Dip, 284
Tortillas and beans

Mediterranean Egg Salad, 308, on a
  whole-grain waffle
Cranapple Sauce, 208

*Tortilla Pizzas, 260
Cantaloupe slices

*Ooey-Gooey Sandwiches, 002
Almond Milk, 271

*Quesadillas with ham, 253
Winter Fruit Salad, 227

Butternut-Apple Soup, 171
Corn muffins with herbed Yogurt
  Cheese, 293

Madame Guedé's Rice Pudding, 280
Whole-wheat cinnamon toast
Cran-raspberry juice

*Corn bran cereal with chocolate milk
Pear Pops, 220

Poached eggs over Polenta, 239
Kiwi halves
Kid's Latte, 278

*Yogurt with raisins in a waffle cone
  with granola on top

Fruit Scoop, 214

The Lunch Bunch

*Pabble on graham crackers, 310
Apple slices
Chocolate milk

Mediterranean Egg Salad, 308, on white
  and dark bread
Mango chunks
Milk

Peanut, Peanut Butter . . . 'n' Honey, 312,
  with banana on English muffin
Pineapple Smoothie, 285
Milk

*Tomato soup
Christine's Broccoli Sandwich, 174
Milkshake

Mini Quiches in Pepper Pots, 309
Apricot halves
Madame Guedé's Rice Pudding, 280

Hummus Dip on pita triangles, 306
Tossed salad with Apricot Vinaigrette, 200

Mt. Everest (My Favorite Potatoes, 179),
   on field of greens (over sprinkles of
   broccoli slaw)
Cheese boulders (cheese cubes)
Jungle Juice Slush, 277

---

*Ham-cheese-mayonnaise-ketchup
   sandwich
Carrot and bell pepper sticks
Robert's Juicy Juice, 222

Vietnamese Noodle Salad with shrimp, 194
Raspberry sorbet with fresh peaches

Spinach salad with strawberries and turkey
   breast slices
Apricot Vinaigrette, 200
Popcorn cakes
Triple-Decker Dessert, 291

---

*Batman-and-Robin Noodles, 167
Frozen grapes (cut in pieces for kids
   under five)

*Creamy Tuna Spread, 301, on wheat
   crackers
Celery and cucumber spears with dip
Strawberry Dream Pops, 224

---

*Tortilla Pizzas, 260
Black Bean Salsa, 168
Surprise on a Stick, 288

Bugs Bunny Soup, 170, with floating
   icebergs (croutons)
Corn muffins
Island Punch, 216

Fish Nuggets with Pink Sauce, 305
Cheesy Potato Casserole, 173
Ranch Slaw, 184

---

*Cheese Sandwich Shapes, 336
Zucchini Dots, 195
Watermelon balls

Triplet sandwiches (three slices of bread;
   1st layer—cream cheese, grated carrot
   and chopped zucchini; 2nd layer—
   tuna or salmon and mayonaise)
Pear Pops, 220

Raspberry Swirl Yogurt Cheese, 293,
   on bagels
Cantaloupe triangles

Martian Soup, 177, with string cheese
   dippers
Whole-wheat crackers
Nicolas's Fruit Blast, 219

Mix-and-Match Lunch Game

Pick a bread on the left plus a filling on the right, and voila—a unique lunchbox stuffer!

Breads	Fillings	Other Toppings
Wheat bread	Mediterranean Egg Salad	Lettuce
Rye bread	Chicken salad	Tomato
Pita bread	Ham and cheese	Cucumber
Wheat crackers	Laughing Cow cheese	Chopped cucumber in yogurt
Saltine crackers	American cheese	Ranch Slaw
Rye Krisp	Mozarella cheese	Confetti Salad
Triscuits	Swiss cheese	Bean sprouts
English muffin	Pabble	Grated carrot
Bagel	Turkey pastrami	
Bagel crisps	String cheese	
Baked chips	Smoked turkey	
Croissant	Refried beans	
Hoagie roll	Hummus Dip	
Tortilla	Chef salad	
	Black Bean Salsa	
	Creamy Tuna Spread	

Curried Chicken Salad on pita bread, 303
Kid-Friendly Frozen Fruit Salad, 218
Sweet Lassi, 289

Spinach Dip with raw veggies, 188
Calzones, 237
Almond Pudding, 272

Macaroni and Cheese, 279
Ranch Slaw, 184
Tooty-Fruity Drink, 226

Carrot sticks
Polenta Triangles, 239, with Black Bean
  Salsa, 168
Frozen Fruit on a Straw, 212

Corn-Barley Salad, 240
Tortilla Wraps, 261
Cranapple Sauce, 208

Lentil Chili, 307, over Baked Tortilla
  Chips, 233
Nicolas's Fruit Blast, 219

▼

Dinner

Plum Good Meatballs, 313
Baked sweet potatoes
Tossed salad

---

*Veggie Tacos, 320
Queso Dip, 284
Pumpkin Pudding, 183

Lentil Chili, 307
Cornbread muffins
Rainbow Fruit Salsa, 221, with Cinnamon
   Tortilla Chips, 207

---

*Tropical Fish, 318
Broccoli Salad, 169
Wheat rolls
Peach Crisp, 217

Salmon Patties, 316, with Pink Sauce, 305
Cheesy Potato Casserole, 173
Limey Tomatoes, 176

Spinach-Stuffed Shells, 189
Garlic bread
Winter Fruit Salad, 227

---

*Cabbage Stir-Fry with angel hair pasta, 172
Grilled chicken
Fresh orange slices
Angel Dessert, 199

Oven-Fried Zucchini Sticks, 180
Salmon Corn Chowder, 315
Fresh fruit with Creamy Fruit Dip, 209

Chicken Chili, 297
Baked Tortilla Chips, 233, with Queso
   Dip, 284
So-Easy Flan, 287, with fresh raspberries

Hummus Dip with pita triangles, 306
Grilled lamb chops
Aladdin's Dinner (Eggplant Bake), 165
Carrot Pudding (Gajar Halwa), 273

---

*Tossed salad with Apricot Vinaigrette, 200
Tuna Twist, 319
Bread sticks
Kiwi Green Goblin Squares, 276

Martian Soup, 177, with swimming aliens
   (Goldfish crackers)
Pork chops
Walnut-Mint Bulgur, 264
Peanutty Rice Krispie Pie, 283

---

*Ranch Slaw, 184
Pasta with White Clam Sauce, 311
Triple-Decker Dessert, 291
Apricot-Mango Fizzy, 201

Dreamsicle Soup, 210
Veggie Cake, 191
Trail-Ride Zucchini Muffins, 262
Tutti-Frutti Drink, 226

Veggie Tacos, 320
Peachy Cloud Tapioca, 281

Raw celery and carrots with Sesame
   Onion Dip, 275
Aladdin's Dinner (Eggplant Bake), 165
Fresh kiwi fruit
Chocolate Malt Tapioca, 281

Mini Quiches in Pepper Pots, 309
Fruited Couscous, 245
Chocolate-Banana Pops, 206

Fish and Tomatoes, 304
Potato Pancakes, 182
Floating Fruits, 211

Spaghetti à la Carbonara, 317
Green beans
Surprise on a Stick, 288

Broccoli Salad, 169
Swiss Cheese Fondue, 290
Bluebird Nests, 204

Simple Seven-Bean Dip, 186
Grilled burgers
Strawberry Dream Pops, 224

---

*Cowboy Beans, 299
Raw veggies
Jungle Juice Slush, 277

Broiled salmon
Barbecued Corn on the Cob, 166
Whole artichokes with lemon butter

Grilled chicken
Fried Rice, 244
Honeydew slices

Raw veggies with Cottage Cream Dip, 275
Chili Mac, 298
Orange slices
Snickerdoodles, 257

Raging Ravioli, 254
Garlic bread
Fruit Soda, 215
Angel Dessert, 199

Oven-Fried Zucchini Sticks, 180
Grilled shrimp
Fruited Couscous, 245
Mexican Bread Pudding, 250

---

*Creamy Fruit Dip, 209, with apples,
   nectarines, and grapes
Quick Veggie Lasagna, 314
Fresh strawberries over frozen yogurt

Macaroni and cheese with Sneaky
   White Sauce, 187
Veggie Pockets, 192
Jungle Juice Slush, 277

Pot Stickers, 181
Vietnamese Spring Rolls with
   Dressing, 194
Triple-Decker Dessert, 291

Mixed green salad
Crepes with Chicken in Cream Sauce, 241
Yummy-but-Healthy Cake with
   raspberries, 265

Spaghetti with Secret Sauce, 185
Bread sticks
Fruit Fondue, 213

Broiled salmon
Cheesy Potato Casserole, 173
Tomato and cucumber salad

Vegetables

Ten Tricky Ways to Get Your Kids to Eat Their Veggies

Vegetables are one of the foods most often refused by children. Here are some tricks to help interest them:

1. *Dip it!* Kids like to dip. Popular dips include ranch dressing, ketchup, salsa, melted cheese dip, and bean dip. Try offering raw veggies with a dip as a first course. A steamed artichoke is an interesting dipping vegetable. Amazingly, both my kids like this funky veggie. Dip artichoke petals in vinaigrette dressing or lemon butter.

2. *Sneak it!* Sometimes parents have to sneak—sneak veggies into their kids' foods, that is! My favorite ways to sneak in veggies:
  • Add grated veggies to cooked pasta sauce.
  • Add puréed cauliflower to twice-baked potatoes.
  • Add cooked carrots to mashed potatoes before whipping.

3. *Leaf it!* Many kids like salads. My son Nicolas is a great example of a veggie hater/salad lover. When we have spinach salad, he often has second and third servings.

4. *Make it more fun!* Serve veggies in a new and fun way:
  • Create veggie kebabs—raw, steamed, or grilled. Be careful with skewers for younger kids. You may want to use a thin coffee straw to poke through steamed veggies.
  • Serve veggies in a veggie bowl. For example, serve flavored acorn squash in a hollowed-out squash half or hollowed-out baby pumpkin. Hollowed-out peppers and tomatoes also make great bowls for veggies or other foods.

5. *Fry it!* Make oven-fried veggies, such as zucchini sticks and eggplant rounds (recipe page 180). If your kids only like "real" fried veggies, that's better than no veggies at all!

6. *Stuff it or wrap it!* Into pita pockets, pasta shells, tortillas, or crepes. Tossed salad with bites of ham and cheese go great in a pita pocket. Pasta shells are wonderful stuffed with a cheese-spinach mixture. (See page 189 for recipe, which includes tofu variation.)

7. *Sauce it!* A sauce often adds just the right touch to appeal to kids. Try easily melted cream cheese or Velveeta sauce, white sauce, or tomato sauce. Mykle Mary loves her broccoli with melted cheese.

8. *Drink it!* Don't overlook the possibility that your kids might like tomato or V-8 juice, even if they don't like tomatoes! If you have a juicer, experiment with combinations of vegetable-fruit juices. Carrot juice is sweet and can be mixed with fruit smoothies. Tip: If your kids participate in the experiments, they are more likely to drink the end result!

9. *Squish it!* Purée vegetables into a creamy soup or purée beans and cheese for a dip.

10. *Grate it!* Some kids like their veggies finely grated, if you please. Try a carrot-and-raisin salad or coleslaw.

Aladdin's Dinner (Eggplant Bake)

Sometimes the trick to getting kids to eat their veggies is not telling them what's in their dinner. Just tell them this is the sort of food Aladdin eats.

Makes: 7 servings

1 eggplant, peeled and cut into ¼-inch lengthwise slices

Salt

2½ cups marinara sauce (preferably low-sodium)

2 cups part-skim mozzarella cheese

1 cup artichoke hearts that have had all the water squeezed out

1. Lay out eggplant slices on paper towels. Salt generously and let sit for 10 minutes. Remove excess water and blot with paper towels. This gets out the bitter taste.

2. Spread ½ cup sauce into an 8-inch square, microwave-safe baking dish.

3. Cover with a layer of eggplant, then ½ cup sauce, ½ cup cheese, ½ cup artichoke, remains of the eggplant, ½ cup sauce, ½ cup cheese, remains of the artichoke, 1 cup of sauce, and ¾ cup cheese.

4. Cook in microwave for 15 minutes on high, rotating half a turn in the middle of cooking. Let sit for 5 minutes before serving.

Each ½-cup child serving provides	**Key Nutrients**
60 calories	*22% calcium*
5 grams carbohydrate	*20% vitamin B_{12}*
5 grams protein	*18% magnesium*
3 grams fat	*18% vitamin A*
1 gram fiber	*17% vitamin C*

Barbecued Corn on the Cob

If you hate shucking corn before you cook it, you'll love this recipe modified from *Quick and Healthy, Volume II,* by Brenda Ponichtera, R.D. (Scaledown Publishing, 1995). Kids will get a kick out of eating corn cooked this way.

Makes: 4 servings

4 ears of corn

1. Start barbecue grill.

2. When grill is hot, place unshucked corn directly on the grill over high heat. Close hood and cook for 15 minutes, turning corn several times while cooking.

3. Remove corn and let sit until cool enough to handle. Pull down husks and use as a handle.

Each ½ ear of corn provides

42 calories
9 grams carbohydrate
1 gram protein
0 fat

Key Nutrients

37% pantothenic acid
16% thiamin
11% folate

Batman-and-Robin Noodles

This super-easy lunch gives your superheroes all the energy they need!

Makes: 2¼ cups

1½ cups + ¾ cup water

1 chicken breast, cut in strips or bite-sized pieces (depending on age of children)

1 cup grated Napa cabbage

½ cup peas, frozen or canned

3-ounce package Ramen noodles, any flavor

1. Pour 1½ cups water in a saucepan.

2. Add chicken and the seasoning packet from Ramen noodle package. Simmer 10 minutes on medium high.

3. Add vegetables and simmer 5 more minutes.

4. Add ¾ cup water and noodles and cook until tender.

Each ¾-cup child serving provides

208 calories
15 grams carbohydrate
24 grams protein
6 grams fat

Key Nutrients

37% niacin
28% selenium

Black Bean Salsa

A different way to eat vegetables!

Makes: 3½ cups

1 cup drained corn

1 cup cooked barley

1 cup cooked black beans, drained

1 finely chopped tomato

1 minced garlic clove

1–3 slices onion, minced

4 tablespoons vinaigrette dressing

1. Mix all ingredients together and serve.

Each ¼-cup child serving provides

59 calories

8 grams carbohydrate

2 grams protein

2 grams fat

1 gram fiber

Key Nutrients

18% magnesium

17% folate

10% manganese

Broccoli Salad

This recipe, modified from *Quick and Healthy, Volume II* by Brenda Ponichtera, makes a great potluck dish. Kids will forget they are eating broccoli!

Makes: 6 ½-cup servings

2½ cups fresh broccoli, chopped (kids may prefer it lightly steamed first)

½ cup raisins

¼ cup sunflower seeds

2 tablespoons red onion, finely diced

2 tablespoons bacon bits or bacon-flavored soy bits

2 tablespoons nonfat plain yogurt

2 tablespoons light mayonnaise

1½ tablespoons sugar

½ tablespoon vinegar

1. Combine broccoli, raisins, sunflower seeds, onion, and bacon or soy bits.

2. Mix together remaining ingredients and add to the broccoli mixture. Toss well to coat.

3. Chill 2 hours or longer to allow flavors to blend.

Each ¼-cup child serving provides

11 calories

8 grams carbohydrate

1 gram protein

1 gram fat

1 gram fiber

Key Nutrients

43% vitamin C

28% vitamin E

Bugs Bunny Soup

This soup is for all the "silly wabbits" in your house!

Makes: about 7 cups

2 tablespoons butter or oil

¾ cup onion, chopped

2 stalks celery, chopped

1½ pounds peeled carrots, sliced (or bagged peeled baby carrots)

1 cup water

3 tablespoons chicken broth mix

½ teaspoon dill

2 cups milk

1. Heat butter or oil in a pot.

2. Add onion and celery and cook until brown and tender.

3. Add carrots and brown for 5 minutes.

4. Add water, broth mix, and dill. Stir until blended. Cover and continue cooking until carrots are tender.

5. Remove from heat and pour half of the mixture into a blender with 1 cup of milk. First blend on low, then on high until puréed; pour into a serving bowl. Repeat with other half of mixture.

6. Mix both batches together and serve.

Each ½-cup child serving provides

60 calories
7 grams carbohydrate
2 grams protein
3 grams fat
1.5 grams fiber

Key Nutrients

350% vitamin A
13% vitamin C
12% calcium

Butternut-Apple Soup

This creamy soup that uses fall's harvest will be sure to please.

Makes: about 5 cups

4 cups butternut squash, cooked

1 cup milk

1 cup applesauce

1 tablespoon butter or margarine

1. Put all ingredients in a blender and purée until smooth.

2. Adjust the amount of milk for a smoother soup.

Each ½-cup child serving provides

65 calories

12 grams carbohydrate

1.5 grams protein

2.5 grams fiber

Key Nutrients

150% vitamin A

35% magnesium

32% vitamin C

Cabbage Stir-Fry

For cabbage lovers only.

Makes: 2 cups

1½ tablespoons vegetable oil
½ teaspoon sesame oil
1 teaspoon garlic, chopped
5 cups cabbage, shredded
2 tablespoons light soy sauce

1. Heat oils in a large nonstick pan.
2. Add chopped garlic and cook for 30 seconds, stirring briskly to prevent burning.
3. Add cabbage and soy sauce; cook, stirring constantly. If cabbage starts to stick you can add a spoon of water at a time.
4. Continue cooking until the cabbage reaches desired texture.

Variation

Add marinated chicken breast strips or tofu cubes to the garlic and stir-fry for a few minutes until cooked before adding the cabbage.

Each ¼-cup child serving provides	Key Nutrients
39 calories	*35% vitamin C*
2.5 grams carbohydrate	*17% vitamin E*
1 gram protein	*13% folate*
3 grams fat	
1 gram fiber	

Cheesy Potato Casserole

A great throw-together recipe that can be doubled.

Makes: 12 servings

1 pound frozen hash browns, thawed

½ can cream of chicken soup

½ cup onion, chopped

8 ounces fat-free sour cream

4 ounces reduced-fat Monterey Jack or cheddar cheese, shredded

1½ cups Complete bran flakes

2 tablespoons butter or margarine, melted

¼ cup parmesan cheese, freshly grated

1. Preheat oven to 350°F.

2. Combine hash browns, soup, onion, sour cream, and shredded cheese. Spread in a baking dish.

3. In a small bowl, combine bran flakes, butter or margarine, and grated cheese. Mix well and spread evenly over the hash-brown layer.

4. Bake for 40 minutes.

Each ¼-cup child serving provides

72 calories

7 grams carbohydrate

3 grams protein

4 grams fat

Key Nutrients

21% vitamin B_6

14% magnesium

13% riboflavin

Christine's Broccoli Sandwich

For all those broccoli lovers, this sandwich provides a nice change from peanut butter and jelly.

Makes: 1 serving

2 slices whole-wheat bread

1 tablespoon dijonnaise or ¼ teaspoon Dijon mustard mixed with 2 teaspoons light mayonnaise

¼ cup steamed broccoli

1 ounce cheese, grated

1. Spread one side of each slice of bread with dijonnaise.

2. Drain broccoli and place on one slice.

3. Top with cheese.

4. Broil in a toaster oven until cheese melts.

5. Cover with remaining slice and serve.

Each child's serving (½ sandwich) provides

133 calories
13 grams carbohydrate
7 grams protein
7 grams fat
4 grams fiber

Key Nutrients

36% vitamin C
32% calcium
25% riboflavin
16% folate

Confetti Salad

When Adree Rojas makes this for her three daughters, Elsa, Sophia, and Lorraine, there are no leftovers! If your kids don't enjoy traditional coleslaw, they might like this. Some kids like it on their tacos instead of lettuce.

Makes: 6 ½-cup servings

3 cups shredded cabbage

¼–½ cup finely chopped parsley, regular or flat Italian (you can also use smaller amounts of cilantro for a bit more zing)

1 fresh tomato, finely chopped

2 tablespoons oil

1 tablespoon fresh lime or lemon juice

½–2 slices onion, very finely chopped (amount varies with hotness of onion and how well your kids tolerate fresh onion)

Salt and pepper to taste

1. Mix all ingredients.

2. Chill briefly and serve. This is best eaten fresh.

Each ¼-cup child serving provides

28 calories
2 grams carbohydrate
< 1 gram protein
2 grams fat
1 gram fiber

Key Nutrients

239% vitamin K
35% vitamin C
11% folate

Limey Tomatoes

The lime gives fresh tomato slices a whole new taste! You may also enjoy the addition of freshly snipped parsley or chives. Expand the recipe as needed.

Makes: 4 servings

4 plum tomatoes
1 small lime
2 teaspoons olive oil
Salt or garlic salt (optional)

1. Thinly slice tomatoes and arrange on platter.

2. Squeeze lime juice over slices.

3. Drizzle with oil. Sprinkle with salt or garlic salt, if desired.

Variation

Use sliced jicama instead of tomatoes.

Each child serving (½ tomato) provides

34 calories
0 grams carbohydrate
0 grams protein
2 grams fat

Key Nutrients

32% vitamin C

Martian Soup

If your child is opposed to eating green things, adding a Martian twist may help! Even the worst vegetable haters like this soup!

Makes: 10 cups

7 medium new potatoes

Water

1¾ pounds fresh spinach or 3 10-ounce packages frozen chopped spinach, thawed (reserve liquid)

1½ cups milk

1 cup cooking liquid from potatoes and spinach

Sour cream or ketchup for garnish (optional)

1. Peel and cut each potato into 1-inch chunks. Place potatoes in a 3-quart pot and cover with water.

2. Cook over medium-high heat until the potatoes are almost done, adding spinach (and spinach liquid if using frozen) the last 5 to 10 minutes of cooking time. Remove pan from heat and drain, reserving cooking liquid.

3. Purée in batches in a blender (make sure each batch has some spinach, potatoes, and enough milk and cooking liquid to blend). Pour batches into a large pot or bowl.

4. When finished, mix well and add salt and pepper to taste. Add more liquid if you would like a thinner soup.

5. Pour into serving bowls. If desired, add sour cream or ketchup to each bowl and swirl with a spoon.

6. Serve with star croutons (see left).

Star Croutons

1. Toast bread in a toaster.

2. With star-shaped cookie cutters, cut out star shapes from the toast.

3. Float on top of soup.

Each ½-cup child serving provides

64 calories
13 grams carbohydrate
2.5 grams protein
0 grams fat
2 grams fiber

Key Nutrients

69% vitamin A
56% magnesium
55% folate
47% vitamin B$_6$
42% vitamin C

Mashed Tater Balls

According to Nicolas, Katie, and Robert, that's what these treats taste like! Great for an after-school snack or to go in a lunch box. Vary the seasonings according to what your family likes.

Makes: 1½ cups

1 tablespoon olive oil

1 large or 2 regular garlic cloves, minced

1-pound can chickpeas (also called garbanzo beans), rinsed and well drained

1. Heat olive oil in a nonstick skillet.

2. Add garlic and chickpeas. Stir-fry on high for 3 minutes.

3. Lower to medium heat and cook, stirring often, for another 7 minutes, or until golden brown.

4. Serve warm or cold. Makes a good addition to salads.

Each ¼-cup child serving provides	**Key Nutrients**
60 calories	*38% vitamin E*
7 grams carbohydrate	*16% magnesium*
2 grams protein	*10% iron*
3 grams fat	
2 grams fiber	

My Favorite Potatoes

This is a favorite at our house, and it's a great way to include more vegetables in your diet (and to get picky children to gobble up their veggies). Vary the amount of carrots for a different flavor and color.

Makes: 18 servings

10 medium potatoes (about 7 ounces each), peeled and cubed

5 medium carrots, peeled and sliced

⅓–½ cup evaporated skim milk

2 tablespoons soft margarine

1 to 2 crushed garlic cloves (optional)

Salt and pepper to taste

1. Place potatoes and carrots in a large pot and cover with water.

2. Cook 45 minutes to 1 hour, or until both are tender.

3. Drain and place the vegetables in a large bowl.

4. Whip with an electric beater; add milk, margarine, and seasonings. Add more milk to reach the desired consistency.

Variation

Add 3 ounces light Velveeta cheese while beating for richer, creamier potatoes.

Each ¼-cup child serving provides

48 calories
9 grams carbohydrate
1 gram protein
1 gram fat
1 gram fiber

Key Nutrients

30% vitamin A
Small amounts of all other nutrients

Vegetables

Oven-Fried Zucchini Sticks

What a great way to eat vegetables! They almost taste too good to be healthy!

Makes: 4 servings

Cooking spray

½ cup Italian bread crumbs

2 tablespoons freshly grated
or canned parmesan
cheese

¼ teaspoon garlic powder

3 medium zucchini

½ cup water or milk

1 cup fat-free or low-fat
spaghetti sauce or ranch
dressing

1. Preheat the oven to 450°F. Spray a cookie sheet with cooking spray.

2. Place bread crumbs, cheese, and garlic powder in a zip-lock bag; shake well to combine. Set aside.

3. Cut each zucchini lengthwise into 8 pieces; cut each piece in half horizontally.

4. Fill a saucer with water or milk. Dip each zucchini stick in water or milk and drop into the bag of crumb mixture. Shake until coated on all sides and place on the coated cookie sheet. Repeat with rest of sticks.

5. Bake for 10 to 15 minutes or until brown and tender.

6. Serve with warm spaghetti sauce or ranch dressing.

Variations

Eggplant: Peel eggplant and slice into rounds, then follow above directions.

Potatoes and Sweet Potatoes: Peel and slice into preferred thickness. Sprinkle with garlic salt or spices and parmesan cheese. Spray with cooking spray and bake.

**Each child serving
(4 sticks) provides**

53 calories
9 grams carbohydrate
3 grams protein
1 gram fat

Key Nutrients

*Small amounts of all
nutrients*

Pot Stickers

Kids can help make these veggie- and meat-stuffed pockets. Get creative with the fillings!

Makes: about 20 pot stickers

1 tablespoon oil

½ *pound lean ground beef or ground pork*

1 medium onion, chopped

3 tablespoons + 1 teaspoon soy sauce

2 teaspoons sesame oil

4 teaspoons garlic, chopped

1 teaspoon fresh ginger, chopped

3 cups coleslaw mix

20 won ton or Gyoza wrappers

1 tablespoon water

1. Heat oil in a large nonstick skillet.

2. Add meat, onion, 3 tablespoons soy sauce, sesame oil, garlic, and ginger. Cook over medium heat until meat is cooked through.

3. Add coleslaw mix and continue cooking until tender.

4. Put a spoonful of mixture on each wrapper, fold over, and seal. (To seal, wet the inside edge of wrapper with a drop of water and fold over.)

5. Place filled wrappers in a skillet. Add 1 tablespoon of water and 1 teaspoon of soy sauce. Cover and cook 5 minutes or until the pot stickers start to brown, turning once.

6. Serve with rice or pasta.

Each child serving (1 pot sticker) provides	Key Nutrients
47 calories	11% vitamin C
5 grams carbohydrate	5% folate
3 grams protein	Small amounts of other
2 grams fat	nutrients

Potato Pancakes

Potato pancakes with a twist!

Makes: 12 pancakes

2 cups grated potatoes

2 cups grated zucchini

2 large eggs

½ cup flour

½ teaspoon garlic sauce

1 teaspoon dehydrated onion

2 tablespoons parmesan
  cheese

1. Mix all ingredients in bowl. Heat pan that has been sprayed with cooking spray or wiped with oil over medium-high heat.

2. Pour ¼ cup of batter onto hot pan, spreading it out to a 5-inch circle with a spoon.

3. Cook several minutes on each side.

4. Serve with ketchup, pasta sauce, or salsa.

Each pancake provides

58 calories

9 grams carbohydrate

3 grams protein

1 gram fat

Key Nutrients

13% magnesium

8% vitamin C

Pumpkin Pudding

The easiest pudding you'll ever make!

Makes: 6 ½-cup servings

2 cups pumpkin pie filling

1⅓ cup plain nonfat yogurt or mashed silken tofu

Whipped topping and Teddy Grahams for garnish

1. Combine pie filling with yogurt or tofu; stir well with spoon.

2. Garnish with whipped topping and Teddy Grahams.

Each ¼-cup child serving provides

61 calories

14 grams carbohydrate

2 grams protein

0 grams fat

Key Nutrients

35% vitamin A

22% riboflavin

14% magnesium

13% calcium

Ranch Slaw

Everything tastes better with ranch dressing, and this recipe proves it!

Makes: 4 ½-cup servings

1¾ cups shredded cabbage
¼ cup grated carrots
3 tablespoons ranch dressing

1. Mix all ingredients together and serve.

Each ¼-cup kid serving provides	Key Nutrients
25 calories	*154% vitamin K*
2 grams carbohydrate	*24% vitamin A*
<1 gram protein	*22% vitamin C*
2 grams fat	

Secret Sauce

Not even the best secret agent will be able to figure out what is in this healthy sauce! The sauce ends up being the same color as tomato sauce that's in canned ravioli that kids love.

Makes: 5 cups

2 tablespoons oil

3 stalks celery, chopped

1 small onion, chopped

10 small cloves of garlic

½ cup chopped parsley

2 red peppers, roasted and chopped

2 teaspoons Italian seasoning

1 8-ounce can tomato sauce

1 28-ounce can diced tomatoes in juice

1 teaspoon sugar

1 teaspoon salt

½ teaspoon pepper

1. Pour oil into large nonstick skillet. Add next 4 ingredients. Cook, stirring occasionally until onion is transparent.

2. Add rest of ingredients and simmer for 30 minutes.

3. Pour into blender and purée. Serve over pasta or ravioli.

Each ¼-cup kid serving provides

38 calories
6 grams carbohydrate
1 gram protein
1 gram fat

Key Nutrients

63% vitamin A
39% vitamin C
17% vitamin B$_6$

Simple Seven-Bean Dip

In our house, this dip is often made as a 2- or 3-ingredient dip, depending on what's available. Layers can be omitted depending on your family's preferences. When my son Robert was only a year old, he started eating this with his hands at a New Year's Eve party!

Makes: about 8½ cups

2 15-ounce cans seasoned refried pinto or black beans

1½ cups prepared guacamole

1 cup salsa or tomatoes, finely chopped

1 cup fat-free or light sour cream

1 8-ounce package reduced-fat cheddar or Monterey Jack cheese, finely grated

2 tablespoons green onions, finely chopped

3 tablespoons black olives, chopped

1. With a spatula, spread beans into a 9- or 10-inch pie plate or a low serving dish.

2. Top with a layer of guacamole.

3. Mix salsa or tomatoes and sour cream and spread on top of guacamole.

4. Sprinkle with cheese, follow with green onions, and end with chopped olives.

Each ¼-cup child serving provides

160 calories
11 grams carbohydrate
0 grams protein
10 grams fat
3 grams fiber

Key Nutrients

36% folate
36% magnesium
17% vitamin C
11% iron

Sneaky White Sauce

Your kids will never suspect this white sauce is made of cauliflower—in fact, you can also sneak it by adults. This versatile sauce can be made into macaroni and cheese or served over chicken or fish. Spice it up by adding tarragon, garlic, or whatever spices your family likes.

Makes: 1¼ cups

½ **cup milk**

2 cups cooked fresh or frozen cauliflower

¼ **to ½ cup cheese (if using sharp cheddar ¼ cup will do)**

Salt and pepper to taste

1. Steam or cook cauliflower in small amount of water until tender. Drain.

2. Place cauliflower in blender with milk. Purée until smooth.

3. Return to saucepan and stir in cheese until melted.

Each ¼-cup serving provides

67 calories
4 grams carbohydrate
5 grams protein
4 grams fat

Key Nutrients

69% vitamin C
25% calcium
23% vitamin B$_6$
21% riboflavin

Spinach Dip

This dip is a great camouflage for spinach.

Makes: about 5 cups

*1 package Knorr leek soup
or Garden Vegetable soup
mix*

8 ounces fat-free sour cream

*8 ounces regular or light
mayonnaise*

*2 10-ounce packages frozen
chopped spinach, thawed
and drained*

*4½-ounce can water
chestnuts, chopped, or ½
cup finely chopped red or
yellow bell pepper
(optional)*

*1 large round loaf of
sourdough bread*

*Cucumber spears, squash
rounds, and other raw or
steamed vegetables*

Thin slices of French bread

1. In a large bowl, combine soup mix, sour cream, and mayonnaise; mix well.

2. Fold in spinach and water chestnuts or bell pepper.

3. Refrigerate at least 1 hour before serving.

4. Scoop out the center of a sourdough bread. Break the scooped-out bread into bite-sized pieces. Reserve.

5. Spoon the dip into the bread bowl.

6. Serve with cucumber spears, squash rounds, any other raw or steamed vegetables, bite-sized pieces of bread (from step 4), and thin slices of French bread.

**Each 2-tablespoon
serving provides**

41 calories
4 grams carbohydrate
1 gram protein
3 grams fat

Key Nutrients

28% vitamin A
12% magnesium

Spinach-Stuffed Shells

This is one spinach recipe both my kids like! The stuffed shells freeze well, so try doubling the recipe and freezing half.

Makes: 4 servings

1 10-ounce package frozen spinach, cooked or thawed, well drained

1 cup low-fat or fat-free cottage cheese

⅓ cup parmesan cheese, preferably fresh

½ cup mozzarella cheese, grated

¼ teaspoon garlic powder, or to taste

½ pound large pasta shells, cooked until still slightly firm or al denté, drained

2½ cups prepared low-fat marinara sauce

Grated mozzarella and parmesan cheese for garnish

1. Preheat the oven to 350°F.

2. In a large bowl, combine all ingredients except shells, sauce, and garnish; mix until well blended.

3. Stuff each shell with some of spinach mixture and arrange the shells in a baking dish.

4. Cover the shells with sauce.

5. Bake for 30 minutes. Sprinkle with a bit of grated cheese just before serving.

Variation Using Tofu

Double the amount of pasta, cottage cheese, and spinach. Drain 1 pound of firm tofu and squeeze out excess water. Put the tofu in a food processor with 2 cloves fresh garlic and a bunch of fresh basil leaves. Process until smooth. Add cottage cheese and process until smooth. Remove from processor bowl and stir in spinach. Stuff and cook shells as directed above.

Each child serving (2 shells) provides

133 calories
18 grams carbohydrate
9 grams protein
3 grams fat
1 gram fiber

Key Nutrients

29% calcium
18% vitamin A
14% thiamin

Valentine Soup (Minute Minestrone)

This soup is sure to warm the hearts of your valentines. Serve with toast cut in the shape of hearts.

Makes: 4 servings

5 ounces frozen spinach, thawed, or cooked in minimal amount of water, not drained

1 8-ounce can tomato sauce

1 14½-ounce can diced tomatoes

1 cup green beans

1 cup garbanzo or kidney beans

¾ to 1 cup cooked pasta

1 cup water

½ teaspoon onion powder

½ teaspoon garlic powder

1 teaspoon Italian spices

½ teaspoon dried basil

1 teaspoon dried or 2 teaspoons fresh parsley

1. Combine all ingredients in a 1½-quart saucepan.

2. Simmer 10 to 15 minutes until heated. Add more water for a thinner soup.

Each ½-cup child serving provides

63 calories
13 grams carbohydrate
2 grams protein
1 gram fat
3 grams fiber

Key Nutrients

76% vitamin A
28% vitamin C
16% iron

Veggie Cake

Almost any vegetable works in a veggie cake, as long as the vegetable is finely chopped or grated. Cauliflower works well because it blends right in with the batter and kids don't even see it! This recipe is especially good for kids "allergic" to green!

Makes: 12 servings

1 cup finely chopped carrots (about 20 baby carrots)

1½ cups finely chopped cauliflower

½ cup finely chopped onion

1 cup grated cheddar cheese

4 eggs

2 cups milk

1 cup biscuit or pancake mix

¾ teaspoon garlic salt

¼ cup parmesan cheese

1. Preheat oven to 400°F. Spray a 9-by-13-inch pan with cooking spray.

2. Sprinkle carrots, cauliflower, and onion evenly over bottom of pan; sprinkle with cheddar cheese.

3. Mix eggs, milk, pancake mix, garlic salt, and parmesan cheese. Pour over vegetables and cheese, distributing with spatula.

4. Bake 30 minutes or until cooked through.

Each serving provides

138 calories
11 grams carbohydrate
8 grams protein
7 grams fat
1 gram fiber

Key Nutrients

233% vitamin K
87% vitamin A
26% vitamin C

Veggie Pockets

Kids will like these various shapes!

Makes: about 12 pockets

2 cups cooked drained
   vegetables (finely chopped
   spinach, broccoli, and
   cauliflower; grated carrots
   and zucchini)

2 ounces light cream cheese

¼ cup feta cheese

½ cup grated mozarella
   cheese

1 teaspoon onion flakes

⅛ teaspoon dill

dash of pepper

6 sheets phyllo dough,
   thawed (Note: Phyllo
   dough needs to thaw in
   refrigerator for 12 hours.)

2 tablespoons oil

1. Preheat oven to 400°F.

2. In medium saucepan, mix vegetables with cheeses, dill, and pepper; cook over low heat until cheese is melted.

3. Prepare pockets (see below).

4. Place pockets on a cookie sheet coated with cooking spray. Spray top of pockets with cooking spray. Bake for 15–20 minutes, until golden brown.

Basic directions to make pockets:

The type of pockets can vary depending on what shape you like. Place one layer of phyllo dough on a flat surface. Brush lightly with oil and top with another sheet. Brush lightly with oil. Place 1–2 tablespoons of filling on top. Fold or roll to desired shape.

Triangle: Cut phyllo sheet lengthwise into 4 equal rectangles. Follow basic directions, arranging the two stacked strips horizontally in front of you. Place 1 tablespoon filling on left end of dough, ½ inch from edges. Fold bottom left corner of dough up over filling forming a triangle. Press top and right edges. Fold triangle over itself to right and then over itself to the bottom; then, to right and top. Continue until all dough is folded up. Press edge to seal.

Veggie Pockets
(continued)

Egg roll: Using 2 narrow rectangles as above and arranged vertically in front of you, place 1-2 tablespoons of filling on bottom of dough, leaving ½ inch border. Roll dough and filling over once. Tuck in sides and continue rolling, pressing edge to seal.

Envelope: Cut phyllo into two wider rectangles and prepare first two layers, as above: Place 1–2 tablespoons of filling in middle of rectangle. Fold bottom of dough over filling, then top dough. Fold over right side and then left side, making an envelope edge by folding under the sides to form an angle.

1 veggie pocket with spinach provides	Key Nutrients
96 calories	*78% folate*
9 grams carbohydrates	*74% vitamin A*
4 grams protein	*32% magnesium*
5 grams fat	*21% calcium*

Vietnamese Noodle Salad

This is one of my favorite Vietnamese meals. It gives kids a different exposure to salad. The dressing is the creation of my nephew, Hao Do.

Makes: 4 to 6 servings and ¾ cup dressing

Salad:
6 ounces dried Asian rice noodles (also called rice sticks)

4–6 cups torn spinach and leaf lettuce or mixed greens

1 cucumber, peeled and finely chopped

2 carrots, peeled and julienned or grated

2 green onions, finely chopped

¼ cup fresh cilantro, finely chopped

3 tablespoons peanuts, coarsely chopped (optional)

12 ounces cooked shrimp, chicken, beef, pork, or tofu (optional)

Dressing:
3 garlic cloves, pressed

2 tablespoons lemon or lime juice

1 tablespoon sugar

4 tablespoons Asian fish sauce

½ cup water

1. Cook noodles 5 minutes. Rinse with cold water; drain.

2. Toss together spinach, lettuce, cucumber, and carrots. Divide among plates.

3. In a small bowl, mix onion and cilantro and sprinkle on vegetables. (Sprinkle just a little on child's serving.)

4. Combine all dressing ingredients and mix well.

5. Toss noodles with most of dressing and spoon noodles over greens. Serve the rest of the dressing on the side.

6. Top with peanuts and shrimp, meat, or tofu, if you like.

To Make Spring Rolls Using Same Ingredients

Cut recipe in half. Using 12 rice papers, dip each individually in bowl of water until soft. On one end, fill with slices of meat; chopped peanuts; pieces of carrot, cucumber, and cilantro; and ¼ cup of cooked noodles. Fold bottom over filling. Tuck in sides and continue rolling. Serve with lettuce or spinach and dipping sauce.

Each ½-cup child serving provides	Key Nutrients
98 calories	43% vitamin K
11 grams carbohydrate	37% vitamin C
7 grams protein	33% vitamin A
3 grams fat	21% vitamin B_6
	19% folate
	18% niacin

Zucchini Dots

This is a recipe even two-year-olds can help with!

Makes: 4 servings

1 uncooked zucchini, sliced thin

⅓ cup Ranch style or other salad dressing

1. Arrange zucchini on a plate, without overlapping.

2. Place a dot of dressing on each slice.

Each half-size child portion provides

30 calories
1 gram carbohydrate
0 grams protein
3 grams fat

Key Nutrients

Small amounts of many nutrients

Fruits

Fruit is as sweet as dessert, but a lot healthier. It's easy to eat, comes in its own biodegradable package, and is full of vitamins and fiber. Fruit (along with vegetables) is known for its ability to decrease the risk of cancer, heart disease, and other illnesses. Now there is evidence that fruit also improves lung function. Children who eat plenty of fresh fruit are likely to have better lung function than those who eat none.[1]

Most kids like fruits, but there are always a few who would rather eat vegetables. Even if your child does like fruits, you may find him eating the same fruit day after day. Fruit jags are common and can have some unexpected results. When my son Nicolas was two, he went through bananas like crazy. Now, at seven, he is finally eating an occasional banana after four years of total boycott! Our younger son Robert had also had a banana jag, but he eased into eating just a few bananas a week without the extended boycott.

To keep your child from fruit burnout, simply run out of the fruit in question, and forget to buy it from time to time. Then it is very easy to say, "We are out of bananas, but look: we have this fuzzy kiwi!" By eating a variety of fruits, you can also avoid eating too much of one pesticide that might be on one type of fruit but not on another. On the next page, you'll find a few ideas for fruit substitutions.

Most families run into ruts in the winter, when only a few fruits are in season in their region. Of course, at large groceries, you can find almost any fruit anytime, shipped from all over the world. Be aware that fruits shipped long distances often contain extra pesticides and preservatives to keep them looking "perfect." (For more information on pesticides, see page 82.) It is best to stick to fruits that are in season in your own area, buy canned or frozen, or can your own next summer!

Fruit Substitutions	
If Your Child Likes:	**He May Also Like:**
Apples	Pears, jicama (a crisp, sweet root vegetable)
Oranges	Grapefruit
Peaches	Apricots, cantaloupe
Raisins, grapes	Blueberries, raspberries
Strawberries	Kiwi

▼

Fifteen Ways to Include More Fruit in Your Family's Diet

1. Don't be afraid to use more canned fruit—for instance, in your child's lunch—especially when some fruits are out of season.

2. Bake canned fruit in a cobbler or crisp during the cold months. (See page 217 for an easy low-sugar recipe.)

3. Put canned fruit together with fresh fruit for a great winter salad. Good choices include peaches, pineapple, banana, apple, grapes.

4. Make a shake from frozen fruit as the beverage for a December "picnic" by the fire. (You can always dream of sunshine!)

5. Try preparing the same fruit in a different way:

• Bake an apple in the microwave.
• Grill a grapefruit under the broiler.
• Cook bananas with brown sugar and orange juice (recipe page 202).
• Freeze bananas or seedless grapes. (They taste like ice cream!)
• Make a melon kebab on a thin straw.

6. Add a new twist to food by making fruit salsas and sauces. (Several recipes follow.)

7. Bring along dried apricots and raisins for great car snacks.

8. Top pancakes or waffles with fresh or frozen berries or cinnamon applesauce.

9. Make an old-fashioned gelatin salad with fruit.

10. Top a whole-grain waffle or angel food cake with fresh fruit and light whipped topping.

11. Serve fruit ready to eat—peeled and sliced or sectioned.

12. Add dried fruits to quick breads, hot cereals, pancakes, bread and rice puddings, cookies, and bars. Try raisins, apricots, dates, mangos, or prunes.

13. Use applesauce, mashed banana, or prune purée instead of oil in cakes, bars, and quick breads. Baby-food fruits also work well.

14. Add chopped apple, pear, mango, or raisins to tuna or chicken salad.

15. Create a fruit sundae with yogurt.

Angel Dessert

The perfect dessert for your little angels!

Makes: 19 1-cup servings

1 angel food cake

1 package (3½ ounces)
lemon pudding mix

1¾ cup milk

3 cups light whipped
topping, divided

12 ounces custard-style
vanilla yogurt

1 quart fresh strawberries,
washed and sliced

1 cup fresh raspberries,
washed and dried

1. Cut cake into 1-inch cubes. Set aside.

2. Prepare pudding according to package directions. Fold in 2 cups of whipped topping.

3. In trifle bowl or other large bowl (preferably transparent), place ⅓ of cake cubes followed by ⅓ of pudding mixture and ⅓ of strawberries. Repeat 2 more times.

4. With remaining cup of whipped topping, spread in thin layer over top, place spoonfuls around edge of bowl, or place in middle. Arrange raspberries decoratively on top. Chill if not serving immediately.

Variations

For Valentine's Day: Use vanilla pudding and cherry or strawberry yogurt. Use cherry pie filling for fruit.

For the Fourth of July: Use strawberries and blueberries. On top, form a flag.

**Each ½-cup
serving provides**

80 calories
16 grams carbohydrate
2 grams protein
2 grams fat

Key Nutrients

30% vitamin C
17% calcium

Apricot Vinaigrette

This mild dressing goes well with tossed salads—even those with grilled meats. The rice vinegar is not as strong as other vinegars. If your children prefer creamy dressings, stir in a tablespoon of mayonnaise, yogurt, or fat-free sour cream.

Makes: 1 cup

1 15¼-ounce can apricots, drained

1 clove garlic, minced

4 tablespoons oil

2 tablespoons seasoned rice vinegar

2 tablespoons water

⅛ teaspoon salt

Pinch of pepper

1. Pour all ingredients into blender and blend on low, then high, until puréed.

Each 2-tablespoon serving provides

47 calories
4 grams carbohydrate
0 grams protein
3 grams fat

Key Nutrients

Provides small amounts of many nutrients.

Apricot-Mango Fizzy

This is the perfect classroom party punch—and it's not as sweet as most punches.

Makes: 22 5-ounce servings

48 ounces canned apricot-mango juice or 12 ounces orange juice (or other juice) concentrate, thawed and prepared

4 cups vanilla frozen yogurt or light ice cream

32 ounces lemon-lime club soda (no sugar added)

1. Place juice and yogurt in a large bowl.

2. Fill with soda.

Great flavor combinations:

- Cran-raspberry juice concentrate, raspberry flavored club soda, raspberry sherbet
- Limeade concentrate, lime-flavored soda, lime sherbet
- Strawberry nectar, plain club soda, rainbow sherbet or vanilla ice cream

Each 5-ounce child serving provides

75 calories
16 grams carbohydrate
2 grams protein
1 gram fat

Key Nutrients

22% vitamin A

Bananas NeeNee

This is a kid version of bananas Foster. It can be eaten alone or served over vanilla ice cream or frozen yogurt.

Makes: 6 servings

3 large bananas

3 tablespoons orange juice concentrate

⅓ cup brown sugar, packed

3 tablespoons water

3 tablespoons light margarine or butter

1. Cut bananas into quarters, then cut each quarter into long slices.

2. Mix orange juice concentrate, brown sugar, water, and butter in a nonstick skillet. Heat until mixed and bubbly.

3. Gently fold in bananas and cook until warm.

Each serving provides

134 calories
28 grams carbohydrate
1 gram protein
3 grams fat
1 gram fiber

Key Nutrients

68% vitamin B$_6$
37% vitamin C

Berry-Orange Sauce

Perfect over pancakes, waffles, or fresh fruit salad with frozen yogurt.

Makes: 3 servings

10-ounce bag unsweetened strawberries or blueberries, thawed

1 tablespoon cornstarch

⅓ cup orange juice (or other juice)

3 tablespoons sugar

1 teaspoon vanilla

1. Strain thawed berries, reserving juice.

2. Heat berry juice in a saucepan until it simmers.

3. Dissolve cornstarch in cold orange juice. Add with sugar to simmering berry juice. Stir occasionally to prevent sticking.

4. Cook until thick and clear.

5. Add vanilla and berries.

6. Serve warm over pancakes, waffles, or ice cream.

Each serving provides

91 calories
23 grams carbohydrate
0 grams protein
0 grams fat

Key Nutrients

55% vitamin C

Bluebird Nests

Kids love these puffy clouds of meringue filled with blueberry "eggs."

Makes: *about 8 nests*

3 egg whites
¼ teaspoon cream of tartar
½ cup sugar
⅛ teaspoon salt
2 cups blueberries

1. Preheat the oven to 225°F.

2. Beat egg whites until foamy.

3. Gradually add sugar and salt and beat until stiff peaks form.

4. Cover a cookie sheet with wax paper or parchment paper. With a spoon or icing bag, form 8 nests.

5. Bake for 1 hour and 45 minutes. Turn oven off and leave meringues in oven an additional 2 hours.

6. Remove nests from cookie sheet and fill with blueberries.

Each nest provides

72 calories
17 grams carbohydrate
2 grams protein
1 gram fiber

Key Nutrients

11% vitamin C
Small amounts of other nutrients

Breakfast Armadillos

If your child has not tried mango, this is a fun way to introduce it.

Makes: 4 servings

2 mangos
8 red seedless grapes

1. Slice the mango in half lengthwise and remove the mango from the pit in two large, flat, curved sections.

2. Being careful not to cut through the skin, make 4 to 6 slices lengthwise through the mango fruit.

3. Make the same number of slices across the mango, creating a checkerboard pattern.

4. Pick up the mango half and gently push on the skin to turn the mango inside out. The skin side will now be curved inward, and the fruit side will stick out, with the checkerboard pattern creating an armadillo-like shell.

5. Insert grapes in the appropriate spots for eyes. (For smaller children, use grape halves.)

Each armadillo provides	Key Nutrients
70 calories	*107% vitamin A*
35 grams carbohydrate	*71% vitamin C*
1 gram protein	
2 grams fiber	

Chocolate-Banana Pops

A cool, fun dessert.

Makes: as much as you like

*Chocolate fondue sauce
(see Fruit Fondue recipe
on page 213) or peanut
butter*

Banana halves

Granola

1. Make recipe for chocolate sauce.

2. Insert a Popsicle stick into each banana half.

3. Roll banana halves in chocolate sauce (or spread with peanut butter).

4. Roll in granola.

5. Place the coated banana pops on a wax-paper-lined plate and freeze until firm.

Each pop provides

*132 calories
24 grams carbohydrate
2 grams protein
4 grams fat
1 gram fiber*

Key Nutrients

*Small amounts of many
nutrients*

Cinnamon Tortilla Chips

Kids love this healthier version of tortilla chips. Serve chips with Rainbow Fruit Salsa (recipe page 221).

Makes: 42 chips

7 small flour or corn tortillas

1 tablespoon sugar

½ tablespoon cinnamon

1. Preheat oven to 450°F.

2. Cut each tortilla into 6 wedges with knife or kitchen shears. Mix cinnamon and sugar.

3. Brush wedges with water and sprinkle with sugar and cinnamon.

4. Bake about 10 minutes or until crisp.

6 chips (1 tortilla) with ½ cup Rainbow Fruit Salsa provides

189 calories
41 grams carbohydrate
3 grams protein
2 grams fat
3 grams fiber

Key Nutrients

91% vitamin C
22% magnesium

Cranapple Sauce

Kids love this naturally pink applesauce.

Makes: 4 ½-cup servings

¾ *cup whole-cranberry sauce*

1½ *cups unsweetened applesauce*

3 *tablespoons Craisins*

1. Mash cranberry sauce in a bowl with a fork.

2. Stir in applesauce and Craisins.

3. Chill before serving.

Each ¼-cup child serving provides

70 calories

19 grams carbohydrate

0 grams protein

0 grams fat

1 gram fiber

Key Nutrients

Small amounts of all nutrients

Creamy Fruit Dip

For all those kids who love to dip.

Makes: 16 ½-ounce servings

8 ounces light cream cheese, softened

⅓ cup fruit juice concentrate, thawed (orange, apple, pineapple-orange, cran-grape, and so on)

Favorite fruits for dipping

1. Combine cream cheese and fruit juice concentrate in a mixing bowl and mix with a wire whisk or mixer until smooth.

2. Clean, peel, slice, and section fruits for dipping, as needed.

3. Dip away with your favorite fresh fruits!

Each ½-ounce serving of dip provides

59 calories
2 grams carbohydrate
1 gram protein
2 grams fat

Key Nutrients

(when made with orange juice concentrate)
18% vitamin C
15% vitamin A

Dreamsicle Soup

This makes a great summer appetizer, especially when served in a hollowed-out cantaloupe! On a scale of 1 to 10, kid taste testers rated this a 1000!

Makes: 5 1-cup servings

1 medium cantaloupe, halved and hollowed out, with fruit coarsely chopped

6 tablespoons orange juice concentrate

1⅓ cups vanilla yogurt

1. Combine fruit, juice, and yogurt in a blender and blend on high until smooth.

2. Serve in hollowed-out cantaloupe halves.

Garnish

Kids will enjoy some blueberries floating on top.

Adults may enjoy some finely snipped chives.

Variation

Serve in hollowed-out orange halves instead.

Each ½-cup child serving provides

67 calories

14 grams carbohydrate

2 grams protein

1 gram fat

Key Nutrients

97% vitamin C

96% vitamin D

66% vitamin A

21% magnesium

16% calcium

Floating Fruits

Sneak fruit into ice cubes!

Makes: as much as you like

Pineapple, pear, and peach, cut into bite-sized chunks (For more color, you might also try cherries, strawberries, raspberries, blueberries, and mandarin oranges.)

Lemon-lime soda or club soda

1. Place chunks of fruit in each section of ice-cube tray.

2. Fill tray with lemon-lime soda.

3. Freeze 3 hours, or until frozen firm.

4. Place fruit cubes in a tall clear glass, then fill glass with lemon-lime soda or club soda.

Variation

Purée the fruit and mix the fruit purée with yogurt. Then pour the fruit-and-yogurt mixture into ice-cube trays and freeze until firm.

Key Nutrients

Nutrients vary according to fruits used.

Frozen Fruit on a Straw

If your kids are tempted by Kool Pops and the like, try this novel idea for serving fruit! A great treat to eat outside on a hot summer day.

Makes: as much as you like

Apple, banana, melon,
pineapple, and/or pear,
cut into medium chunks

Grapes, cut in half

Whole strawberries

Coffee stirring straws

1. Thread fruit chunks onto straw. Freeze.

2. Serve outside for a cool snack.

Key Nutrients

Nutrients vary according to
ingredients used.

Fruit Fondue

Kids will feel very grown-up when they dip their strawberries, pear slices, and grapes into this chocolate sauce. This also makes a special teacher's gift.

Makes: 6 2½-teaspoon servings

⅓ cup milk chocolate or white chocolate chips

2 tablespoons milk

Strawberries, pear slices, and grapes for dipping

1. Heat milk in a medium saucepan; make sure the milk doesn't boil.

2. Add chocolate chips and stir until the chips melt.

3. Pour the sauce into a small bowl and let the kids dip strawberries, pear slices, and grapes.

Each 2½-teaspoon serving of sauce provides

49 calories
6 grams carbohydrate
1 gram protein
3 grams fat

Key Nutrients

Small amounts of all nutrients

Fruit Scoops

A refreshing way to eat fruit.

Makes: as much as you like

Favorite fresh fruit, chopped or crushed

Favorite flavor yogurt

Waffle cones

1. Mix any combination of fresh fruit with any flavor of yogurt.

2. Put ½ cup of the fruit-yogurt mixture into a baggie and twist the baggie until the fruit mixture forms a ball about 2 inches in diameter. Tie the bag with a twistie.

3. Freeze overnight. Serve in a waffle cone.

Key Nutrients

Nutrients vary according to fruits used.

Fruit Soda

If your kids like commercial soda, try this!

Makes: 6 cups

*1 12-ounce can fruit juice
concentrate, any flavor,
thawed*

*1 32-ounce bottle club soda,
plain or flavored, but
unsweetened*

1. Pour juice concentrate in a 2½-quart pitcher.

2. Slowly add club soda. Stir gently and serve immediately.

**Each ½-cup child
serving provides**

*55 calories
14 grams carbohydrate
0 grams protein
0 grams fat*

Key Nutrients

*Nutrient content varies
depending on type of
juice, but most will pro-
vide 50–100% of the
RDA for vitamin C.*

Island Punch

On the island of Maui, some streets are dotted with pink from the guavas that have fallen on the road. You seem to be able to find guava in everything in Hawaii. Here on the mainland, the closest we usually get to this luscious fruit is guava nectar, but it can still add an island touch to drinks.

Makes: as much as you want

Guava nectar
Apple juice

1. Mix equal parts of juices together.

Each 4-ounce child serving provides

60 calories
15 grams carbohydrate
0 grams protein
0 grams fat

Key Nutrients

65% vitamin C

Katie and Nicolas's Fruit Crisp

So easy, your kids could probably make it! Watch them gobble it up!

Makes: 6 servings

2 cups fresh or canned fruit, drained

1 tablespoon brown sugar

1½ tablespoons flour

1 cup low-fat granola

2 tablespoons light margarine or butter, melted

1. Preheat the oven to 350°F.

2. Put fruit, sugar, and flour in a 2-quart baking dish or bowl. Mix well.

3. In a separate bowl, stir together granola and margarine; spread evenly over top of fruit.

4. Bake for 30 to 40 minutes until golden brown.

Each ½-cup child serving provides

62 calories

11 grams carbohydrate

1 gram protein

2 grams fat

1 gram fiber

Key Nutrients

Small amounts of all nutrients

Kid-Friendly Frozen Fruit Salad

This salad is refreshing in the summer and makes a perfect outdoor snack!

Makes: about 12 ½-cup servings

8-ounce can pineapple bits

1 can mandarin oranges, drained

16-ounce can peaches, drained

2 bananas, sliced

2 cups seedless grapes

3 tablespoons cran-grape concentrate (or any other flavor)

1. Combine all ingredients in a large bowl. (Fruit can be finely chopped for smaller eaters.)

2. Place mixture in a large zip-lock bag. Place baggie in freezer until the fruit mixture is slushy, or freeze until firm, then thaw 20 to 30 minutes before serving.

Variations

- Spoon fruit into paper muffin liners or into individual paper cups. Freeze until firm, then remove paper and store the fruit cups in zip-lock bags until ready to serve.
- Add sliced strawberries, blueberries, or any other favorite fruits to the mix.

Each ¼-cup child serving provides

30 calories

8 grams carbohydrate

0 grams protein

0 grams fat

1 gram fiber

Key Nutrients

25% vitamin C

16% vitamin B_6

Nicolas's Fruit Blast

Kids and adults will love this refreshing sorbet.

Makes: 4 servings

15¼-ounce can crushed pineapple, frozen

1 grapefruit, peeled and sectioned, with membranes removed (This is easy to do if you cut the grapefruit in half and section it with a knife.)

1. Take can of pineapple out of the freezer; let thaw until the fruit is soft enough to spoon out in partially frozen chunks.

2. Spoon the pineapple into a blender and add grapefruit sections. Blend until smooth.

3. Serve immediately or refreeze for serving later. If refreezing, blend the fruit mixture again before serving.

Each ¼-cup child serving provides

55 calories
14 grams carbohydrate
0 grams protein
0 grams fat
1 gram fiber

Key Nutrients

48% magnesium
42% manganese
40% vitamin C

Pear Pops

Pears are smooth and creamy when frozen.

Makes: 4 pops

16-ounce can pear slices or halves, drained

8-ounces low-fat yogurt with fruit, any flavor

1. Pour fruit and yogurt into blender and blend until smooth.

2. Divide mixture among Popsicle molds or paper cups; insert sticks.

3. Freeze until firm, about 3 hours.

Variations

Place bits of fruit or whole blueberries in the mold before pouring in pear mixture. Experiment with chocolate chips or sprinkles.

Each pop provides

106 calories
21 grams carbohydrate
3 grams protein
1 gram fat
2 grams fiber

Key Nutrients

25% riboflavin
18% calcium

Rainbow Fruit Salsa

Young kids may not like tomato salsa, but they dig into this! Serve this fun-and-fruity salsa with Cinnamon Tortilla Chips (recipe page 207).

Makes: about 3½ cups (7 ½-cup servings)

2 medium red delicious or granny smith apples, peeled and chopped

1 cup strawberries, fresh or frozen, chopped

1 kiwi, peeled and chopped

1 orange, peeled, seeded, and chopped

1 cup peaches, fresh or canned; peeled, pitted, and chopped

2 tablespoons apple, apricot, or strawberry jelly or jam

2 tablespoons brown sugar

½ cup orange juice, preferably freshly squeezed

Note: The fruit ingredients can be chopped individually or placed in a food processor and pulsed until the consistency of salsa.

1. Make sure fruit is well washed and finely chopped; place in bowl.

2. Mix jelly with brown sugar and orange juice. Mix into fruit mixture.

3. Serve with Cinnamon Tortilla Chips.

½ cup fruit salsa with 6 Cinnamon Tortilla Chips (1 tortilla) provides

189 calories
41 grams carbohydrate
3 grams protein
2 grams fat
3 grams fiber

Key Nutrients

91% vitamin C
22% magnesium

Robert's Juicy Juice

My son Robert concocted this recipe.

Makes: as much as you want

Apple-grape juice
Guava nectar
Apricot nectar

1. Mix equal parts of juices together.

Each 4-ounce child serving provides

89 calories
22 grams carbohydrate
0 grams protein
0 grams fat

Key Nutrients

45% vitamin C
20% vitamin A

Sip of Sunshine

A serving of this juice will feel like sunshine on a cloudy day.

Makes: 8 4-ounce servings

16 ounces apricot nectar
16 ounces pineapple juice

1. Mix and chill, or serve over ice.

Each serving provides

64 calories
16 grams carbohydrate
0 grams protein
0 grams fat

Key Nutrients

18% vitamin A
16% vitamin C

Strawberry Dream Pops

A treat that's full of fiber and vitamin C.

Makes: 8 3-ounce pops

10-ounce package frozen sweetened strawberries, thawed

2 cups plain nonfat or low-fat yogurt

1. Purée fruit and yogurt in a blender.
2. Divide puréed mixture among Popsicle molds or paper cups; insert sticks.
3. Freeze 3 hours or until firm.

Variation

Place bits of fruit or whole blueberries in the mold before pouring in strawberry mixture.

Each pop provides

66 calories
14 grams carbohydrate
3 grams protein
3 grams fiber

Key Nutrients

38% vitamin C
23% calcium

Surf's-Up Punch

A great drink to sip by the beach or pool.

Makes: as much as you want

Apple-peach juice
Pineapple juice
Club soda

1. Mix equal amounts of juices together.

**Each 6-ounce
serving provides**

64 calories
16 grams carbohydrate
0 grams protein
0 grams fat

Key Nutrients

10% vitamin C

Tutti-Frutti Drink

This drink appeals to all ages.

Makes: *as much as you want*

Pineapple juice
Apricot nectar
White grape-peach juice

1. Mix equal parts of juices together.

**Each 4-ounce
serving provides**

68 calories
17 grams carbohydrate

Key Nutrients

37% vitamin C

Winter Fruit Salad

If your family gets tired of the fresh fruit selection available in the winter, try this.

Makes: 6 cups

1 large can (28 ounces) sliced peaches, drained

2 cups frozen blueberries, thawed

1. Mix ingredients in bowl and serve.

Each ½-cup child serving provides

32 calories
8 grams carbohydrate
0 grams protein
0 grams fat
1 gram fiber

Key Nutrients

11% vitamin A
7% vitamin C

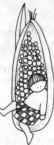

Grains

Tips for Including More Whole Grains in Your Family's Diet

Eating whole grains has never been easier! The wide variety of whole-grain foods, many of them quick-cooking, make it simple for your family to include them in every meal. Here are a few tips on going for the grain.

1. If you start your kids eating whole grains at an early age, they will accept different types of whole grains more easily. If whole grains are something new to your family, they may be met with some hesitation and even protest! If this is the case, try to introduce them gradually. For example:

• Buy or make breads that contain some whole grain. (such as wheat berry and/or whole-wheat or other whole-grain flour), though not as the first ingredient.

• You could also try making sandwiches with one piece of white bread and one piece of wheat bread.

Some whole-grain breads are lighter than others. Experiment until you find one your family likes.

2. Add whole grains to quick breads, muffins, cookies, and pancakes. In most recipes for quick breads and cookies, you can replace at least ¼ to ½ white flour with whole-grain flour. For recipes that require finer flour, you can use whole-wheat pastry flour or oat flour. Check out the bulk section of a natural-foods market to buy small amounts of different flours for experimenting. Hint: Wheat germ and bran can also be added to many recipes (even meatballs). Just add a few tablespoons, and you will be adding important nutrients missing from processed flours.

3. Mix whole grains with white grains. For example, you might mix bulgur, quinoa, or whole-wheat couscous with

white rice or mix whole-wheat pasta with white pasta.

4. Don't overlook salads as a way to mix in some grains. Mix whole-wheat pasta in your pasta salads, whole-kernel corn in a marinated salad, and brown rice in any salad that includes rice.

5. Introduce your kids to whole-grain cereals. To start, mix them with your child's current favorite cereal. You will find many whole-grain cereals in the natural-food aisle at the grocery store. Others are listed below.

6. Buy quick-cooking whole grains, such as bulgur and whole-wheat couscous.

▼

Some Common Whole-Grain Foods

Cereals

Bran Chex
Cheerios
Crunchy Corn Bran
Frosted Mini Wheats
Granola made from whole oats
Honey Nut Mini Wheats
Life Cereal
Old-fashioned oatmeal
Puffed rice
Puffed wheat
Quaker Oat Squares
Wheat Chex

How Can You Tell It's Whole Grain?

Keep in mind that many products seem to be made from whole grain but aren't, which makes selection difficult for the consumer. To determine a product's whole-grain goodness, look carefully at the list of ingredients. Whole-grain flour—such as whole-wheat flour, whole-oat flour, whole-corn flour—should be listed as the first ingredient, and a statement that it is "from the whole grain" should follow.

Grain Side Dishes

Barley
Brown rice
Bulgur (cracked wheat, very quick cooking)
Whole-kernel corn
Whole-wheat couscous (small, quick-cooking pasta)

Bread and Flour Products

Any bread that has whole-grain flour listed as the first ingredient
Corn tortillas
Krusteaz Oat Spice and Honey Wheat Pancakes
Nutrigrain Waffles
Pasta made with whole-wheat or other whole-grain flour
Tortilla chips made from whole-grain cornmeal
Whole-grain granola bars (read the label carefully)
Whole-wheat crackers
Whole-wheat tortillas

Grain (1 cup dry)	Cups Liquid	Approximate Cooking Time (in minutes)	Approximate Yield (cups cooked)
Amaranth	3	20–25	2½
Barley	3	75	3½
*Brown rice	2	55–60	3
*Bulgur	2	15–20	2½
Cornmeal	4	25–30	3
Couscous	1½	5	3⅓
Cracked wheat	2	25	2⅓
Hominy grits (quick)	3½–4	7–10	4½
Millet	3	45	3½
Oat bran	4	2	4
Quinoa	1⅔	10–15	2½
Rolled oats	2	5	3
*Wheat berries	3	60	2⅔

*Quick-cooking types also available

Great Grains

Are you stuck in a rut when it comes to the starchy side dish on your plate? Fortunately, some popular whole grains, formerly only found in bulk in natural-food stores, are making their way into grocery stores. To introduce new grains to your family, try mixing them with something familiar first, like rice or corn. Use the handy guide above for cooking grains. You'll never be at a loss about quantities, cooking times, and yields for each type of grain!

Apple Cider Pancakes

A new rendition of an old favorite, this recipe is modified from *Quick &
Healthy, Volume II* by Brenda Ponichtera, R.D. (Scaledown Publishing, 1995).

Makes: 8 pancakes

Vegetable cooking spray

¼ cup old-fashioned oats

*1 cup whole-grain pancake
    mix (such as Krusteaz)*

¾ cup apple cider

1. Spray a griddle or heavy skillet with vegetable
cooking spray.

2. With a wire whisk, blend all ingredients in a bowl
until smooth.

3. Pour slightly less than ¼ cup batter per pancake on a
hot griddle or skillet. Cook about 1½ to 2 minutes per
side or until golden.

Each child serving (1 pancake) provides	**Key Nutrients**
75 calories	*57% manganese*
17 grams carbohydrate	*44% magnesium*
3 grams protein	*14% selenium*
0 grams fat	*10% iron*
2 grams fiber	

Baked Tortilla Chips

Chips don't have to come out of a bag! Let your kids help you with these. Corn tortillas provide an extra nutritional bonus–they are surprisingly high in calcium. You can also use pocket pita bread that has been split into two rounds.

Makes: 8 servings

8 small corn tortillas
Vegetable cooking spray
Garlic salt, cinnamon sugar, or other spices

1. Preheat oven to 450°F.
2. With clean scissors or knife, cut each tortilla into 4 wedges.
3. Lay the wedges out on a cookie sheet that has been sprayed with cooking spray.
4. Spray tops of tortillas with spray.
5. Sprinkle with garlic salt, cinnamon sugar, or other spices.
6. Bake 6 to 10 minutes or until golden.

Each serving provides	**Key Nutrients**
67 calories	*24% magnesium*
11 grams carbohydrate	*18% vitamin B₆*
2 grams protein	*10% selenium*
1 gram fat	*8% calcium*
2 grams fiber	

Basic Grain Pilaf

Vary the grain and the vegetables for any number of delicious and healthy combinations.

Makes: as much as you like

2 teaspoons oil

1 cup any combination of the following: celery, chiles, garlic, green onion, mushrooms, olives, onion, parsley, red or green sweet pepper, shallots, zucchini (all finely chopped); capers, grated carrots, frozen peas, raisins

Tarragon, chives, or thyme (½–1 teaspoon dried or 1 tablespoon fresh)

Liquid (see chart on page 231 for amount)—use water, plain or flavored with soy sauce or wine, or chicken, beef, or vegetable broth

Grain of choice (see chart, page 231)

1. In large saucepan, heat oil and sauté vegetables for 5 minutes.

2. Add herbs, liquid, and grain; cover and simmer until tender (see chart on page 231 for time).

Variation

If you like, use fruit juice for half of the required liquid.

Spanish Variation

Brown chopped onion in oil for 5 minutes. Add bulgur or other grain, browning for 2 more minutes. Stir in vegetables and herbs, adding ½ teaspoon cumin. Replace part of the required liquid with chopped stewed tomatoes and juice, plain or with chiles.

Each ¼-cup child serving of bulgur provides

55 calories
11 grams carbohydrate
2 grams protein
1 gram fat
2 grams fiber

Key Nutrients

21% magnesium
12% vitamin B_6
8% chromium

Blueberry Coffee Cake

This recipe, modified from *Quick & Healthy Recipes and Ideas* by Brenda Ponichtera, R.D. (Scaledown Publishing, 1994), makes a 9-by-12-inch pan. If you like, halve the recipe for a 9-by-9-inch pan. Or make 12 muffins and a small coffee cake. This recipe freezes well.

Makes: 24 squares or muffins

Cake:
Vegetable cooking spray

1 cup whole-wheat flour

1⅔ cup unbleached flour

2 cups oats (quick or old-fashioned)

1 cup brown sugar, firmly packed

2 tablespoons baking powder

1 teaspoon salt (optional)

1 teaspoon cinnamon

½ teaspoon ground cloves

2 cups milk

2 eggs

⅓ cup + 1 tablespoon oil

2 cups fresh or frozen blueberries, thawed

Topping:
2 tablespoons firmly packed brown sugar

¼ teaspoon cinnamon

1. Preheat the oven to 375°F. Spray a 9-by-12-inch baking pan with vegetable cooking spray.

2. Mix topping ingredients and set aside.

3. In a large bowl, combine flours, oats, sugar, baking powder, and spices.

4. In a separate bowl, mix milk, eggs, and oil. Add to dry ingredients and mix quickly, just until moistened.

5. Fold in blueberries.

6. Pour into baking pan and spoon on topping mixture.

7. Bake for 35 to 40 minutes or until golden brown.

Each child serving (½ square) provides

93 calories
18 grams carbohydrate
3 grams protein
1 gram fat
2 grams fiber

Key Nutrients

44% manganese
26% magnesium
22% thiamin

Bread Pudding

In Louisiana this pudding is often served with a warm bourbon sauce. For kids, try it with a bit of warm maple syrup or Bananas NeeNee (page 202).

Makes: 8 servings

4 cups stale wheat bread, torn into pieces (about ½ loaf French bread or 7 pieces sliced whole-wheat bread)

2 cups milk

½ cup chopped dates or raisins

3 eggs

⅔ cup sugar

4 tablespoons margarine, melted

1 tablespoon vanilla

2 teaspoon cinnamon

1. Preheat the oven to 350°F.

2. Put bread, milk, and dates or raisins into a large bowl and let soak 15 minutes.

3. In a separate bowl, mix together the rest of the ingredients. Stir into bread mixture and pour into a greased 8-by-8-inch pan.

4. Bake for 40 to 50 minutes.

Each ½-cup child serving provides	Key Nutrients
102 calories	29% selenium
18 grams carbohydrate	21% magnesium
3 grams protein	14% chromium
0 grams fat	10% calcium
2 grams fiber	

Calzones

If your family loves pizza, they'll also go for calzones.

Makes: 4 calzones

1 wheat pizza crust or frozen whole-wheat bread dough, thawed

16 ounces ricotta or cottage cheese

2 cups grated mozzarella (or a prepackaged, seasoned pizza-cheese mix)

24 ounces pasta sauce (or tomato sauce mixed with tomato paste)

1. Preheat oven to 400°F.

2. Divide crust or bread dough into 4 to 6 pieces, depending on the size of calzone you want. Shape each piece into a ball, then roll out to a circle about ½-inch thick.

3. Mix cheeses together.

4. Spread ½ to ¾ cup of pasta sauce onto one side of each round of dough.

5. Top with ¾ cup of the cheese mixture.

6. Fold over plain side of dough to within ½ inch of edge of dough with filling, forming a half-moon shape. Fold edge of bottom dough over top dough and seal, crimping edges.

7. Bake for 12–18 minutes.

Each ⅛ calzone provides	**Key Nutrients**
209 calories	42% calcium
34 grams carbohydrate	33% vitamin A
14 grams protein	28% vitamin C
8 grams fat	
3 grams fiber	

CooCoo Crunchies

Like the chocolate-covered cereals kids love, but healthier.

Makes: 3¼ cups

2 cups puffed wheat or
   kamut cereal

1 cup rolled oats (not
   instant)

¼ cup wheat germ

2 tablespoons chocolate milk
   mix

2 tablespoons honey

2 teaspoons oil

2 teaspoons water

1. Preheat oven to 300°F.

2. Mix first 3 ingredients in large bowl.

3. Place chocolate milk mix, honey, oil, and water in a separate microwave-safe bowl or saucepan. Heat in microwave 10 seconds on high, or on stove top, until mixture can be easily mixed. Stir and fold into cereal mixture.

4. Pour cereal mixture onto cookie sheet or cake pan and cook 10 minutes, stirring once.

Each ¼-cup child serving provides

59 calories

10 grams carbohydrate

2 grams protein

1 gram fat

1 gram fiber

Key Nutrients

56% manganese

25% magnesium

Corn Jello (Cheesy Polenta)

The recipe couldn't be simpler—and the serving possibilities are endless!

Makes: 4 servings

⅓ cup stone-ground cornmeal

1 cup chicken broth

½ teaspoon chopped garlic

¼ cup grated cheese, any type

Vegetable cooking spray

1. Stir cornmeal and garlic into chicken broth. Bring to a simmer and cook 10 minutes, stirring frequently.

2. Stir in cheese until melted and remove from heat.

3. Spray a dinner plate or pie plate with cooking spray. Spread polenta in pan, smoothing out the top. Let cool.

> *Note:* Set polenta can be cut into special shapes for kids. Use a cookie cutter or knife to create triangles for pizza or diamonds for kites.

To serve:

Polenta can be served alone as a side dish in place of rice or pasta. Or it can be the base of an entrée, as pasta or rice often are. Here are a few ideas:

- Top with sautéed mushrooms and chicken strips.
- Top with Black Bean Salsa (recipe page 168).
- Top with grilled vegetables, such as zucchini or eggplant.
- Serve with stir-fried tofu and vegetables.
- Top with pasta sauce with ground beef or turkey.

Each ½ portion provides	Key Nutrients
32 calories	*Small amounts of all nutrients*
4 grams carbohydrate	
1 gram protein	
1 gram fat	
1 gram fiber	

Corn-Barley Salad

This is a salad your kids will want more of.

Makes: 2 cups

1 cup drained corn

1 cup cooked barley

2½ tablespoons vinaigrette dressing

1. Mix all ingredients and serve.

Each ¼-cup child serving provides

60 calories

9 grams carbohydrate

1 gram protein

2 grams fat

1 gram fiber

Key Nutrients

12% selenium

11% magnesium

Small amounts of many other nutrients

Crepes

French fries and French dressing aren't really French–but crepes sure are!
Sold on street corners in France, they're French fast food. Crepes are quite
versatile: Fill them with butter and sugar for breakfast or chicken in cream
sauce for dinner. You will find some filling ideas following the recipe.

Makes: about 12 crepes

**Vegetable cooking spray or a
little oil**

1 egg

Few shakes of salt

1 tablespoon oil

1¾ cups milk

¼ cup water

½ cup whole-wheat flour

½ cup white unbleached flour

**For sweet crepes, add 3
teaspoons sugar and 2
teaspoons vanilla.**

**For savory crepes, add herbs,
such as dill, basil, or
tarragon.**

1. Prepare a 10-inch nonstick skillet or griddle by
   spraying with cooking spray or wiping with a slightly
   oiled paper towel. It is essential to have a pan that is
   in good shape without nicks or scratches.

2. In a large bowl, mix together egg, salt, and oil.

3. Add 1 cup milk and beat well. Stir in rest of milk and
   water.

4. If desired, add sugar and vanilla for sweet crepes, or
   add herbs for savory crepes.

5. Gradually stir in flours. Beat until smooth.

5. Let stand several minutes. Batter should resemble
   very thin pancake batter.

6. Heat the oiled skillet or griddle. Ladle about ¼ cup of
   batter onto the pan and quickly rotate pan so batter
   covers whole surface of pan.

7. Cook over medium to medium-high heat until
   underside starts browning. With a pancake turner,
   gently lift edge of crepe, shaking pan slightly to help
   loosen center. Grasp edge with fingers and turn over.
   (The very skilled can flip the crepe over with a flip of
   the wrist!) Cook briefly on other side. Note: It is
   important to stir up the batter a bit between each

Crepes
(continued)

crepe, since the wheat bran in the flour has a tendency to sink to the bottom of the bowl. For thinner crepes, add a bit more water.

8. Fill immediately (see fillings below), or place between pieces of wax paper to use a little later or to freeze.

Tip: Unused batter may be kept in the refrigerator for several days. Before using, let the batter sit at room temperature a few minutes, then beat well or shake.

Fillings:

Breakfast
Applesauce and cinnamon
Berries and strawberry fruit spread or powdered sugar
Fresh fruit and yogurt
Ham and cheese
Margarine and sugar or honey
Peanut butter and banana

Lunch or Dinner
Boursin cheese
Chicken and mushrooms, topped with thick cream of mushroom soup
Ham and Swiss cheese, topped with a Dijon sauce
Ratatouille and mozzarella cheese
Salmon pâté with cucumber yogurt sauce
Sautéed or steamed shrimp and scallops with white sauce
Spinach filling from Spinach-Stuffed Shells (page 189)

Dessert
Chocolate frozen yogurt topped with raspberries
Fresh fruit topped with vanilla yogurt
Margarine and sugar or honey
Peaches with caramel sauce
Vanilla frozen yogurt topped with Bananas NeeNee
  (page 202)
Vanilla frozen yogurt and blueberries with heated
  strawberry all-fruit spread

Each crepe (without filling) provides

61 calories
11 grams carbohydrate
3 grams protein
1 grams fat
1 grams fiber

Key Nutrients

24% riboflavin
19% thiamin
19% magnesium
13% calcium

Flying Saucers

These healthy, edible spaceships will be flying off the plate.

Makes: about 10 to 12 4-inch pancakes

1 cup "complete" pancake mix

½ cup instant uncooked oats (you can use old-fashioned, but the texture will be a bit more chewy)

½ cup toasted wheat germ

1½ cups evaporated skim milk or regular milk

1. Mix together dry ingredients. Stir in milk.

2. Pour about ¼ cup batter per pancake on nonstick skillet and cook over low to medium-high heat until bubbles form on top. Turn and cook another minute or two.

Each pancake provides

161 calories

28 grams carbohydrate

8 grams protein

2 grams fat

2 grams fiber

Key Nutrients

52% magnesium

31% calcium

15% zinc

15% iron

Fried Rice

The zucchini, onion, and cabbage are well camouflaged with the rice, so even veggie haters may eat this!

Makes: 4 cups

1 tablespoon oil

½ small onion, finely chopped

3 cloves garlic, finely chopped

½ cup each: grated carrot, grated cabbage, and grated zucchini

2 tablespoons light soy sauce

3 cups leftover brown or white rice

2 eggs, beaten

1. In large nonstick skillet, heat oil.
2. Add onion and garlic and sauté until transparent.
3. Add vegetables and soy sauce. Stir-fry until tender.
4. Add rice and eggs, and cook, stirring over medium heat, until eggs are cooked through.

Each ½-cup child serving provides

140 calories
20 grams carbohydrate
5 grams protein
4 grams fat
2 grams fiber

Key Nutrients

59% manganese
58% vitamin A
50% magnesium

Fruited Couscous

Though often mistaken for a grain, couscous is actually itty-bitty pasta. This easy version can top a main-dish salad or go beside chicken or pork. The recipe is modified from *The Phytopia Cookbook* by Kim Pierce and Barbara Gollman (Phytopia, Inc., 1998).

Makes: 7 ⅓-cup servings

1½ cups apple juice or chicken broth

⅓ cup dried fruit, such as golden raisins, chopped prunes, or cranberries

1 cup whole-wheat couscous

¼ teaspoon allspice

½ teaspoon cinnamon

Salt to taste

1. Bring apple juice or chicken broth to boiling.

2. Add fruit, couscous, allspice, and cinnamon. Cover, remove from heat, and let stand about 10 minutes. (Or microwave in a microwave-safe dish on low for 1 to 2 minutes, until the liquid is absorbed.)

3. Fluff with a fork, add salt to taste, and serve.

Each ⅓-cup child serving provides

152 calories
37 grams carbohydrate
3 grams protein
0 grams fat
3 grams fiber

Key Nutrients

28% selenium
14% iron
13% magnesium

Granola

If your kids like granola, you can make your own, tailoring it to what your family likes.

Makes: 2½ cups

2 cups rolled oats

3 teaspoons toasted sesame seeds

⅓ cup wheat germ

¼ cup slivered almonds, finely chopped

¼ cup honey

2 tablespoons brown sugar

1 tablespoon oil

Pinch salt

½ cup dried fruit

1. Preheat oven to 300°F.

2. Mix oats, sesame seeds, and wheat germ in a medium bowl.

3. In a microwave-safe bowl or saucepan, mix honey, sugar, oil, and salt. Microwave on high for 30 seconds or cook over medium-low heat until mixture is thin. Stir and pour onto grains, mixing gently until combined.

4. Spread granola onto light-colored cookie sheet (dark cookie sheets brown food faster) and bake 15 to 20 minutes until golden brown, stirring several times during cooking.

5. Remove from oven and stir in dried fruit of your choice—raisins, chopped dates, dried blueberries or cranberries, or chopped mixed fruit. Store in tightly covered container.

Each ¼-cup child serving provides	Key Nutrients
158 calories	61% magnesium
26 grams carbohydrate	28% thiamin
5 grams protein	14% folate
5 grams fat	13% iron
2 grams fiber	

Grinchmeal

The grinch had to eat a very hearty breakfast to carry all those toys up and down the mountain! This chewy version of oatmeal has more calories than regular oatmeal and is great for kids who cannot finish a larger serving.

Makes: 3 cups

1 12-ounce can evaporated milk (skim, low-fat, or whole)

1½ cups granola

¼ cup dried fruit

1 tablespoon margarine

1 cup milk

1. Bring milk, granola, and fruit to a boil in a saucepan. Lower to a simmer and cook over medium heat, stirring frequently until preferred consistency is reached.

2. Let stand to cool and thicken for several minutes. Serve with a dab of margarine and extra milk.

Each ½-cup child serving provides

188 calories
30 grams carbohydrate
7 grams protein
5 grams fat

Key Nutrients

57% magnesium
49% selenium
37% calcium
16% vitamin A

Make-Ahead Batter for Bran Muffins

No time for baking in the morning? No problem with this make-ahead batter that can be kept in the fridge for up to 6 weeks! This recipe was modified from *Simply Colorado* (Colorado Dietetic Association, 1989).

Makes: 5 dozen muffins

2 cups boiling water

2 cups shreds of whole bran cereal

5 cups flour

5 teaspoons baking soda

2 teaspoons salt

2 cups sugar

1 cup margarine, softened

1 cup egg substitute

1 quart low-fat buttermilk

4 cups whole bran cereal buds

Vegetable cooking spray

1. Pour boiling water over shreds of whole bran cereal and set aside.

2. Sift together flour, baking soda, and salt in separate bowl and set aside.

3. Cream together sugar and margarine in a mixing bowl until light and fluffy. Add egg substitute and beat well.

4. Blend in buttermilk, bran cereal buds, and the soaked whole bran cereal.

5. Stir in dry ingredients until moistened. Store in a tightly covered container in refrigerator. Batter will keep for up to 6 weeks.

To make muffins, fill standard-size muffin pan cups coated with cooking spray to ⅔ full with batter (don't stir batter). Bake at 400°F for 20 minutes or until done.

Note: In order to keep this recipe as safe as possible during storage time, egg substitute, which is made with pasteurized eggs, is used. This also cuts down on the fat and cholesterol in the recipe.

Each muffin provides	Key Nutrients
90 calories	52% riboflavin
13 grams carbohydrate	44% magnesium
3 grams protein	44% vitamin B_6
4 grams fat	
2 grams fiber	

Meusli

Traditionally eaten in Switzerland, this version is adapted for kids—and kids love it. You may want to double the recipe! *(Note:* Grains can be purchased in small amounts in the bulk section of natural-food stores.)

Makes: about 4 cups

¾ cups quick oats
¼ cup rolled spelt flakes
¼ cup rolled wheat flakes
2½ cups flaked cereal such
as corn flakes or Wheaties
2 tablespoons brown sugar
½ cup dried fruit

1. Mix all ingredients and store in airtight container.

**Each ½-cup child
serving provides**

123 calories
28 grams carbohydrate
3 grams protein
1 gram fat
2 grams fiber

Key Nutrients

25% folate
22% iron
19% vitamin B₆

Mexican Bread Pudding

My neighbor Elvira Johnson brought this dish over for us to try. It is traditionally served as a dessert during Lent. Unlike bread pudding that is made with milk and cooked in the oven, this pudding cooks quickly and is great for people allergic to milk. Also, this dish is very flexible; add whatever fruits you like!

Makes: 15 servings

9 pieces whole-wheat bread or 6 Mexican Bollio rolls

2 tablespoons light butter or margarine

5 cups of water

2 cinnamon sticks

1 cup dark brown sugar

1 cup raisins

3 bananas, sliced

2 apples, peeled, cored, and chopped

½ cup peanuts

½ cup coconut (optional)

¾ cup grated mozzarella or Monterey Jack cheese (optional)

1. Spread a thin layer of butter or margarine on one side of each bread slice and toast in oven at 325°F for 15 minutes.

2. Boil water with cinnamon sticks for 5 minutes. Remove cinnamon stick, add brown sugar, and cook until dissolved.

3. Reduce heat and add bread. Stir until liquid is absorbed.

4. Add raisins, bananas, apples, peanuts, and coconut; continue to stir until everything is heated through.

5. Stir in cheese (if desired) and serve warm.

Hint: The liquid can be increased or decreased depending on how moist you like your pudding.

Each ½-cup child portion provides	Key Nutrients
99 calories	21% magnesium
18 grams carbohydrate	16% vitamin B_6
2 grams protein	12% chromium
3 grams fat	8% iron
2 grams fiber	

Plum Oat Squares

These delicious bars make a great snack!

Makes: 24 2-inch squares

1 cup all-purpose flour

¼ teaspoon salt

¼ teaspoon baking soda

1 teaspoon cinnamon

1½ cups brown sugar, firmly packed

1 egg or 2 egg whites

2 tablespoons vegetable oil

15-ounce can plums, drained, pitted, and finely chopped

2 cups uncooked rolled oats

¼ cup dried currants or raisins

½ cup chopped walnuts (optional)

Vegetable cooking spray

1. Preheat the oven to 350°F.

2. Combine flour, salt, baking soda, and cinnamon; set aside.

3. In a large mixing bowl, beat together sugar, egg, and oil. Add plums, oats, currants, and walnuts and stir until thoroughly mixed.

4. Add dry ingredients, stirring only until combined.

5. Spread evenly in a 9-by-13-by-2-inch pan coated with vegetable cooking spray.

6. Bake for 28 minutes until browned and a wooden pick inserted in center comes out clean. Cool completely before cutting.

Each 2-inch square provides

150 calories
30 grams carbohydrate
3 grams protein
2 grams fat
2 grams fiber

Key Nutrients

54% manganese
31% magnesium
15% iron

Puffy-Peanutty Granola

If your little one likes peanut butter, she'll love this stick-to-your-ribs cereal!

Makes: 4 cups

1½ cups rolled oats
¼ cup wheat germ
2 cups puffed cereal
¼ cup peanut butter
¼ cup + 1 tablespoon honey

1. Preheat oven to 300°F. Mix together cereals in bowl; set aside.

2. In microwave-safe bowl or saucepan, mix peanut butter and honey. Heat on high 45 seconds, or on stove top, until easy to mix.

3. Mix peanut butter mixture into cereal until well blended.

4. Spread mixture on cookie sheet. Bake 20 minutes or until golden brown, stirring several times during baking.

Each ¼-cup child serving provides

195 calories
30 grams carbohydrate
7 grams protein
6 grams fat

Key Nutrients

120% manganese
76% magnesium
14% folate

Quesadillas

A whole-grain, calcium-rich food that your children will love!

Makes: 4 quesadillas

8 small corn tortillas

1 cup grated reduced-fat Monterey Jack or any other favorite cheese, grated

Optional additions:
Sliced chicken

Ham

Sautéed mushrooms, peppers

Cooked chopped broccoli, spinach, or artichoke hearts, well drained

1. Place 4 corn tortillas in large frying pan over medium heat. Cook 1 to 2 minutes and turn tortillas.

2. Top each tortilla with ¼ cup cheese and any optional ingredients. Top each with another tortilla and turn over.

3. Cook another few minutes until tortillas are warm and cheese is melted.

4. Remove from pan and cut into quarters. Serve with salsa and fat-free sour cream.

Each quesadilla provides

214 calories
26 grams carbohydrate
12 grams protein
8 grams fat
3 grams fiber

Key Nutrients

39% magnesium
36% vitamin B$_6$
17% calcium

Raging Ravioli

Whip this up when there's not much time to cook! Using the Secret Sauce makes it the same color as canned ravioli.

Makes: 6 servings

4 cups Secret Sauce (recipe page 185), or other pasta sauce

½ cup water

1 25-ounce package frozen cheese ravioli, thawed (we like Rosetto brand)

1 cup (8 ounces) grated part-skim mozarella cheese

1. Mix sauce and water in saucepan or skillet.

2. Add ravioli and bring to a slow simmer, stirring gently, until ravioli is cooked through–about 10 minutes.

4 pieces of ravioli with sauce provides	Key Nutrients
95 calories	*87% vitamin A*
12 grams carbohydrate	*52% vitamin C*
4 grams protein	*19% calcium*
4 grams fat	
2 grams fiber	

Roasted Red Pepper Sauce

Many kids will enjoy the mild, sweet taste of red pepper; parents will like the fact that it's packed with vitamin C!

Makes: 1½ cups

½ green onion, chopped

1 heaping cup roasted red bell peppers (can be bought in a jar)

2 tablespoons white wine vinegar (plain or flavored)

⅓ cup parsley or 2 fresh spinach or lettuce leaves

Dash cayenne pepper (optional)

⅓ cup low-fat yogurt or reduced-fat sour cream.

1. Place all ingredients except yogurt or sour cream into a food processor or blender; purée until smooth.

2. Place the mixture into a microwave-safe dish and heat for 2 minutes on medium-high.

3. Fold in yogurt or sour cream. Return to microwave for 30 seconds on high.

4. Stir and serve over Savory Corn Griddle Cakes (recipe page 256) or with roasted or grilled veal or beef.

2 tablespoons sauce provides

10 calories
2 grams carbohydrate
1 gram protein
0 grams fat

Key Nutrients

98% vitamin C

Savory Corn Griddle Cakes

These cakes can be served for brunch, dinner, or as a snack. Serve with salsa or Roasted Red Pepper Sauce (page 255). The recipe is modified from *The Phytopia Cookbook* by Kim Pierce and Barbara Gollman (Phytopia, Inc., 1998).

Makes: 4 servings

¾ cup unbleached flour

½ cup cornmeal

1 teaspoon baking soda

½ teaspoon salt

1 tablespoon sugar

1 egg, slightly beaten

1¼ cups buttermilk

1 tablespoon oil

¾ cup frozen corn, thawed

1 red jalapeño chili pepper without seeds and membrane, finely chopped (optional)

2 tablespoons cilantro, chopped (optional)

Vegetable cooking spray

1. Combine flour, cornmeal, baking soda, salt, and sugar in a mixing bowl.

2. In a separate bowl, whisk together egg, buttermilk, and oil; stir into the flour mixture along with the corn, jalapeño, and cilantro.

3. Coat a griddle or heavy skillet with vegetable cooking spray and place over moderately high heat.

4. For each griddle cake, pour about ¼ cup batter onto the hot griddle, forming a 4- to 5-inch round.

5. Turn griddle cakes when bubbles form on the top and the bottoms are golden. Continue to cook on the second side until cooked through, another 3 or 4 minutes. Keep cakes covered in a warm oven on lowest setting until ready to serve (up to 15 minutes).

Each child half-serving provides	**Key Nutrients**
117 calories	*31% riboflavin*
22 grams carbohydrate	*38% biotin*
4 grams protein	*19% chromium*
1 gram fat	*7% iron*
1 gram fiber	

Snickerdoodles

A whole-wheat version of my very favorite cookie from *Simply Colorado* (Colorado Dietetic Association, 1989).

Makes: 3½ dozen

1 cup sugar

½ cup margarine

1 egg

2 tablespoons skim milk

1 teaspoon vanilla

1 teaspoon baking powder

½ teaspoon baking soda

½ teaspoon nutmeg

½ teaspoon salt

1 tablespoon grated lemon peel or orange peel (optional)

2 cups whole-wheat flour

½ teaspoon cinnamon

2 tablespoons sugar

1. Preheat oven to 375°F.

2. Cream sugar and margarine together. Add egg, milk, vanilla, baking powder, baking soda, nutmeg, salt, and lemon peel. Stir in flour. *Hint:* Do not overmix—it causes flat cookies!

3. Shape dough into 1-inch balls. Combine cinnamon and sugar in saucer.

4. Roll each ball in cinnamon-sugar mixture; place 2 inches apart on ungreased cookie sheet.

5. Bake 10 minutes or until very lightly browned.

Each cookie provides

58 calories

9 grams carbohydrate

1 gram protein

2 grams fat

1 gram fiber

Key Nutrients

Small amounts of many nutrients

Soft Pretzels

A great activity for a rainy day! These pretzels also make a perfect school snack. Teachers might want to make the first initial of each child in the class. This recipe was developed by Debbie Russell.

Makes: 16 pretzels

2 packages quick-rise dry yeast

1½ cup warm water

4 cups all-purpose flour

1 tablespoon sugar

1–2 teaspoons salt

2 eggs (used separately)

Vegetable cooking spray

Coarse salt

2 tablespoons sesame seeds

1. Preheat the oven to 425°F.

2. In a large bowl, dissolve yeast in warm water.

3. In another bowl, combine flour, sugar, and salt.

4. Add flour mixture and 1 beaten egg to yeast. Mix well.

5. Put a little oil or flour on hands. Form dough into ball. Knead 20 times, turning a quarter turn after each time.

6. Divide dough into 16 equal parts. Roll each piece into a rope. Make a traditional pretzel shape, letters, animals, or holiday shapes. Transfer to cookie sheet sprayed with vegetable cooking spray.

7. Beat the other egg in a small bowl. Brush beaten egg on pretzel shapes, then sprinkle with coarse salt and sesame seeds.

8. Bake for 10 to 15 minutes.

Each pretzel provides	**Key Nutrients**
124 calories	*54% manganese*
24 grams carbohydrate	*43% thiamin*
5 grams protein	*37% niacin*
1 gram fat	*32% magnesium*
3 grams fiber	*14% selenium*

Spiced Heart Scones

About 4:00 P.M. is the time to relax with a "spot of tea" and some small cookies or pastries. Try these scones with the fruity cream below. For a special treat, serve your children decaffeinated tea in fine china cups. Developed by Debbie Russell.

Makes: about 20 scones

1½ cups all-purpose flour

1 cup whole-wheat flour

1 tablespoon sugar

4 teaspoons baking powder

1½ teaspoons pumpkin pie spice

5 tablespoons butter or margarine

½ cup milk

1 egg, beaten

2 tablespoons blackstrap molasses

Fruity Cream
1 cup fat-free sour cream (Land O' Lakes or Dean's)

¼ cup strawberry preserves

---

1. Preheat the oven to 400°F.

2. In a large bowl, combine flours, sugar, baking powder, and pumpkin pie spice; mix well.

3. Using a pastry blender, 2 knives, or fork, cut in butter or margarine until crumbly.

4. Combine milk, egg, and molasses in a small bowl; mix with flour mixture just until moistened.

5. Place dough on a lightly floured surface; knead gently 8 times. Add more flour if dough is too sticky. (*Option:* Dough can be refrigerated to ease cutting.)

6. Roll lightly or pat dough to ¼-inch thickness.

7. Cut with a 2½-inch heart-shaped cookie cutter. Place on ungreased cookie sheet.

8. Bake for 8 to 10 minutes or until golden brown. Serve warm with fruity cream.

Each scone (without cream) provides

99 calories
15 grams carbohydrate
2 grams protein
3 grams fat
1 gram fiber

Key Nutrients

23% manganese
14% magnesium
16% riboflavin

Tortilla Pizzas

The perfect lunch when you're out of bread but have tortillas! You may want to double the recipe as this is a big favorite with kids and parents.

Makes: 4 servings

4 10-inch whole-wheat flour or corn tortillas

½ cup pasta sauce

1 cup low-fat mozzarella cheese, grated

2 slices ham or turkey lunch meat, cut into pieces

1. Preheat oven to 375°F.

2. Place tortillas on a cookie sheet. On each tortilla, spread 2 tablespoons of sauce, ¼ cup cheese, and ¼ of the ham or turkey pieces.

3. Bake 15 minutes or until cheese is melted and bottom is slightly crispy.

Each pizza provides	Key Nutrients
262 calories	*37% calcium*
31 grams carbohydrate	*21% magnesium*
15 grams protein	*19% vitamin C and vitamin A*
9 grams fat	
4 grams fiber	*11% zinc*

Tortilla Wraps

There are two great things about tortillas: They are whole-grain and they can be rolled up, making them portable. Oh, make that three—the rolled tortilla can also be sliced into small pinwheels for snacks. To increase your whole grains, try the ideas below, being sure to use either corn or whole-wheat tortillas. And remember, the fresher the tortillas, the better they wrap!

Makes: as much as you want

Corn or whole-wheat tortillas, fresh
Filling of your choice

Italian: Low-fat turkey pepperoni, grated mozzarella cheese, pasta sauce

Mexican: Refried beans, avocado slices, chopped tomato or salsa

All-American: Egg salad, chopped lettuce

Santa Fe Chicken: Leftover grilled chopped chicken, Monterey Jack cheese, black beans

French: Ham, Swiss cheese, dijonnaise (Dijon mustard + mayonnaise)

Seaside: Popcorn shrimp and cream cheese

Each corn tortilla with 1 ounce of cheese and ham provides

177 calories
14 grams carbohydrate
15 grams protein
2 grams fiber

Key Nutrients

91% selenium
48% vitamin B$_{12}$
45% calcium
18% zinc

Trail-Ride Zucchini Muffins

This recipe (modified from *Simply Colorado*) gives your little tyke all the energy she needs for ridin' the trail . . . or sidewalk.

Makes: 18 muffins

Vegetable cooking spray or cupcake liners

1 cup whole-wheat flour

1 cup flour

2 teaspoon baking soda

¼ teaspoon baking powder

1 tablespoon cinnamon

1 egg, beaten

⅓ cup oil

¾ cup sugar

½ cup nonfat dry milk

2½ cups grated zucchini

2 teaspoons vanilla

1 teaspoon lemon extract

½ cup dried fruit such as raisins, dates, cranberries, blueberries

1. Preheat oven to 350°F.

2. Spray muffins tins with cooking spray or fill cups with cupcake liners.

3. Sift flours, baking soda, baking powder, and cinnamon together in a medium bowl; set aside.

4. Combine egg, oil, sugar, dry milk, zucchini, vanilla, and lemon extract in a separate large bowl; beat thoroughly.

5. Stir flour mixture into egg mixture just until smooth (avoid over-stirring). Fold in dried fruit.

6. Bake 20 minutes or until done.

Each muffin provides	Key Nutrients
140 calories	*23% magnesium*
23 grams carbohydrate	*21% thiamin and*
3 grams protein	*riboflavin*
5 grams fat	*10% calcium*

Waffle Sundae Clouds

This recipe works equally well for breakfast or a hearty after-school snack.

Makes: 4 servings

6 ounces fruit-flavored
yogurt

¾ cup light whipped topping

1 cup sliced fresh fruit

⅓ cup fruit syrup or 6
tablespoons fruit jam,
melted

4 whole-grain waffles

1. Fold whipped topping into yogurt. Gently stir in fruit.

2. Toast waffles and top with ¼ of yogurt mixture. Drizzle each with syrup.

Each waffle
sundae provides

264 calories
50 grams carbohydrate
5 grams protein
6 grams fat
3 grams fiber

Key Nutrients

23% iron
46% vitamin B$_6$
19% calcium

Walnut-Mint Bulgur

Bulgur is to the Middle East what corn is to us—a staple. It's great served alongside grilled meat, such as pork and lamb. This recipe is modified from *The Phytopia Cookbook* by Kim Pierce and Barbara Gollman (Phytopia, Inc., 1998).

Makes: about 4 ½-cup servings

1½ *cup apple juice or water*

½ *teaspoon salt*

1 *cup bulgur wheat*

1 *large shallot, finely minced (a shallot is bigger than garlic and sweeter than an onion)*

2 *tablespoons mint, minced*

2 *teaspoons walnut oil or olive oil*

*2 tablespoons finely chopped walnuts, toasted

Freshly ground pepper

*Note: Nuts are a choking hazard for children under 5, so make sure to finely chop them.

1. Bring juice or water and salt to a boil in a small saucepan.

2. Stir in bulgur; reduce heat, cover, and cook over low heat until liquid is absorbed, about 10 to 12 minutes.

3. Transfer bulgur to a medium bowl, fluff with a fork, and cool completely.

4. Stir in shallot, mint, oil, and toasted walnuts.

5. Season to taste with salt and pepper.

Each ¼-cup child serving provides

104 calories
19 grams carbohydrate
3 grams protein
3 grams fat
4 grams fiber

Key Nutrients

17% vitamin B_6
15% niacin

Yummy-but-Healthy Cake

A great-tasting and healthy treat! The molasses and whole grains really boost the nutrient content.

Makes: 12 servings

1¼ cups whole-wheat flour

½ cup oatmeal

¼ cup cornstarch

1 teaspoon baking soda

1 teaspoon each ground ginger and cinnamon

½ teaspoon ground cloves

½ teaspoon salt

1 large egg

2 tablespoons canola oil

½ cup blackstrap molasses

1¾ cups applesauce (use the type fortified with vitamin C)

1. Preheat oven to 325°F.

2. In a large bowl, mix together all dry ingredients and spices.

3. In a separate bowl, combine egg, oil, molasses, and applesauce.

4. Gradually add egg mixture to dry ingredients.

5. Pour batter into a greased and floured 9-by-9-inch pan. (In a pinch you can also use a 9-inch pie plate.)

6. Bake for 45 minutes, or until a knife inserted into the middle comes out clean. Let cool on a wire rack.

Each serving provides	Key Nutrients
148 calories	*52% selenium*
27 grams carbohydrate	*37% magnesium*
3 grams protein	*30% iron*
3 grams fat	*20% calcium*
3 grams fiber	

Dairy

Dairy products are especially important for growing children. Without them, children don't have the necessary calcium to build their bones. And calcium is not just for bones; it is also important for:
- blood clotting;
- release of chemicals that send messages between nerves;
- control of muscle contractions;
- production and activity of enzymes and hormones; and
- growth and maturing of lining cells throughout the body.

In addition:
- Research released in 1998 shows that chronic calcium deficiency may be a cause of premenstrual syndrome.
- A calcium-rich diet helped people with abnormal colon cells (which sometimes lead to cancer) have normal cell growth.
- The Dietary Approaches to Stop Hypertension (DASH) study showed that a diet rich in low-fat dairy products along with plenty of fruit and vegetables significantly lowered blood pressure.
- Women given calcium supplements during pregnancy had children whose blood pressure remained lower than average for at least the first seven years of life (thus lowering the risk of developing hypertension later).
- Milk is fortified with vitamins A and D, which may be important for children who don't get those vitamins from other sources.

Unfortunately, milk is not necessarily the drink of choice for today's kids and teens. Forty percent of teen girls consume less than one serving of dairy products a day.[1] Sodas, flavored teas, and juice drinks often replace milk. But those drinks provide nothing in the nutrient department, unless they're fortified.

How much calcium do we need? Two government agencies have slightly differing recommendations. (See the charts below.)

The chart on the next page will help you choose calcium-rich foods.

Milk

Your child either is a milk drinker or isn't. I have one of each. If milk is the only factor, my younger son has the strongest bones on the block. My other son needs lots of encouragement to finish a glass, so I give him calcium supplements from time to time. If your child dislikes milk, try the tips below.

- Add some type of flavoring to white milk. Ovaltine and Nestlé's Quik can turn white milk to chocolate in a flash. My kids are also fond of flavored coffee syrups. Their favorite is amaretto, followed by hazelnut, raspberry, and strawberry. They also like mixing syrups to come up with their own flavoring.

- Make other foods that include milk, such as creamed soups, milkshakes, pudding, custards, and sauces.

National Academy of Sciences Dietary Reference Intakes	
Age	**Calcium (in milligrams)**
0–6 months	210 (from human milk)
7–12 months	270 (from human milk and solid foods)
1–3 years	500
4–8 years	800
9–18 years	1300
19–50 years	1000
51 years and older	1200
Pregnancy/Lactation:	
18 and younger	1250
Over 18	1000

National Institutes of Health (NIH) Recommendations	
Age	**Calcium (in milligrams)**
0–6 months	400
6–12 months	600
1–5 years	800
6–10 years	800–1200
Adolescents/ young adults	1200–1500
Men 25–65	1000
Women 25–50	1000
Pregnant/ Nursing	1200–1500

Source: NIH Consensus Development Panel on Optimal Calcium Intake

Getting Your Calcium from Food	
Food/Amount	**Calcium (in milligrams)**
Plain nonfat yogurt, 1 cup	452
Plain low-fat yogurt, 1 cup	415
Swiss cheese, 1½ ounces	408
Chocolate milkshake, 8 ounces	299
Milk, any type, 1 cup	300
Chocolate milk, 1 cup	280
Soft serve ice cream, ½ cup	88
2% reduced-fat cottage cheese, ½ cup	78
You can also find calcium in smaller amounts in other foods:	
Salmon with bones, 3 ounces	167
Almonds, ⅓ cup	120
Frozen kale, cooked, ½ cup	90

Note: Some foods are now fortified with calcium—for example, Tropicana and Minute Maid juices and some breads and cereals.

Cheese

Cheese provides a good source of calcium, though it is high in fat and saturated fat. The fat content of cheese shouldn't be a problem unless your child eats more than a couple of servings daily, or if your family has a history of high cholesterol. Most common cheeses are available in low-fat and fat-free varieties, though these are more expensive. Be aware that although fat-free cheese works well when cooked within something, it doesn't melt well when cooked on something.

There are many ways to include cheese in foods. Following are a few examples:

- Cheese enchiladas
- Cheese fondue
- Cheese sauce
- Cheese soup
- Egg dishes (quiches, omelets, and so on)
- Grilled cheese sandwiches
- Homemade macaroni and cheese
- Lasagna or stuffed shells

Yogurt

Yogurt is a great way to get calcium, and it may provide many more health benefits, too! The active cultures in yogurt are believed to help restore and maintain a healthy environment in the intestinal tract for the bacteria essential to good digestion. (That's why it's a good idea to eat yogurt while on antibiotics.) The cultures are also believed to reduce the incidence and duration of some types of diarrhea.

Lactose-intolerant people can usually tolerate yogurt because the active cultures in yogurt help break down lactose.

Yogurt can be used in:

- cakes;
- dips;
- parfaits;
- pies;
- popsicles;
- sauces; and
- with cereal instead of milk.

If someone in your family can't or won't drink milk, see the following ways to sneak calcium into your family's diet.

Twenty Ways to Sneak Calcium into Your Family's Diet

1. Serve creamy soups (homemade or canned) made with milk or evaporated milk.

2. Use evaporated milk (which has twice the calcium of regular milk) in food preparation, such as when making mashed potatoes, pudding, cream sauces, and so on.

3. Eat dairy-based desserts, such as frozen yogurt, milkshakes, pudding, Triple-Decker Dessert (page 291), or Strawberry Dream Pops (page 224).

4. Add low-fat cheese to mashed potatoes, pasta, sandwiches, sauces, and vegetables.

5. Add molasses to pancakes, quick breads, cookies, and cakes—such as Yummy-but-Healthy Cake (page 265).

6. Add sesame seeds and almonds to cakes, cookies, dips, granola, pudding (see Almond Pudding, page 272), salads, snack bars, and vegetables.

7. Add nonfat milk powder to prepared soups, pancake and cake batter, milkshakes, cream sauces, and yogurt shakes.

8. Let your child have a milkshake instead of a cola at your next fast-food outing.

9. Make dip out of yogurt, adding your own herbs and spices, or use a packaged dip mix with plain yogurt.

10. Add a yogurt-based sauce to fruit salad.

11. Use calcium-rich tofu in your dips.

12. Serve fish with small bones. Salmon Patties (page 316) pack an even greater calcium punch if topped with cheese.

13. Serve milk-based quiche, So-Easy Flan (page 287), or Bread Pudding (page 236).

14. Eat more vegetables, which are good sources of calcium.

15. Instead of buying regular orange juice, choose Minute Maid Calcium-Fortified Orange Juice or Tropicana Pure Premium Orange Juice with Calcium. One cup of either juice contains 350 milligrams of calcium.

16. Buy other foods fortified with calcium, such as Wonder Bread, Total or Product 10 cereal, and Carnation Instant Breakfast.

17. Offer low-fat cheese on sandwiches.

18. For those who prefer water over milk, look for a mineral water with a high calcium content.

19. Serve frozen yogurt instead of ice cream—the yogurt has more calcium.

20. Don't forget cheese as a snack—by itself, with crackers, or in dips such as Queso Dip (page 284).

Almond Milk

Almond-flavored coffee syrup makes morning milk more enjoyable!

Makes: *as much as you want*

Milk, warm or cold

Amaretto- or almond-flavored coffee syrup, 1 to 2 teaspoons per cup of milk

1. Mix flavoring into milk.

2. Serve milk, warm in mugs or cold in glasses.

Each 1-cup serving of almond milk provides

132 calories
12 grams carbohydrate
8 grams protein
3 grams fat

Key Nutrients

37% calcium

Almond Pudding

This pudding is a treat in Turkey. It's calorie-rich, but also nutrient-dense.

Makes: 4 heaping ½-cup servings

1 cup water
½ cup slivered almonds
2 cups milk, divided
¼ cup nonfat dry milk powder
⅓ cup sugar
1 tablespoon cornstarch
¼ cup water
1 teaspoon vanilla

1. Put 1 cup water and almonds in a small saucepan and bring to a boil; boil for 1 minute.

2. Drain almonds and place in a blender with 1 cup milk. Blend for 3 minutes.

3. Pour the mixture back into the saucepan; add 1 cup milk, milk powder, and sugar. Simmer for 2 minutes, stirring constantly. Be careful not to let it boil over.

4. Mix cornstarch and water in a separate bowl and add to the pudding. Cook over low heat 3 minutes or until thickened. Allow to cool a few minutes, then add vanilla.

5. Spoon into dessert cups and refrigerate before serving.

Each ¼-cup child serving provides

115 calories
15 grams carbohydrate
5 grams protein
5 grams fat
2 grams fiber

Key Nutrients

44% magnesium
41% riboflavin
25% calcium

Carrot Pudding (Gajar Halwa)

This is a popular dish in India in the winter, when carrots are fresh. It is traditionally made with milk and cream. Here is a quick, lower-fat version, modified from *Lite and Luscious Cuisine of India,* by Madhu Gadia, M.S., R.D. (Piquant Publishing, 1997).

Makes: 8 ½-cup servings

2 pounds carrots, grated

2 cups skim milk

12-ounce can skim evaporated milk

15-ounce carton part-skim ricotta cheese

1 cup sugar

4 cardamom pods

1. Place grated carrots and skim milk in a heavy skillet on medium heat. Bring just to a boil, reduce heat, and simmer for 20 minutes. Stir periodically to avoid burning on the bottom.

2. Add evaporated skim milk and continue to cook until most of the milk evaporates.

3. In the meantime, cook ricotta cheese in a separate nonstick frying pan on medium heat for 8 to 10 minutes until most of the liquid evaporates. Stir periodically to avoid burning on the bottom, but do not stir too much. The cheese should become slightly crumbly.

4. Add ricotta cheese and sugar to the carrots; mix. Continue to simmer, cooking until most of the liquid evaporates. The halwa should be moist, not dry, and crumbly. Remove from the heat.

5. Remove the seeds from cardamom pods and crush with a mortar and pestle. Add the crushed seeds to the halwa.

6. Transfer to a serving platter. Serve warm or cold.

Each ¼-cup child serving provides

135 calories
23 grams carbohydrate
6 grams protein
3 grams fat
2 grams fiber

Key Nutrients

418% vitamin A
40% riboflavin
37% calcium
28% magnesium

Cocoa Mocha

A variation on a favorite drink of kids.

Makes: 4 7-ounce servings

3 cups fat-free skim or 1% low-fat milk

1½ tablespoons Nutella chocolate-hazelnut spread or 3 tablespoons chocolate chips

½ cup decaffeinated coffee

Ground cinnamon to taste (optional)

1. Heat milk and hazelnut spread in a microwave oven or in a saucepan, stirring frequently, until the mixture starts to steam; do not boil.

2. Blend in coffee and pour into 4 serving cups.

3. Sprinkle with cinnamon, if you like.

Each 4-ounce child serving provides

69 calories
8 grams carbohydrate
5 grams protein
2 grams fat

Key Nutrients

27% riboflavin
24% magnesium
20% calcium

Cottage Cream Dips

You can make a high-protein base for dips simply by putting cottage cheese in a food processor with milk. Then get creative with the many possibilities!

Makes: 8 2-tablespoon servings

Dip Base

16 ounces cottage cheese (regular or low-fat)

2 tablespoons milk

1. Combine cottage cheese with milk in a food processor and process on high until smooth and creamy.

Sesame Onion Dip

2 teaspoons toasted sesame seeds

1 cup dip base

2 teaspoons dehydrated onion

1 teaspoon soy sauce

1. Toast sesame seeds in oven or toaster oven for 1 to 2 minutes, watching constantly to avoid burning.

2. Combine all ingredients in a bowl, mix well, and refrigerate at least ½ hour before serving.

Pesto Dip

1 tablespoon pesto sauce (basil-garlic-cheese mixture purchased in produce section)

1 cup dip base

1. Combine in a bowl and mix well.

Dressing Dip

1 tablespoon favorite dry dip mix (good options include ranch and Good Seasons Italian)

1 cup dip base

1. Combine in a bowl and mix well.

Spinach Dip

1 cup chopped frozen spinach, thawed

2 cups cottage cheese

½ cup fresh Parmesan cheese

1 teaspoon garlic powder

1. Purée spinach with cottage cheese.

2. Add Parmesan cheese and garlic powder; mix well.

Each 2-tablespoon serving provides approximately

30 calories
5 grams protein
1 gram fat

Key Nutrients

Small amounts of many nutrients

Goblin Squares

Just the thing to eat after carving a jack-o'-lantern—or for the preschool Halloween or harvest party. Modified from *Simply Colorado* (Colorado Dietetic Association, 1989).

Makes: 18 servings

2 cups cooked pumpkin

½ cup sugar

1 teaspoon ground ginger

½ teaspoon nutmeg

½ gallon nonfat or low-fat vanilla frozen yogurt

4 dozen gingersnaps

1. Combine pumpkin, sugar, and spices in a medium-large bowl; stir in yogurt.

2. Line bottom of 9-by-13-by-2-inch pan with gingersnaps. Pour half of pumpkin mixture over gingersnaps. Repeat layers and freeze.

3. To serve, remove from freezer, let set at room temperature for 5 minutes, and cut into squares.

Each serving provides

202 calories

38 grams carbohydrate

5 grams protein

3 grams fat

1 gram fiber

Key Nutrients

155% vitamin A

27% calcium

11% iron

Jungle Juice Slush

This treat will give your child energy for swinging across the jungle gym.

Makes: 4 8-ounce servings

1 cup milk

1 teaspoon coconut extract

⅓ cup frozen orange juice concentrate (½ of a 6-ounce can)

1 ripe medium banana, cut into chunks

8-ounce can crushed pineapple (packed in juice), frozen

1 cup low-fat vanilla ice cream

1. In a blender, combine milk, coconut extract, and juice concentrate.

2. Add fruits and ice cream. Blend until smooth.

Each ½-cup child serving provides

100 calories
8 grams carbohydrate
3 grams protein
2 grams fat
1 gram fiber

Key Nutrients

48% vitamin C
29% vitamin B$_6$
17% calcium
15% folate

Kid's Latte

Kids can now have their own latte to sip as they browse over the cartoons.

Makes: 3 servings

3 cups fat-free skim or 1% low-fat milk

3 tablespoons sugar

½ cup decaffeinated coffee, brewed (or ½ cup strong cocoa)

Cocoa powder or ground cinnamon (optional)

1. Heat milk and sugar in a microwave oven or in a small saucepan over the stove just until it starts to steam and a few bubbles appear; don't let it boil.

2. Divide the coffee and then the heated milk among 3 mugs.

3. Dust each latte with cocoa powder or cinnamon, if you like.

Serving option: Try small cereal bowls in place of mugs; kids might enjoy dipping toast into their latte.

Variation

Mocha Capucooler: Mix half of milk with sugar. Pour into an ice-cube tray and freeze solid. Mix remaining milk, coffee, and 2 teaspoons chocolate syrup in a small pitcher. Place milk-sugar ice cubes in 3 small glasses. Pour mocha-milk liquid over ice and serve.

Each ½-cup child serving provides	Key Nutrients
62 calories	37% riboflavin
4 grams protein	27% calcium
1 gram fat	22% vitamin D

Macaroni and Cheese

Sometimes you've just got to make the real thing.

Makes: Approximately 5 cups

2½ tablespoons light butter

2 tablespoons flour

1 cup low-fat milk or evaporated milk

4 ounces sharp cheddar cheese, grated, reserving 2 tablespoons for garnish

5 cups cooked macaroni

1. In medium saucepan on low heat, melt butter and stir in flour until it makes a paste.

2. Gradually stir in milk until smooth. Cook until thickened.

3. Add cheese and cook until melted.

4. Stir in macaroni. Pour into serving dish and top with reserved cheese.

Each ½-cup child serving provides

181 calories
21 grams carbohydrate
7 grams protein
8 grams fat
1 gram fiber

Key Nutrients

30% riboflavin
23% calcium
23% magnesium

Madame Guedé's Rice Pudding

A French family recipe, this is a favorite of ours that is great for breakfast!

Makes: 3 cups

1 cup medium-grain rice, uncooked

4 cups milk

⅓ cup sugar

Pinch salt

1–2 tablespoons vanilla

1. Place rice, milk, and sugar in large saucepan on stove top. Stir. Turn heat to high and watch carefully until milk starts to foam; then turn down to low.

2. Simmer 45 minutes to 1 hour, stirring occasionally until rice is thick and almost a purée consistency. During cooking, it may be necessary to add milk to keep the rice moist.

3. When rice gets to preferred consistency, remove from heat and stir in vanilla. Pour into a serving dish or small bowls.

Each ⅓-cup child serving provides

149 calories
30 grams carbohydrate
5 grams protein
1 gram fat

Key Nutrients

57% vitamin B$_{12}$
38% ribloflavin
28% magnesium
27% calcium

More-Milk Tapioca

Just like the kind my grandmother used to make (and like the commercially prepared kind now packaged in individual plastic cups) but with less sugar and fat—all the better for you!

Makes: 6 ½-cup servings

⅓ *cup sugar*

3 tablespoons quick-cooking tapioca

1 12-ounce can low-fat evaporated milk

1¼ cups milk

1 egg, well beaten

1 teaspoon vanilla

½ teaspoon each: any favorite spices (optional)

1. Mix sugar and tapioca together in a saucepan.

2. Stir in all milk and well-beaten egg. Let stand 5 minutes.

3. Stirring constantly, bring to a full boil over medium heat.

4. Remove from burner and stir in vanilla and any other spices you like.

5. Simmer 20 minutes while stirring.

6. Spoon into dishes or a serving bowl and refrigerate.

Variations

Chocolate Malt Tapioca: After you take tapioca from the heat, add ½ cup of Ovaltine Chocolate Malt. Stir well and continue cooling.

Peachy Cloud Tapioca: Preheat oven to 350°F. While tapioca is cooling, mix in 1 cup chopped peaches. Pour the pudding into a 1½- or 2-quart baking dish. In a separate bowl, beat 2 egg whites until stiff. Add 2 tablespoons of sugar. Spread the beaten egg whites gently over the tapioca mixture and place the baking dish in the oven for 10 to 15 minutes or until lightly browned. Return to refrigerator until cooled.

More-Milk Tapioca
(continued)

Tropical Tapioca: Use ½ cup drained juice from pineapple and oranges in place of ½ cup of milk in recipe. Mix 1 11-ounce drained can of mandarin oranges, ½ cup drained crushed pineapple, and 2 tablespoons of coconut (or 1 teaspoon coconut extract) into cooling tapioca.

Volcano Tapioca: Cook tapioca according to basic instructions. After removing from the refrigerator, mound servings of tapioca in a bowl and shape like a mountain. Drizzle 1 teaspoon of grape or other red fruit concentrate over the top. Serve immediately.

Each ¼-cup child serving of plain tapioca provides

87 calories
12 grams carbohydrate
4 grams protein
2 grams fat

Key Nutrients

31% riboflavin
23% calcium
20% vitamin D

Peanutty Rice Krispie Pie

This easy treat, modified from *Simply Colorado* (Colorado Dietetic Association, 1989), is a big favorite with kids and adults.

Makes: 10 servings

⅓ cup corn syrup

½ cup creamy peanut butter, at room temperature

2 cups Rice Krispies

1 quart nonfat frozen yogurt of choice

Sliced fresh fruit or chocolate syrup (optional)

1. Mix corn syrup, peanut butter, and Rice Krispies together. Press into a 9-inch pie pan.

2. Spoon frozen yogurt into Rice Krispie crust; freeze.

3. If desired, top with fresh fruit or chocolate syrup before serving.

Each serving provides

187 calories
27 grams carbohydrate
7 grams protein
6 grams fat

Key Nutrients

28% calcium
Small amounts of other nutrients

Queso Dip

If your definition of queso is the yellow stuff that comes on top of chips at an amusement park, wait until you try this! This treat is actually easier to make than using processed cheese, and it tastes better, too!

Makes: 4 2-tablespoon servings

2 tablespoons salsa, any style or hotness (or 1 tablespoon chopped, cooked onions and 1 tablespoon chopped chili peppers)

1 cup grated cheese (Monterey Jack or Mexican blend)

Baked tortilla chips or vegetables

1. In a small nonstick pan, heat salsa until bubbly.

2. Add grated cheese and stir constantly until cheese melts (less than 1 minute.)

3. Serve with baked tortilla chips or vegetables. Watch out, this disappears fast—you might want to double or triple the recipe!

Each 2-tablespoon serving provides

108 calories
1 gram carbohydrate
7 grams protein
9 grams fat

Key Nutrients

42% calcium
26% vitamin B$_{12}$
22% riboflavin

Smoothies

With these simple fruit shakes, you are only limited by your imagination and what's on hand.

Makes: 3 servings

Choose a fruit in one of the following forms:

15-ounce can fruit in light syrup or in its own juice (undrained, frozen)

2 cups frozen fruit, unsweetened

2 cups frozen fruit, sweetened

2 cups fresh fruit, cut in chunks and frozen

Or choose any combination totaling 2 cups.

Choose one or more of the following liquids, totaling 1 cup:

fruit juice or nectar

low-fat yogurt—vanilla, plain, or fruit-flavored

milk

Choose one flavoring (optional):

1 teaspoon vanilla or other extract

2 teaspoons fruit jam

1 tablespoon flavored coffee syrup

1. If you are using canned fruit, freeze the can overnight or for 3 hours. When frozen, put the can in a large bowl and fill with hot water until the can is covered. Let sit in water 7 minutes for a 15-ounce can, 5 minutes for an 8-ounce can. Pour out water, open can, and pour fruit and liquid into a bowl. With a fork, separate the fruit into 3 or 4 big chunks.

2. Put liquid and flavoring of your choice into a blender and add frozen fruit in chunks. (Don't forget to cover the blender before turning it on!)

3. Blend on low speed for 30 seconds, then on high speed for 30 seconds, or until smooth.

4. Pour into 3 glasses. Drink and enjoy!

Smoothies
(continued)

Flavor Combinations:

- 16-ounce package frozen sweetened strawberries + plain or vanilla yogurt
- 8-ounce can chunk pineapple in its own juice + 1 banana + vanilla yogurt + ½ teaspoon coconut extract
- 15-ounce can frozen pears + vanilla yogurt + 1 tablespoon caramel-flavored syrup
- 1 cup frozen unsweetened strawberries + 1 cup frozen unsweetened blueberries + vanilla yogurt
- 15-ounce can Del Monte Raspberry-Flavored Sliced Peaches + raspberry yogurt

Each serving provides	Key Nutrients
(when made with light peaches and raspberry yogurt)	*32% riboflavin*
111 calories	*23% calcium*
23 grams carbohydrate	*21% vitamin A*
4 grams protein	*22% magnesium*
1 gram fat	
1 gram fiber	

So-Easy Flan

This is a variation of my friend Minerva's recipe—it's a snap to put together. And what a delicious way to get your calcium!

Makes: 9 servings

⅓ *cup sugar*

1 12-ounce can skim or low-fat evaporated milk

1 14-ounce can sweetened condensed milk

½ *cup milk*

5 eggs

2 teaspoons cornstarch

2 teaspoons vanilla

1. Preheat oven to 350°F.

2. Pour sugar into saucepan and cook over medium heat, shaking occasionally. Sugar will start to turn into a syrup; continue shaking until sugar has turned into golden brown syrup.

3. Remove from heat and pour syrup into an 8-inch-square baking dish.

4. Place remaining ingredients in a blender. Blend on low, then high, until well mixed.

5. Pour egg mixture into baking dish. Cover with foil. Put inside larger baking pan or dish. Pour hot water into outer dish to a depth of 1 inch.

6. Bake for 50 to 60 minutes until knife inserted in middle comes out clean.

7. Remove carefully and let cool.

8. Place a serving plate or platter on top of flan dish and turn over, so that flan comes out on serving plate with syrup side up.

Each child-size half-portion provides	Key Nutrients
123 calories	*44% riboflavin*
18 grams carbohydrate	*26% calcium*
5 grams protein	*16% magnesium*
3 grams fat	

Surprise on a Stick

Kids will love to help you make this treat.

Makes: 6 servings

1 small package of pudding mix, any flavor

2 cups milk

1 cup finely chopped fruit— banana, strawberries, pears

6 5-ounce paper cups

6 Popsicle sticks

1. Prepare pudding according to package directions. Stir in fruit.

2. Pour into cups and insert Popsicle sticks. Cover with foil (poking stick through foil) and freeze until firm.

Flavor Ideas:

- Chocolate and banana
- Lemon and strawberry or blueberry
- Vanilla and grape
- Vanilla and peach

One treat provides	Key Nutrients
(made with vanilla pudding and banana)	*30% riboflavin*
112 calories	*20% calcium*
24 grams carbohydrate	*17% vitamin D*
0 grams protein	
1 gram fat	

Sweet Lassi

Sweet lassi is a very popular drink in India, especially on a hot summer day. It's perfect for kids who are lactose intolerant. Modified from *Lite and Luscious Cuisine of India,* by Madhu Gadia, M.S., R.D. (Piquant Publishing, 1997).

Makes: 2 6-ounce servings

⅔ cup plain nonfat yogurt
⅔ cup cold water
1 tablespoon sugar
2–3 ice cubes

1. Place everything in a blender and blend until frothy.

**Each 6-ounce
serving provides**

64 calories
12 grams carbohydrate
4 grams protein
0 grams fat

Key Nutrients

50% vitamin B₁₂
35% riboflavin
29% calcium

Swiss Cheese Fondue

Every country seems to have a melted-cheese dish, and the Swiss are no exception. This dish is popular in France and Germany, too. Perfect on a cold winter night with hunks of crusty French bread.

Makes: 10 servings

Vegetable cooking spray

1 clove garlic, cut in half

1½ pounds Swiss cheese*, grated

2 tablespoons flour

2 tablespoons kirsch (cherry liqueur)

30 slices French bread, cut into cubes

Raw or steamed vegetables (optional)

*The Swiss generally use Swiss, Gruyere, and Comte. But use what you can find.

1. Spray a nonstick fondue pot with vegetable cooking spray.

2. Put garlic in pot and heat for several minutes, allowing the pot to absorb the garlic flavor. Remove pot from heat and remove garlic.

3. Place grated cheese and flour into pot and mix. Add kirsch.

4. Over low heat, melt cheese with kirsch, stirring constantly.

5. Using fondue forks, dip bread into cheese. If you like, use raw or steamed vegetables for dipping as well.

Each child portion (1½ slices of bread, 1¼ ounces cheese) provides

278 calories
28 grams carbohydrate
15 grams protein
12 grams fat

Key Nutrients

76% calcium
62% magnesium
50% thiamin

Triple-Decker Dessert

It's pretty to see and yummy for the tummy!

Makes: 5 cups (8 servings)

2 8-ounce containers yogurt, vanilla or fruit-flavored

1 cup light whipped topping

2 cups fresh or frozen fruit, defrosted

Chopped nuts or granola

1. Mix yogurt with whipped topping.

2. In a see-through glass bowl or parfait dishes, layer yogurt and fruit.

3. Top with chopped nuts or granola.

Great Flavor Combinations:

- Blueberry or lemon yogurt with strawberries and/or blueberries
- Piña colada yogurt with crushed pineapple and banana slices
- Strawberry or vanilla yogurt with chopped kiwi
- Vanilla yogurt with seedless grapes

Each ½-cup child serving provides

(made with low-fat vanilla yogurt and blueberries)
89 calories
16 grams carbohydrate
3 grams protein
3 grams fat
1 gram fiber

Key Nutrients

12% vitamin C
18% calcium

Yogawiches

Your kids won't turn down these cool sandwiches!

Makes: 1 serving

¼ cup frozen yogurt or
sherbet, any flavor

2 graham cracker squares,
any flavor, or gingerbread
cookies

Colored or chocolate
sprinkles, chopped nuts,
or granola (optional)

1. Spread frozen yogurt or sherbet on 1 graham cracker.

2. Top with other graham cracker. Press lightly, so that yogurt extends just slightly beyond edges of crackers.

3. If you like, dip each side in sprinkles, nuts, or granola. Repeat until finished.

4. Cover each Yogawich with plastic wrap and freeze until ready to eat!

Some Good Flavor Combinations:

Frozen Yogurt/Sherbet	Graham Crackers
Neapolitan	Plain
Chocolate	Cinnamon
Chocolate swirl	Chocolate
Raspberry sherbet	Chocolate
Cookies and creme	Plain
Rainbow sherbet	Plain
Vanilla	Chocolate, cinnamon, or plain

Each sherbet serving provides	Key Nutrients	Each yogurt serving provides	Key Nutrients
123 calories	20% riboflavin	122 calories	32% riboflavin
25 grams carbohydrate	13% magnesium	17 grams carbohydrate	14% magnesium
2 grams protein		0 grams protein	10% calcium
2 grams fat		5 grams fat	

Note: Nutrition information is for servings without candy sprinkles, nuts, or granola.

Yogurt Cheese

Another fun make-your-own recipe.

Makes: 1 cup

2 cups plain yogurt without gelatin

1. Line a colander with cheesecloth; a fine-weave fabric, such as an old, clean pillowcase; or coffee filters.

2. Pour in yogurt. Cover with plastic wrap. Set colander over larger bowl to collect draining liquid. Refrigerate 24 hours.

3. Discard liquid. Scrape cheese from colander and refrigerate.

Variations

- *Raspberry Swirl Cheese:* Swirl 2 tablespoons of raspberry jam through ½ cup yogurt cheese.
- *Fresh Herb Spread:* Snip 2 teaspoons each of fresh dill and fresh basil. Stir herbs and ½ teaspoon salt into 1 cup of yogurt cheese.

Each tablespoon of plain yogurt cheese provides approximately

11 calories
1 gram carbohydrate
1 gram protein
0 grams fat

Key Nutrients

10% calcium
Small amounts of other nutrients

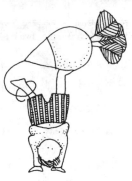

CHAPTER EIGHTEEN

Protein

Protein plays a crucial part in growth and development. However, protein needs are not as high as most people think. So rest assured, even if your child won't touch her meat, she is more than likely receiving more than enough protein.

For example, the Recommended Dietary Allowance (RDA) for protein for one- to three-year-olds is sixteen grams. Your child would receive that much protein in just two cups of milk. The RDA for four- to six-year-olds goes up to twenty-four grams. That much protein would be in one egg, three pieces of bread, one ounce of cheese, and one cup of milk.

So, don't worry too much about protein! In fact, most health organizations are encouraging us to move toward a plant-centered diet. What's that? A plant-centered diet is simply one that features beans, grains, and veggies more than meat and other animal products.

Your child learns by your example. A good goal might be to opt for a few meatless meals a week to make room for some of those grains and veggies! If you're still worried that your child may not be getting enough protein, here are some other ways for including protein in her diet.

Ten Ways to Sneak Protein into Your Child's Diet:

1. Don't forget the cheese—it has as much protein per ounce as meat. Choose low-fat cheeses. Macaroni and cheese (especially homemade) provides protein and calcium—and most kids love it!

2. Bean dips are a great way for kids to "dip" their protein. Try seasoned refried beans with a bit of melted cheese or Hummus Dip (page 306).

3. Remember, yogurt is a great source of protein and calcium.

4. Use tofu in puddings, dips, and sauces.

5. Peanut butter (and other nut butters, like tahini) and nuts also provide protein. (Be careful, though; unless finely chopped, nuts are a choking hazard for young children.)

6. Purée chicken into soup, such as Chicken Chili (page 297).

7. Try textured vegetable protein (TVP). Its texture is similar to that of ground meat, and it may please the palate of kids who don't like the texture of nonground meats. TVP can be bought in bulk at health-food stores or frozen at the grocery store. (Try Morningstar Farms Recipe Crumbles.)

8. Grain-based veggie burgers may also appeal to kids who don't like the texture of meat.

Protein Content of Kid-Friendly Foods		
Food	**Amount**	**Protein**
Bean and cheese burrito	1	7 grams
Cheddar cheese	1 ounce	7 grams
Cheese pizza	⅛ of 12-inch	8 grams
Cheese, processed American	1 ounce	5.6 grams
Cheeseburger with bun	1	15 grams
Chicken leg	1	14 grams
Chicken nuggets	6	17 grams
Dried beans	½ cup	5–7 grams
Fish sticks	2	9 grams
Hot dog	1	10 grams
Milk, protein-fortified	1 cup	10 grams
Milkshake	10 ounces	10 grams
Milk, white or chocolate, any fat content	1 cup	8 grams
Peanut butter	1 tablespoon	4 grams
Soy protein crumbles	½ cup	10 grams
Tuna, in water	1 ounce	7 grams
Veggie burger	1	11 grams
Yogurt	4 oz	5 grams

9. Don't overlook mild-tasting fish (watch for bones) and shellfish. Make a dip using cream cheese and shrimp or crab.

10. Milk is also high protein, though it doesn't supply the iron and zinc that meats do.

Chicken Chili

A great source of protein and calcium.

Makes: about 10 cups

1 large onion, chopped

3 large garlic cloves, chopped

1 teaspoon margarine or butter

4 boneless, skinless chicken breasts

2 teaspoons ground cumin

1 teaspoon seasoned salt

2½ cups water

2 10¾-ounce cans condensed cream of chicken soup

2 12-ounce cans skim evaporated milk

2 14-ounce cans (3 cups) northern white beans, drained

Monterey Jack cheese and tortilla chips, broken into pieces, for garnish (adults may enjoy a teaspoon of salsa as well)

1. Sauté onion and garlic in margarine over medium heat. (Add a tablespoon of water if it gets too dry.)

2. Add chicken, cumin, salt, and water. Simmer over medium heat, uncovered, until chicken is cooked through, about 10 to 15 minutes.

3. Remove chicken to platter and cut into large pieces.

4. Pour half of cooking liquid into a blender.

5. Add half of chicken. Blend on low and high speed until smooth.

6. Add rest of chicken and broth and repeat.

7. Pour chicken broth mixture back into the pan. Add cream of chicken soup and milk. Mix with a wire whisk.

8. Add beans and cook until warm.

9. Pour into bowls and top with cheese and tortilla chips.

Each ½-cup child serving provides

(without chips and cheese)
124 calories
11 grams carbohydrate
11 grams protein
4 grams fat
1 gram fiber

Key Nutrients

35% magnesium
34% niacin
27% folate
25% vitamin B_6

Chili Mac

This is my friend Sue Reitzel's recipe for a family favorite.

Makes: 8½ cups

½ pound lean ground beef

1 tablespoon minced onion

1 large garlic clove

½ teaspoon Italian seasoning

2 tablespoons Taco Bell
   Chicken Fajita Seasoning
   Mix

1 15-ounce can diced
   tomatoes

2 cups water

¼ teaspoon mild chili powder

½ teaspoon sugar

1 8-ounce package dry
   macaroni

8 ounces light Velveeta
   cheese, cut into chunks.

1. Brown ground beef with onion, garlic, and seasonings.

2. Add tomatoes, water, chili powder, and sugar. Cook over medium heat.

3. Boil macaroni according to package directions in separate pan. Drain and add to beef mixture.

4. Blend cheese into beef and cook over medium heat, stirring often, until cheese is melted.

Each ½-cup child serving provides	Key Nutrients
157 calories	36% magnesium
18 grams carbohydrate	19% calcium
10 grams protein	18% iron
5 grams fat	15% zinc

Cowboy Beans

Feed your cowboys and cowgirls these beans, and they'll be ready to ride!
(In other words, if you need a quick meal before baseball practice, this is it!)

Makes: 4½ cups

8 ounces turkey kielbasa

½ small onion, minced

1 teaspoon oil

¾ cups ketchup

3 tablespoons molasses

2 15-ounce cans Great
   Northern Beans, drained

1. Slice sausage and cook in microwave or on stove top according to package directions. Drain off fat and set aside.

2. Sauté onion in oil. Add ketchup and molasses and stir until well blended. Stir in beans and sausage. Warm on low heat until ready to eat.

**Each ½-cup child
serving provides**

180 calories

29 grams carbohydrate

11 grams protein

3 grams fat

6 grams fiber

Key Nutrients

62% magnesium

48% folate

25% iron

Creamy Herbed Chicken

Forgot to take something out of the freezer to cook for dinner? No problem with this recipe, which starts with frozen chicken breasts.

Makes: 4 servings

4 boneless, skinless chicken breasts, frozen

¾ cup water

½ teaspoon each: salt, thyme, tarragon, basil

¼ teaspoon dill

1 teaspoon garlic, chopped

Dash of pepper

2 tablespoons butter

2½ tablespoons flour

2 cups milk

1. Put frozen chicken breasts, water, salt, herbs, garlic, and pepper in a pan and cover. Cook for 15 minutes over medium heat, stirring occasionally.

2. Remove chicken from pan.

3. Add butter to the pan juices; heat until melted.

4. Stir in flour until blended.

5. Gradually add milk and cook over low heat until thickened.

6. Place chicken back in the pan and mix with sauce. Simmer 5 minutes.

7. Serve with pasta or rice.

Each 2-ounce child serving provides

129 calories
7 grams carbohydrate
16 grams protein
6 grams fat

Key Nutrients

100% niacin
68% selenium
35% magnesium
34% riboflavin
17% calcium

Creamy Tuna Spread

Even kids who are turned off by tuna will eat these sandwiches up!

Makes: 4 whole sandwiches

4 ounces light cream cheese

⅛ teaspoon dill

¼ teaspoon seasoned salt

6-ounce can tuna, packed in water, drained

8 pieces whole-wheat bread

Lettuce and tomato (optional)

1. Place cream cheese in a small bowl and stir to soften.

2. Blend in seasonings.

3. Add tuna, mixing until well blended.

4. Spread on 4 slices bread. Top with lettuce and tomato, if you like.

5. Add bread, slice sandwiches in half, and serve.

Variations

Also try this spread on crackers, baked chips, popcorn cakes, or pita bread quarters.

Each ½ sandwich provides

113 calories
13 grams carbohydrate
10 grams protein
2 grams fat
3 grams fiber

Key Nutrients

170% selenium
43% magnesium
42% niacin
11% iron

Crispy Chicken

A healthier and less messy stand-in for fried chicken.

Makes: 4 servings

1½ cups bran flakes

3 tablespoons Parmesan cheese

1 teaspoon curry powder

¼ teaspoon garlic powder

2 tablespoons wheat germ

2 heaping tablespoons parsley, chopped

½ teaspoon each salt and pepper

1 frying chicken, cut in pieces

½ cup milk or 1 egg, beaten

Vegetable cooking spray

1. Preheat oven to 425°F.

2. Crush bran flakes by placing them in a bag and pounding with a hard object. Transfer to a shallow bowl or to a large zip-lock bag.

3. Add Parmesan cheese, curry, garlic powder, wheat germ, parsley, salt, and pepper. Stir (or shake bag), mixing ingredients well.

4. Dip each chicken piece in either milk or egg and roll through (or shake in) the crumb mixture. Repeat with rest of chicken pieces.

5. Place coated chicken pieces on a baking sheet sprayed with vegetable cooking spray. Bake 45 to 60 minutes, or until golden brown.

Each 2-ounce child serving provides

115 calories
9 grams carbohydrate
14 grams protein
3 grams fat
1 gram fiber

Key Nutrients

101% niacin
80% vitamin B_6
45% riboflavin
20% iron

Curried Chicken Salad

Kids of all ages (and adults, too) love the flavor of this mild curried salad. The mango adds a bit of color as well as some vitamins.

Makes: 6 servings

¼ *cup mayonnaise*

½ *cup fat-free sour cream*

½ *teaspoon garlic salt*

½ *teaspoon curry*

½ *teaspoon onion powder*

4 cooked, boneless, skinless chicken breasts, chopped

1 mango, seeded, peeled, and chopped (approximately ⅔ cup)

6 whole-wheat pita pockets

Shredded lettuce or sprouts for garnish

1. In a large bowl, combine mayonnaise, sour cream, garlic salt, curry, and onion powder. Mix well.

2. Fold in chicken and mango.

3. Serve in pita pockets with lettuce or sprouts. Can also be served on top of mixed greens.

Variations

- Use chopped peaches or raisins in place of mango.
- Adults and some children may enjoy the addition of chopped celery and green onion.

Each ½ sandwich provides

112 calories

12 grams carbohydrate

7 grams protein

4 grams fat

Key Nutrients

50% niacin

26% vitamin B₆

17% vitamin A

Fish and Tomatoes

The tomatoes give flavor and just a touch of spice. A great meal when you have frozen fish fillets on hand. You can also use Italian-spiced tomatoes.

Makes: 5 servings

1 tablespoon oil

½ medium-small onion, finely chopped

5 filets white fish (catfish, cod, and so on)

1 14- to 16-ounce can diced tomatoes with jalapeños (mild or medium hot)

1. Heat oil in a large frying pan. Add onion and cook until soft.

2. Add fish and cook 5 minutes.

3. Add tomatoes. Cover and cook 5 to 10 minutes until fish is opaque through (rule of thumb: 10 minutes per inch of thickness at 425–450°F). Serve.

Each 2-ounce child serving of fish with sauce provides

Key Nutrients

85 calories

4 grams carbohydrate

13 grams protein

2 grams fat

65% vitamin B_{12}

47% selenium

36% magnesium

35% vitamin B_6

Fish Nuggets

These are much healthier than the usual fish sticks, and they are quick to make, too. Double the recipe and freeze half for another time.

Makes: 4 servings

1 large egg or 2 medium eggs

2 tablespoons milk

1 pound white fish, cut into pieces

½ heaping cup seasoned fry mix

Vegetable cooking spray

1. Preheat the oven to 400°F.

2. Beat egg with milk.

3. Pour fry mix into a zip-lock bag or into a bowl.

4. Dip fish pieces in the egg mixture, then place them in the bag with mix and shake until coated (or roll in the mix in bowl).

5. Place the coated fish nuggets on a cookie sheet sprayed with vegetable cooking spray. Bake 10 to 15 minutes, or until golden brown. Serve with Pink Sauce.

Pink Sauce: Mix equal parts mayonnaise and ketchup. Some prefer the sauce more ketchup-y or more mayo-y; adjust accordingly.

Each 2-ounce child serving provides

77 calories
5 grams carbohydrate
11 grams protein
1 gram fat

Key Nutrients

54% B_{12}
25% vitamin B_6
24% magnesium
22% niacin

Hummus Dip

This is Minerva Al Tabaa's recipe for a Middle Eastern dip.

Makes: about 2 cups

1 15-ounce can chickpeas
  (garbanzo beans)

3 tablespoons sesame tahini
  (sesame seed butter)

Juice of 1 lemon

2 cloves garlic, crushed

Salt to taste

Pita wedges, baked tortilla
  chips, celery, and carrot
  sticks for dipping

1. Drain chickpeas, reserving liquid.

2. Place chickpeas in a blender with ¼ cup of reserved liquid; add tahini, lemon juice, garlic, and salt. Blend until smooth.

3. Serve with pita wedges, baked tortilla chips, celery, and carrot sticks.

**Each ¼-cup child
serving provides**

93 calories
11 grams carbohydrate
3 grams protein
5 grams fat
3 grams fiber

Key Nutrients

45% magnesium
16% vitamin C
15% iron

Lentil Chili

An easy recipe that's meatless.

Makes: 8 servings

1 pound lentils, rinsed

5 cups water

1 1-ounce packet dry onion soup mix

1 to 1½ teaspoons chili powder

1 teaspoon cumin

16 ounces tomatoes or tomato sauce

1. In a large saucepan, bring lentils and water to a boil.

2. Add soup mix and simmer for 30 minutes.

3. Add the rest of the ingredients and simmer 30 minutes more.

4. Serve in a bowl with cornbread, or use as a taco filling or dip. For a smoother dip, purée in blender.

Each ½-cup child serving provides

108 calories
19 grams carbohydrate
8 grams protein
0 grams fat

Key Nutrients

99% folate
41% magnesium
30% vitamin B$_6$
29% iron

Mediterranean Egg Salad

This dish provides an excellent way to sneak in a vegetable while stretching your eggs.

Makes: 4 servings

3 eggs, hard-boiled

1 cup quartered artichoke hearts, water squeezed out

2 tablespoons mayonnaise

Green or black olives, chopped (optional)

1. Place eggs in a bowl and stir slightly with fork.

2. Add remaining ingredients and mix well.

3. Serve between whole-grain bread, on top of a popcorn cake, in a hollowed-out tomato, or on top of a green salad.

Each serving provides	Key Nutrients
104 calories	*46% vitamin B$_{12}$*
6 grams carbohydrate	*36% magnesium*
6 grams protein	*24% folate*
7 grams fat	*17% vitamin A*

Mini Quiches in Pepper Pots

Most kids like the mild taste of red or yellow peppers.

Makes: 4 servings

4 medium yellow or red
   sweet peppers

1 cup grated coleslaw mix or
   finely chopped broccoli or
   frozen mixed vegetables,
   thawed

4 eggs

½ cup milk

1 teaspoon garlic powder

½ teaspoon tarragon

1. Preheat oven to 325°F.

2. Cut off tops of peppers and remove seeds. With a knife, scallop or zigzag the edges of the pepper, if desired. Stand peppers in custard cups or muffin tins.

3. Spoon ¼ cup of vegetable mixture into each pepper.

4. In a bowl, beat together eggs, milk, and seasonings. Pour ¼ of mixture into each pepper.

5. Bake for 60 to 70 minutes, or until a knife inserted near center comes out clean.

Microwave Directions:

Place custard cups on a microwave-safe plate. Microwave on high for 6 minutes. Rotate plate. Cook on 50 percent power, rotating plate every 3 minutes until a knife inserted near center comes out clean (about 10 to 14 minutes).

Each child serving (½ pepper) provides	Key Nutrients
65 calories	81% vitamin C
5 grams carbohydrate	30% selenium
4 grams protein	28% vitamin B_6
3 grams fat	

Pabble

A great spread for lunch or snacks!

Makes: 12 tablespoons

⅓ cup natural style peanut butter

⅓ cup unsweetened applesauce

2 tablespoons honey

¼ teaspoons cinnamon

Crackers, bread, graham crackers, apples, or celery

1. Combine peanut butter, applesauce, honey, and cinnamon; mix well.

2. Serve on crackers, bread, graham crackers, apples, or celery.

Each table-spoon provides

55 calories

5 grams carbohydrate

2 grams protein

4 grams fat

1 gram fiber

Key Nutrients

17% niacin

16% magnesium

Pasta with White Clam Sauce

Surprisingly, clams have more iron than red meat! This is a delicious sauce over pasta.

Makes: 4 servings

½ *small onion, chopped*

3 *teaspoons garlic, chopped*

2 *tablespoons olive oil*

1 *14-ounce can chopped baby clams*

3 *tablespoons parsley, chopped*

Cooked pasta

⅓ *cup Parmesan cheese, freshly grated*

1. Sauté onion and garlic in olive oil for 3 to 4 minutes until tender.

2. Add clams, clam juice (from can), and parsley. Cook until simmering.

3. Serve over warm pasta and top with Parmesan cheese.

Each ½-cup child serving of pasta with sauce provides

153 calories
18 grams carbohydrate
8 grams protein
6 grams fat

Key Nutrients

28% iron
25% riboflavin
22% vitamin B₆
22% niacin

Peanut, Peanut Butter, . . . 'n' Honey!

If you've got a food processor, making peanut butter is easy—and it's great fun for the kids to watch. Nuts provide healthy monounsaturated fat, as well as trace minerals. You can try the same recipe with cashews or walnuts.

Makes: 1¾ cups

3 cups roasted unsalted spanish peanuts

5 teaspoons oil

4 tablespoons honey

1/4 teaspoon salt

1. Put processor bowl and blade in place and lock into position. Place all ingredients in bowl.

2. Process on high until mixture is a smooth peanut butter. Scrape down sides occasionally with a spatula.

Store peanut butter in an airtight container in the refrigerator.

Variation

Instead of honey, use ¼ cup or more of canned fruit such as peaches, apricots, or applesauce.

Each table-spoon provides

105 calories
4 grams carbohydrate
4 grams protein
9 grams fat
1 gram fiber

Key Nutrients

50% chromium
32% magnesium
25% folate

Plum Good Meatballs

The plum sauce is finger-lickin' good!

Makes: 42 meatballs

Meatballs

1 pound extra lean ground
    beef

1 egg, optional

½ cup cooked bulgur, rice, or
    oatmeal

1 tablespoon soy sauce

3 cloves garlic, minced

3 tablespoons onion, minced

Plum Sauce

1 15-ounce can plums in
    heavy syrup, drained and
    pitted

2 tablespoons light soy sauce
    or 1 tablespoon regular
    soy sauce

2 tablespoons brown sugar

2 tablespoons ketchup

Pinch each of garlic and
    onion powder

Meatballs

1. Mix all ingredients in bowl. Form into small meatballs, using about 1 tablespoon mixture for each.

2. Brown in nonstick skillet for 5 minutes over medium-high heat, turning halfway through cooking. Cover and cook 4 more minutes.

Plum Sauce

1. Place all ingredients in blender. Blend on low and then high speed until puréed.

2. Drain meatballs and add sauce, stirring gently to coat. Heat over low heat or in microwave until warm.

Each meatball provides

26 calories

7 grams carbohydrate

0 grams protein

0 grams fat

Key Nutrients

Small amounts of all
nutrients

Quick Veggie Lasagna

I love lasagna, but I hate fussing with the noodles! This recipe cuts prep time and hassles in half, since you don't precook the noodles. The layers of noodles nicely hide a few veggies, too!

Makes: 12 servings

Vegetable cooking spray

15-ounce container low-fat ricotta cheese

1 cup mashed firm tofu or low-fat cottage cheese

1 teaspoon garlic, chopped

½ teaspoon dried basil

½ cup freshly grated Parmesan cheese

4 cups spaghetti sauce

12 lasagna noodles (¾ pound)

2 cups (8 ounces) grated part-skim mozzarella cheese

1¼ cups steamed chopped broccoli or other chopped veggie

1. Preheat oven to 350°F.

2. Spray a 9-by-13-inch pan with cooking spray.

3. Mix together ricotta, tofu, garlic, basil, and Parmesan.

4. Assemble ingredients in this order:

1 cup sauce, spread on the bottom of the pan	Rest of cheese mixture
4 noodles, touching	Rest of veggies
½ of cheese mixture	⅔ cup mozzarella
⅔ cup mozzarella	1 cup sauce
½ of veggies	4 noodles
1 cup sauce	1 cup sauce
4 noodles	⅔ cup mozzarella on top

5. Cover the pan tightly with foil and bake 1 hour to 1 hour and 20 minutes.

Each child half-serving provides	Key Nutrients
121 calories	33% calcium
11 grams carbohydrate	27% vitamin A
8 grams protein	22% vitamin C
5 grams fat	

Salmon Corn Chowder

Make this chowder from staples in your pantry, and you won't have to call out for pizza when there's nothing in the fridge for dinner!

Makes: 10 1-cup servings

2 cans condensed cream of celery soup

1 onion, chopped

1 cup celery, chopped

1 can creamed corn

1 can whole-kernel corn, drained

14¾-ounce can salmon, with skin removed

2 cups evaporated skim milk

1. Combine all ingredients in a large saucepan. Cook until warmed through.

2. Serve with cornbread.

Each ½-cup child serving provides

95 calories

12 grams carbohydrate

67 grams protein

3 grams fat

1 gram fiber

Key Nutrients

89% vitamin B$_{12}$

48% selenium

28% magnesium

25% calcium

Salmon Patties

Salmon provides essential fats (of which we don't get enough) that are important for brain development.

Makes: 4 servings

14¾-ounce can pink salmon, with skin removed

½ green onion, chopped

4 tablespoons wheat germ

½ cup plain bread crumbs

1 tablespoon oil

2 eggs

½ teaspoon dill

½ teaspoon garlic salt

1. In a bowl, combine all ingredients and mash with a fork. Form into burger patties.

2. Cook over low-medium heat for 7 minutes each side or bake in oven at 425°F for 10 to 15 minutes.

Variation

Shape the mixture into small balls or fish shapes. These make good finger food for toddlers.

½ patty provides	**Key Nutrients**
131 calories	*73% niacin*
13 grams protein	*48% magnesium*
6 grams carbohydrate	*24% calcium*
6 grams fat	*7% zinc and iron*
1 gram fiber	

Spaghetti à la Carbonara

This is a big favorite for kids who aren't big meat eaters.

Makes: 8 to 10 servings

1 pound spaghetti, angel hair, or other pasta

Vegetable cooking spray

8 ounces lean ham, sliced and cut into strips (you can also use turkey ham or turkey breast)

4 eggs

1¼ cups fat-free sour cream, divided

1 cup fresh Parmesan cheese, grated

1. Bring a large pot of water to boil and cook pasta according to package directions until firm, but tender.

2. Meanwhile, spray a pan with vegetable cooking spray and cook ham for 2 to 3 minutes over medium heat, stirring frequently. Remove from pan and set aside.

3. In a bowl, mix eggs, ½ cup sour cream, and cheese.

4. Pour egg mixture into the same pan used for the ham and cook, stirring constantly, until thickened and heated to 160°F. Turn heat down to low.

5. Stir in rest of sour cream and warm through.

6. In a large bowl, toss pasta with sauce and serve with extra freshly grated Parmesan cheese.

Variation

During last 5 minutes of cooking pasta, add a package of frozen vegetables. Suggested additions: broccoli, peas, mixed vegetables.

Each child half-serving provides	Key Nutrients
164 calories	*66% thiamin*
18 grams carbohydrate	*37% niacin*
9 grams protein	*42% riboflavin*
6 grams fat	*19% calcium*

Tropical Fish

Families who love fish will want to double this simple recipe!

Makes: 4 4-ounce servings

*1 pound white fish filets
(trout, cod, orange roughy,
and so on)*

*⅓ cup fresh-squeezed lime
juice*

Garlic salt to taste

1 tablespoon butter

3 cloves garlic, minced

1. Put fish filets in a large zip-lock bag together with lime juice.

2. Sprinkle with garlic salt.

3. Close bag and shake to ensure that all the fish is covered with juice and salt.

4. Roll over the bag so juice and fish are in the bottom end of bag; refrigerate.

5. Mince garlic.

6. Heat butter in a large frying pan; add garlic and sauté several minutes, stirring often.

7. Add fish. Cook for 5 minutes per side.

**Each 2-ounce child
serving provides**

*84 calories
1 gram carbohydrate
11 grams protein
3 grams fat*

Key Nutrients

*22% magnesium
20% riboflavin
11% iron*

Tuna Twist

A surprising way to serve canned tuna.

Makes: 4 1½-cup servings

6-ounce can tuna, drained

2 cups pasta sauce

*4 cups cooked pasta:
    spaghetti, shells, or rotini*

*Parmesan cheese, freshly
    grated*

1. In a blender, mix tuna and sauce.

2. Heat and serve over pasta.

3. Top with Parmesan cheese.

Variation

Adults may enjoy the addition of capers and/or sliced green or black olives to the finished sauce.

**Each ½-cup serving
pasta with ¼ cup
sauce provides**

143 calories

22 grams carbohydrate

9 grams protein

2 grams fat

2 grams fiber

Key Nutrients

60% vitamin B$_{12}$

48% niacin

40% magnesium

29% thiamin

Veggie Tacos

This meal can be made in a matter of minutes . . . and it's healthy, too! Kids cannot tell the ground beef is missing. This mixture can also be used as a nacho topping or dip, with the cheese cooked into it.

Makes: 6 tacos

1 teaspoon oil

½ cup onion, finely chopped

1 clove garlic, chopped

2 cups Green Giant Soy Crumbles or extra lean ground beef, cooked and drained

15-ounce can refried beans, any flavor

½ teaspoon cumin

½ cup mild salsa

6 corn tortillas or taco shells

Shredded lettuce

Chopped tomato

½ cup cheese

Guacamole

1. Heat oil in nonstick pan. Sauté onion and garlic until translucent.

2. Add soy crumbles (but not beef) and heat 3 minutes.

3. Stir in refried beans, cumin, and salsa. Cook over medium heat until heated through. (If using ground beef instead of soy crumbles, add the cooked beef now.)

4. Fill tortillas or taco shells and serve as soft or crispy tacos. Provide small dishes of lettuce, tomato, cheese, and guacamole so all can garnish their tacos as they like.

Each child serving (½ taco) provides	**Key Nutrients**
104 calories	*27% folate*
10 grams carbohydrate	*15% iron*
9 grams protein	*13% vitamin A*
3 grams fat	
3 grams fiber	

Fun Snacks for Home and School

"Mom, I'm hungry!" The snack call happens many times during the day. The after-school snack call is probably the loudest.

Whether your child is six or sixteen, the dilemma is the same: What can you give your kids for an after-school snack that won't fill them so much that they won't eat dinner, but will fill them enough to stop them from asking for more?

And it's one thing to have good intentions, but sometimes another thing to get your kids to follow through on your ideas! As children get older, it may be even more challenging to get them to eat healthy snacks. Here are a few tips.

Ten Ways to Encourage Kids to Eat Healthy Snacks

1. Display the foods you want your kids to eat.

2. Try to keep foods out of the house (or well hidden) that you don't want your kids to eat for snacks on a regular basis (chips, cookies, candy).

3. Make healthy foods easy to eat: the apples peeled and sliced, the oranges cut into sections, the cantaloupes and pineapples in bite-sized cubes.

4. Get your child involved in snack preparation, for example, in making a dip for veggies or cutting cheese into shapes with a cookie cutter.

5. Stick to whole, simple foods as much as possible: fruit, vegetables, cheese, milk. Often the less preparation, the better.

6. Have your child help pick out snack options at the grocery store or fruit stand.

7. Make it fun! Turn snack eating into a game by trying to go through the alphabet and eating a snack beginning with every letter. Or do the same with colors. In the spirit and challenge of the game, kids might be quite happy to eat healthy snacks that fit the next letter or color.

8. For young children, have snacks ready to eat by snacktime–this will prevent impulse eating.

9. You are more likely to get older kids to go for your snack if you have it ready when they walk in the door from school. They won't have a chance to think about other (less healthy) alternatives.

10. Give your child choices: "Do you want a bowl of cereal or cheese and crackers?"

▼

Planning Healthy Snacks

When planning snacks, the Food Guide Pyramid is a great place to start.

Grains

The bottom of the Food Guide Pyramid– grains–should be the basis of healthy snacking. However, your kids will argue that potato chips, snack crackers, and cupcakes also fit into the grain category! Here are some ideas for including grains that will make you both happy:

- Bagel with melted cheese
- Baked tortilla chips (such as baked Tostitos)
- Cereal (preferably whole-grain, like Cheerios) and milk
- Snack mix made with pretzels, bran Chex, and nuts
- Whole-wheat toast with butter and jam

Fruits and Vegetables

The fruit and vegetable group follows, and with a little creativity, can provide many great snacks. Don't remind your child that this sort of snack is good for him, and he'll be more likely to eat it!

- Baby carrots and ranch dip
- Fresh fruit, sliced and ready to eat (always a hit at my house)
- Fruit shake or smoothie made with frozen fruit (put in hot water for a few minutes) and a cup of milk or yogurt
- Salsa and baked chips (Did you know that salsa is packed with vitamin C?)
- Vegetable soup (This is great in the winter for kids who love veggies.)

Protein

Protein gives energy that will stick with your child. If a fat, juicy steak comes to mind, keep thinking! Most kids don't need any extra saturated fat. Snacktime is a good opportunity to give your child beans–a great, cheap protein food. Kid-appealing ideas include:

- Refried bean dip (Get spiced refried beans in the can and serve them plain or mixed with low-fat grated cheese. Make a quick layered dip by adding cheese, salsa, or chopped tomatoes, and low-fat or fat-free sour cream.)
- Bean burritos (For more fun, make "burrito bites." After tightly rolling up the burritos, cut them into bite-sized pieces.)

Dairy

Dairy—most kids don't get enough! Use snacktime as a way to boost calcium intake. Besides a cold glass of milk or chocolate milk, try these ideas:

- Cheese is a good source of calcium but tends to be high in fat, so look for low-fat versions.
  - –Melt low-fat cheddar over baked chips.
  - –Melt some low-fat Velveeta and stir in some Ro-Tel tomatoes for a dip.
  - –Simply serve sliced cheese with sliced apples or pears.
- Yogurt is liked by many kids, mine included. Younger kids tend to enjoy the new custard-style yogurt—and parents enjoy it because it really doesn't spill out of the spoon! You can do other things with yogurt, too:
  - –Try it as a dip or topping for fresh fruit.
  - –Layer with fruit and light whipped topping in a pretty glass for a parfait.

Fats and Sugars

The group at the top of the pyramid (fats and sugars) is what your kids probably clamor for at snacktime. It's your job to skillfully substitute one of the healthier ideas above. If that doesn't work, don't despair! It's possible to make even this group healthier!

- Nuts are high-fat but contain other nutrients. They can make a good snack, provided your child can use the extra fat. The good news is that nuts have monounsaturated fat, which is heart-healthy. Peanut butter on wheat crackers or bread is also a popular snack.
- A milkshake made with ice cream still has milk in it, as do pudding and custard.
- On the cookie front, oatmeal-raisin and peanut-butter cookies do have more nutrients than most cookies. Quick breads are sweet and can be high-fat. However, if they are made with some healthier ingredients, like zucchini or pumpkin, you can feel better about serving them to your kids.

Snacks can represent a significant part of your child's diet. Make them count! Throughout this book you can find many foods that may be used as snacks. The ones listed above and in the following recipes are just some of the options.

Apricot Bread

My friend Alicia Barrera first brought us this bread as a Christmas goodie—
we loved it!

Makes: 12 slices

1 cup water

⅔ cups dried apricots,
  chopped

1 egg

¾ cup sugar

2 tablespoons melted butter
  or oil

1¾ cups flour

¼ cup wheat germ

1 tablespoon baking powder

½ teaspoon salt

¼ teaspoon baking soda

¼ cup water

½ cup orange juice

½ teaspoon orange rind

½ cup chopped nuts
  (optional)

1. Preheat the oven to 350°F.

2. Bring 1 cup of water to a boil. Add apricots, turn off
heat, and let sit 15 minutes.

3. Beat egg in a medium bowl and stir in sugar and
butter.

4. In a separate bowl, combine dry ingredients and add
alternately with water and orange juice to egg
mixture. Stir until moistened.

5. Drain apricots and stir into the batter. Add orange
rind and nuts.

6. Pour into 9-by-5-by-3-inch loaf pan and bake for 1
hour or until a wooden pick inserted in center comes
out clean. Let cool in pan 10 minutes, then remove
from pan; finish cooling on a wire rack.

Each ½-slice child serving provides

63 calories

11 grams carbohydrate

2 grams protein

2 grams fat

1 gram fiber

Key Nutrients

Small amounts of all
nutrients

Cheerio Treats

An all-time favorite with kids of all ages.

Makes: 12 squares

3 tablespoons light margarine

1 tablespoon water

4 cups miniature marshmallows

4 cups Cheerios or multigrain Cheerios

¼ cup chocolate chips

Vegetable cooking spray

1. Melt margarine, water, and marshmallows over low-medium heat in a large saucepan. Stir.

2. Add Cheerios and chips and stir gently until well mixed.

3. Spray an 8-by-8-inch pan with vegetable cooking spray. Press mixture evenly into pan. Refrigerate before serving.

Each bar provides

113 calories

22 grams carbohydrate

2 grams protein

3 grams fat

Key Nutrients

16% magnesium

15% iron

Crunch-Munch Mix

A quick, yummy snack for the Snack Leader to bring.

Makes: about 15 cups

2 bags popped light popcorn
5 cups small pretzel twists
1 tablespoon olive oil
1 tablespoon ranch-flavored
  dressing mix

1. In a very large bowl, toss popcorn and pretzels.

2. Slowly drizzle half of oil and mix with spoon. Repeat with rest of oil.

3. Sprinkle with half of dressing mix. Toss with 2 big spoons or hands.

4. Repeat with remaining dressing mix.

5. For handy individual snacks, divide the snack mix into zip-lock bags.

**Each 1-cup
serving provides**

101 calories
19 grams carbohydrate
2 grams protein
2 grams fat

Key Nutrients

Small amounts of all
  nutrients

Dirt or Sand Cake

This was a class favorite when my son Nicolas first started preschool. The recipe can be cut in half if you use it just for your family. Dirt cake uses chocolate pudding and cookies; sand cake uses butterscotch pudding and graham crackers.

Makes: 24 ⅓-cup servings

2 large packages instant chocolate or butterscotch pudding, prepared with skim or 1% milk

2 cups light whipped topping

2 cups chocolate cookie crumbs or graham cracker crumbs (to make crumbs, put cookies or crackers in a paper or plastic bag and crush with a rolling pin or meat mallet)

16 gummy worms or gummy bugs

1. Prepare pudding according to package directions.

2. Stir in whipped topping.

3. Spoon pudding into individual serving dishes. Or, for a really dirty or sandy look, spoon all the pudding into a large, clean ceramic pot or child's sand pail lined with foil or plastic wrap.

4. Top pudding with chocolate cookie crumbs or graham cracker crumbs.

5. Place gummy worms halfway into the pudding.

Each ⅓-cup child serving provides

114 calories
24 grams carbohydrate
1 gram protein
2 grams fat

Key Nutrients

Small amounts of all nutrients

Honey Bear Snack Mix

This is Sandy Russell's recipe for a "beary" good snack.

Makes: 3 cups or 6 ½-cup servings

1 cup honey bear-shaped graham snacks

1 cup Honey Nut Cheerios

1 cup honey-roasted mixed nuts

1. Combine all ingredients and mix well.

2. Store in an airtight container.

3. Serve in paper cups.

Each ½-cup child serving provides

162 calories
20 grams carbohydrate
4 grams protein
8 grams fat

Key Nutrients

Small amounts of all nutrients

Honey Bran Bars

If your little honey loves honey and molasses, try this.

Makes: 24 bars

Vegetable cooking spray

4 cups Complete Bran Flakes

½ cup sunflower seeds or chopped nuts

½ cup raisins

⅓ cup reduced-fat margarine

⅓ cup honey

⅓ cup brown sugar, firmly packed

1. Spray a 9-by-9-inch baking pan with vegetable cooking spray.

2. In a large bowl, toss together cereal, seeds or nuts, and raisins. Set aside.

3. In a pot, stir together margarine, honey, and brown sugar and bring to a boil stirring constantly. Boil gently for 5 minutes, stirring. Pour over cereal mixture and mix.

4. Press cereal mixture into baking pan. Let stand for 1 hour, then cut into bars.

Each bar provides

80 calories

13 grams carbohydrate

2 grams protein

0 grams fat

1 gram fiber

Key Nutrients

44% iron

30% magnesium,

19% folate

10% zinc

Kashi Balls

What is Kashi? It's a brand of organic cereal made from seven whole grains plus sesame seeds. Kashi has a bit more substance than regular puffed cereals, and it contains fiber. Find it in the regular cereal aisle or in the natural-foods section of your grocery.

Makes: 40 small balls

¼ cup light margarine

3 cups miniature marshmallows

½ cup natural-style peanut butter

3 cups Kashi (or puffed or ring cereal)

1 cup raisins, chopped dates, apricots, or other dried fruit

1. Over medium-low heat, melt margarine in a large saucepan.

2. Add marshmallows and stir until melted, then mix in peanut butter.

3. Gently stir in cereal and fruit until mixed well. Let cool slightly.

4. With clean hands, form cereal mixture into Ping-Pong-sized balls. Press hard while forming balls. Store in an airtight container.

Each Kashi ball provides

48 calories
8 grams carbohydrate
1 gram protein
2 grams fat

Key Nutrients

Small amounts of most nutrients

Kiwi Green Goblin Pudding

Kiwi provides the hair and eyes for this fun snack–or it could be the bumps of an alligator! It's okay to eat the furry skin; just wash it well.

Makes: 6 ⅓-cup servings

1 3½-ounce package instant vanilla pudding mix

2 cups milk

Green food coloring

4 kiwi fruit, sliced

½ cup raisins

1. Prepare pudding with milk according to package directions, adding green food coloring until desired shade is reached.

2. Spoon the green pudding into individual dessert bowls or custard cups.

3. Cut 2 kiwi slices into quarters and place on the pudding as eyes.

4. Line the edges of bowls with kiwi slices, peel side up.

5. Use raisins to make mouths.

Each ⅓-cup serving provides

125 calories

27 grams carbohydrate

3 grams protein

1 gram fat

2 grams fiber

Key Nutrients

126% vitamin C

32% riboflavin

23% calcium

Ooey-Gooey Sandwiches

Your kids will find these to be *m-m-m* good!

Makes: 4 sandwich halves

4 slices whole-grain bread

3 teaspoons peanut butter

16 milk chocolate chips
(about 2 teaspoons)

1. Spread a thin layer of peanut butter on 2 slices of bread.

2. Top each with 8 chocolate chips.

3. Cover with other slice of bread.

4. Heat the sandwiches in a toaster oven or in a nonstick pan until chips start to melt.

Each ½ sandwich provides

103 calories
14 grams carbohydrate
4 grams protein
4 grams fat
3 grams fiber

Key Nutrients

Small amounts of all nutrients

Robert's Snack Mix

My son Robert came up with this recipe. You can use any of your children's favorite cereals, but this recipe includes some of the healthier ones.

Makes: 11 ½-cup servings

2 cups Life cereal
2 cups Corn Bran cereal
½ cup peanuts or mixed nuts
1 cup dried fruit

1. Combine all ingredients and mix well.
2. Keep in an airtight container.

**Each ½-cup
serving provides**

128 calories
23 grams carbohydrate
3 grams protein
3 grams fat
3 grams fiber

Key Nutrients

50% iron
35% folate
14% zinc

Taco Crunch Snack

A perfect snack for the Cub Scout den.

Makes: 10 cups

3 tablespoons olive oil or melted butter

4 cups cheese Goldfish crackers

4 cups popped popcorn

2 cups pretzel sticks

1 to 2 tablespoons taco seasoning mix

1. Mix Goldfish, popcorn, and pretzels in a large bowl.

2. Drizzle with part of the oil and toss. Repeat with the rest of the oil.

3. Slowly sprinkle with taco mix, a small bit at a time, tasting as you go. Season to taste.

Each ½-cup serving provides

66 calories
12 grams carbohydrate
2 grams protein
2 grams fat

Key Nutrients

Small amounts of all nutrients

▼

Other Fun Snack Ideas

Let your imagination run wild!

Pizzas

Basic Pizza
Take something round (English muffin, pita bread, tortilla, rice or popcorn cake), then add some sauce and cheese and you've got pizza!

Pizza Face
Make a face using sliced olives for eyes, a bell pepper slice a for mouth, and a carrot slice for a nose.

Mexican Pizza
Top this pizza with salsa and refried beans!

Clock Pizza
Use low-fat turkey pepperoni as the numbers.

Mouse-Face Pizza
Use oval-shaped cheese for eyes and nose, olives on top of that, and bell pepper strips for mouth and whiskers. Use oval zucchini slices for the ears, which you place slightly under cheese so they stick out above crust.

Stars and Stripes Pizza
Cut out cheese in shapes of stars, and use red pepper slices to make stripes.

Boats

Baked Potato Boats
First cut baked potatoes in half and carefully scoop out potato without breaking the skin. Mix scooped-out potato with a little milk and cheese, then put it back inside the skin. Cut triangles out of cheese for the sail and attach them with toothpicks or coffee stirrers. Make a deck with red pepper or plum tomato slices. Make a rowboat using carrot sticks as the oars and grapes as the heads of people.

Bread Boats
Put your favorite sandwich topping on each bread or bun half. Use the tips for making the potato boat (above) to make a bread boat. Serve on top of a green sea (shredded leaf lettuce) with lots of fish (Goldfish crackers) swimming by.

Cucumber Boats
Cut cucumber in half lengthwise. Scoop out middle. Fill with ranch dip or cream-cheese dip. With other cucumber half and carrots, make long oars. Serve with oars resting against boat.

Tasty Critters

Fire Ants on a Snow-Covered Log
Spread celery sticks with light cream cheese. Top with ants (dried cranberries).

Spiders
Make peanut butter sandwiches with round whole-grain crackers. Insert pretzel sticks into peanut-butter filling to make legs.

Orange Octopus
Spread one side of a round whole-grain cracker with pimiento spread or cream cheese. Using a vegetable peeler and a raw

carrot, make four long carrot shavings. Drape shavings across middle of cracker and spread, making eight octopus tentacles. Top with another cracker.

Sandwich Shapes

Kids love these for lunch, and they also make a great snack to bring for the class. All you need are your favorite cookie cutters, bread, and sandwich fillings. Cut bread with cookie cutters and fill with your favorite sandwich makings. If you are using sandwich fillings that are not spreadable, like ham or cheese, cut those into shapes as well.

Eating on the Run

Once you have children, it seems you're always on the go—sometimes grabbing snacks to keep you going until you get home to eat a real meal. Because some of our homemade snacks aren't necessarily portable, it's best to know which healthy foods work well for taking on the go. Here are some ideas that have worked for our family over the years:

For Toddlers
For the Car or Stroller:
Apple slices
Bananas
Cheerios
Goldfish crackers
Graham crackers
Grape halves
Pretzels
Puffed cereal or other small shaped cereal
Raisins, dates, dried apricots, Craisins, dried mango slices

Ideas for Sandwich Fillings	
Savory	**Sweet**
Cheese	Apple butter
Cream cheese with cucumber slices	Cream cheese mixed with mashed banana
Egg salad	Cream cheese with blueberries
Ham/lunch meat	Jam
Hummus	
Peanut butter and jelly	
Pimiento cheese	

String cheese or cheese slices
Teething crackers
Wheat crackers

More Suitable for Older Kids
(because of choking hazards for younger kids or just because they take a little more coordination)
For the Car:
Carrot and celery sticks
Go-Gurt (yogurt in a tube)
Granola bars
Nutrigrain bars
Nuts
Peanut butter crackers
Popcorn
Whole grapes
Whole pieces of fruit
Yogurt

At the Mall:
Bread sticks with marinara sauce
Fresh-squeezed lemonade
Fried rice with vegetables

Frozen yogurt
Milkshake
Refried beans with cheese
Sherbet
Smoothies
Soft pretzels

Drinks

It's wise to carry squeeze bottles in the car for the "thirsties," especially in the summer months. If you'll be out running errands for a while, frozen juice boxes or frozen water bottles will defrost quickly and provide a refreshing drink.

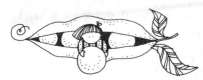

Eating Out

This chapter answers questions such as:

• *Taking my toddler to a restaurant sometimes frazzles my nerves. How can I make the experience more enjoyable?*

• *What can I do? My youngest child doesn't like the food at two of the restaurants where the rest of our family enjoys eating.*

• *We're planning to take our three-year-old to an authentic Chinese restaurant. What menu selections might appeal to her?*

• *Which fast-food restaurants have the healthiest kids' meals?*

• *What measures are taken to inspect the meats used in fast-food restaurants?*

• *How do the calories compare for typical fast-food choices?*

• *My child complains of an itchy throat every time we eat at a certain restaurant. Why?*

More and more Americans are eating out, according to the U.S. Department of Agriculture's latest nationwide food consumption survey *What We Eat in America.*

"In 1994–95, 57 percent of Americans consumed meals and snacks away from home on any given day, accounting for about half of their daily calorie and fat intake on average," said Catherine E. Woteki, Acting Under Secretary for Research, Education, and Economics. "Seventeen years ago, by comparison, 43 percent of Americans ate away from home for just over 40 percent of daily calories and fat. Given the prevalence of two-career families, the lack of time available for home cooking, and the wide variety of choices available for meals away from home, the increase is not surprising." And fast-food establishments, including pizza parlors, have passed restaurants as the most frequent source of outside food.

These statistics hold true even for families with children. When you have kids in tow, you may opt for more fast food, pizza, or take-out. But occasionally you may want your kids to enjoy finer dining. Getting your children used to eating out at an early age gives you an opportunity to teach manners for eating out as well as a chance to introduce new and unusual foods. To make your dining experience the best it can be, follow the tips below:

Tips for an Enjoyable Restaurant Experience

1. Make sure your child is not overly hungry. Children have a very low tolerance for waiting when they're hungry—which means waiting for a table, and for food, will not be an enjoyable experience. Since eating out is often a spur-of-the-moment idea, usually little or no time is avail-

able to plan ahead. So grab an apple, some animal crackers, or pretzels, and head out the door. Munching on a snack will give your child something to do while waiting. Set a limit on the amount of predinner snacks, however, to make sure your child is still hungry when dinner arrives!

2. If the outing is planned, make sure your child is well rested. If the family has been running nonstop all day, you can be sure that your child won't be her usual angelic self if you choose to go out to eat that evening!

3. Choose a restaurant that has some diversion for children (or bring your own). Restaurants are getting wise to the fact that families with children eat out, and they need something for their children to do. The most creative I've seen (and the favorite with my kids) was at an Italian restaurant. After we were seated, out waiter brought each child a saucer containing a small amount of pizza dough—a chance to play with food without getting into trouble! In fact, it also kept my husband occupied! After dinner the kids sat at the bar and watched pizza come out of the brick oven.

Most restaurants have crayons and a outline to color, toys, or a table with beads. If your child is not overly interested in this sort of entertainment, bring your own. Things we have found useful include books, small cars, small animals, and action figures for pretend play. As a last resort, almost anything can be turned into a plaything. Packets of sugar can be used to make a picture or stack. A handful of straws can be used for a game of pick-up sticks. A game of I-Spy is always entertaining for kids over two years.

3. If your child is unlikely to make a meal from items on the menu, bring some of your own food. Restaurants usually don't mind and completely understand that children have special needs—especially babies and picky eaters. In addition, you may want to discuss the dining-out adventure in advance so your child will know what kind of foods to expect.

4. Decide on your philosophy about eating before you leave home. Many restaurants have kids' menus from which you can choose the usual burger, grilled cheese, or hot dog. Sometimes, though, I get tired of my kids eating a burger every time we go out! I'd like them to experience and learn to enjoy foods from other cultures. So I selectively let them know what the menu is, using some foods from the regular menu. At a Mexican restaurant, for example, I'll say: "Let's see . . . you can have a cheese quesadilla or enchilada, a bean burrito, or a chicken taco." (I slyly leave out the fact they could also have a burger or hot dog!) This approach works until your children learn to read well.

Also make your plan for drinks. Kids' meals usually include a drink. After about the age of five for my older son and three for my younger, we decided to let them splurge with their drinks and order a lemon-lime soda. Since they don't drink such things at home, it was an honest splurge. Sometimes I veto the sodas and get water, milk, or juice for them. Be careful if you get them a sweet drink; let them have only a few sips before dinner, or the drink will be their dinner!

You may choose to continue ordering milk or juice for your child. Another way to make the usual drinks special is to ask for chocolate milk or juice with a splash of soda. We often concoct our own fruit punch by asking for half cranberry and half orange juice.

5. If your child is in her "terrific twos," this is the probably the toughest time to take her out. You will spend most of the evening chasing her and trying to get her to sit down. For that age group, if going out isn't enjoyable, stick to a kid-oriented place like Chuck-E-Cheese—or get a baby-sitter!

6. If your child is a light eater and not too picky, order her a side dish or let her eat part of the food on your own plate. This will save money and aggravation.

▼

Suggested Selections for Restaurant Dining

If you can steer your child away from the children's menu, following are some healthy ideas for main and side dishes. Often something from the appetizer or side dish menu is the perfect size for your little diner.

American Style
Restaurants like Friday's, Bennigan's, and Chili's usually have something for everyone:

Main dishes: Peel-and-eat shrimp, veggie burgers, fajitas, teriyaki or grilled chicken, pasta primavera, sandwiches, quesadillas

Side dishes: Salads, black beans, baked potato, soup

Desserts: Sorbet, frozen yogurt

Breakfast and Coffee Shops
In the mood for breakfast at dinnertime? No problem with restaurants like Denny's, House of Pancakes, and Village Inn. Breakfast is a favorite with kids just about anytime:

Main dishes: Cold or hot cereal, blueberry pancakes, Belgian waffle with fruit sauce, eggs any style, French toast

Side dishes: Ham; whole-grain English muffins, toast, bagels, muffins; fresh fruits

Drinks: Milk and a variety of juices

Chinese
If your child loves vegetables, she will like almost any Chinese food. If not, stay with these simple dishes:

Main dishes: Velvet chicken (chicken with snow peas, water chestnuts, and bamboo shoots), shrimp or beef with broccoli, moo shu shrimp (shrimp with vegetables served with thin pancakes to stuff), any lo mein noodle dish (noodles with beef, shrimp, pork, or vegetables)

Side dishes: Egg drop soup, corn velvet soup, steamed rice, vegetable fried rice, lychees (a tasty, unusual, nutlike fruit)

Italian

Main dishes: Any kind of pasta—plain or with red sauce, tortellini, canneloni (pasta filled with cheese and spinach), ravioli

Side dishes: Salad, minestrone soup, pasta e fagiole soup (pasta with beans)

Japanese

Japanese food is similar to Chinese food in that they both use a lot of vegetables:

Main dishes: Yakitori chicken, teriyaki chicken, beef, salmon, seafood, shabu-shabu (sliced beef and vegetables with noodles cooked at the table with sauces)

Side dishes: Steamed dumplings, egg rolls, tempura (Though deep-fried, it may be an interesting way to eat foods like yam, mushroom, and broccoli. Ditto for egg rolls.)

Soups: Miso (made out of soybean paste and tofu), su-udon (noodle soup), yaki-udon (noodle soup with stir-fried vegetables)

Mexican

Main dishes: Bean burrito, cheese quesadillas, or cheese enchilada with mild sauce

Side dishes: Refried beans, Spanish rice, tortilla chips with guacamole and mild salsa (After the first basket of chips, don't ask for more!)

Pizza

Main dishes: Cheese or ham pizza, pasta with marinara sauce

Side dishes: Salad, fruit from salad bar, bread sticks

Eating Out and Fast Food

Eating fast food frequently can present a nutritional challenge. Typical fast food (burger and fries) contains little fruits and vegetables or fiber. However, if your child eats out only occasionally—say twice a month—she might as well enjoy it!

If your child is like most, she may like the food at your local drive-thru, but what she really likes is the toy that comes with it. The fast-food giants have learned how to market to kids—in a big way. Collecting the toys that come with kids' meals has become a big phenomenon. Since habits of all kinds start early, regular trips to Burger Land may settle your child in an unhealthy routine that she'll find hard to change when she's older. So go easy on the fast food.

If the burger makers spent as much time coming up with nutritious sandwiches for kids as they do inventing "have-to-have" toys, our kids would have much healthier diets. Let's look at what's available in a couple of typical kids' meals.

- McDonald's Happy Meal with cheeseburger, small fries, and small Sprite: 640 calories, 23 grams fat, 995 milligrams sodium
- McDonald's Chicken Nuggets, small fries, and small Sprite: 510 calories, 21 grams fat, 515 milligrams sodium

Nutrient values for kids' meals with burgers and chicken nuggets at other fast-food eateries

Five Healthiest Fast-Food Restaurants for Families

1st Place: Wendy's offers burgers, grilled chicken, baked potatoes, chili, and a salad bar—something healthy to please every family member!

2nd Place: Taco Bell also has a variety of meals to please a variety of appetites. Most noteworthy is the availability of refried beans, a big plus for vegetarians and those wishing to cut down on meat.

3rd Place: Subway has sandwiches available on a wheat bun; they use turkey lunch meats; and they offer a variety of vegetables. Many salads and a few soups are also available.

4th Place: KFC has been trying for a long time to get a healthy baked chicken on its menu. Now they have the Tender Roast chicken. KFC also gets an A+ for offering healthy side dishes, such as Mean Greens, baked beans, corn, and mashed potatoes.

5th Place: Arby's offers lean roast beef and roasted chicken sandwiches as well as burgers, potatoes, and soups. However, watch the sodium.

are very similar to those at McDonald's.

Obviously a typical trip to most burger restaurants gives your family an unhealthy dose of fat, saturated fat, and sodium, not to mention an absence of fruits and vegetables. But sometimes eating fast food is inevitable. You're at the mall with a baby in the stroller and a toddler beside you who is whining that she's hungry. Who has time to figure out which eatery has the healthiest food for tots? Often the fast-food restaurants with the best choices are the ones that have something besides burgers.

- If you must eat fast food regularly, vary the restaurants.
- If your child won't drink milk, order her a milkshake for dessert.
- Don't feel compelled to order the kid's meal. You can always buy the "must-have" toy separately.
- Set limits on how often you eat fast food, and on how often you go to a certain place. Let your child know why you set limits.
- Set a good example by ordering one of the healthier items from the menu.

▼

Make the Best of Fast Food

- On days that your family eats fast food, make sure to compensate by having more snacks of fruits and vegetables.

▼

Best Kids' Meals from Fast-Food Eateries

Taco Bell
The best bet from all fast-food outlets is a burrito meal. At Taco Bell you can get a bean

burrito with cheese and nachos plus a toy and a drink. Your child will not only skip the meat and saturated fat in a burger, she will also get a healthy dose of fiber and other nutrients from the beans. And I know from experience that your little one will barely get through the burrito, much less the nachos.

Subway

At Subway you can get a kid's meal that doesn't have anything fried in it, thanks to Baked Lay's potato chips. Subway is lowest on the fat totem pole for kids' meals, though the sodium in the meats does add up.

KFC

A fried chicken leg and baked beans have less fat and more fiber than a burger and fries.

▼

The "Best of the Menu" from Other Fast-Food Eateries

Arby's offers a Junior Roast Beef Sandwich, which provides a break from the burger routine. Arby's also has a good selection of soups, including Clam Chowder, Cream of Broccoli, and Lumberjack Mixed Vegetable. For small children, soup can be a meal when accompanied by milk and perhaps part of a baked potato or fries.

Blimpie's has several best bets: a Grilled Chicken Sub, Roast Beef Sub, and Turkey Sub, all weighing in with less than ten grams of fat.

Boston Market, a different kind of fast-food eatery, offers diners more of a balanced meal. Foods that may appeal to kids (and nutrition-conscious parents) include Grilled Chicken Sandwich, Butternut Squash, Green Bean Casserole, Barbecue Baked Beans, and Fruit Salad. For soup eaters, there is Chicken Soup and Chicken Tortilla Soup.

Carl's Jr. offers a Grilled Chicken Sandwich and a hamburger that has almost half the fat of competing burgers.

Chick-Fil-A has chicken nuggets and waffle fries on its kids' menu, for a total of seventeen grams of fat, making it a better choice than McDonald's Chicken Nuggets. Two choices that can help round out the meal are coleslaw and carrot-and-raisin salad. The menu offers other great choices too: chargrilled Chicken Deluxe Sandwich, Chicken Salad Sandwich (on whole wheat), and Hearty Breast of Chicken Soup. If your child likes salad, the chargrilled Chicken Garden Salad or Chicken Salad plate are both good choices. Chick-Fil-A also appears to give promotional toys aimed at promoting family values. Past toys have included a Richard Scarry book and Focus on the Family's "Adventure in Odyssey" tapes.

Church's chicken leg and mashed potatoes have less fat than a burger by itself, making it an okay choice.

Domino's or Little Caesar's thin crust pizza can also offer a fairly balanced meal, especially if you order plain cheese, cheese and ham, or some pineapple or a vegetable. Two slices contain less fat and sodium than a burger.

Food Safety and Fast Food

Rare is the parent who orders a burger for their child without thinking twice about the danger of the E. coli bacteria. After several outbreaks and deaths from the E. coli illness, the government and food industry have been doing their part to step up meat inspection, resulting in several recalls of ground beef. One company that seems to be doing its part is Jack in the Box, operated by Foodmaker, Inc.

"The fact is, not all hamburger meat is created equal," said David Theno, Ph.D., vice president of quality assurance, research and development, and technical services at Foodmaker, Inc., operator and franchisor of Jack in the Box restaurants. "There are food companies out there that are doing the right things to ensure the safety of hamburger meat in the food chain. Central to their food safety efforts is microbial testing to control and eliminate the O157:H7 bacteria. Today, there are hamburger manufacturers out there doing microbial testing every fifteen minutes to test for O157:H7. If it is found, that lot is destroyed and removed from the food chain."

In 1993, Jack in the Box restaurants instituted the restaurant industry's most comprehensive HACCP (hazard analysis critical control points) food-safety program. Patterned after the National Aeronautics and Space Administration's program to ensure safe food for astronauts in the 1960s, the company's HACCP system has been called the gold standard in food safety systems by the U.S. Department of Agriculture (USDA), Food and Drug Administration, and the Center for Science in the Public Interest. Dr. David Theno has been appointed to the USDA's National Advisory Committee on Meat and Poultry Inspection. Theno was chosen as the fast-food industry's exclusive representative on the sixteen-member committee.

Hardee's offers the typical burger and a chicken breast sandwich. However, Hardee's also offers some healthier side dishes, such as baked beans and mashed potatoes.

Jack in the Box has the usual burger and chicken nugget kids' meals. Jack in the Box also has a few other healthy entrées: the Chicken Teriyaki Bowl and the Chicken Fajita Pita. The Chicken Teriyaki Bowl is strips of teriyaki-marinated chicken breast, fresh broccoli, and carrots on a bed of steamed rice. It gets a thumbs-up for its inclusion of grains, lean protein, and vegetables, but a thumbs-down for its high sodium content. The dish may be a good one to share with Mom or Dad. The Chicken Fajita Pita also gets a thumbs up for its inclusion of grilled onions, tomatoes, and two kinds of lettuce.

KFC gives kids a choice. Its kids' meal includes a chicken leg (roasted or fried) or chicken strips and choice of a side dish. The side dishes can really help round out the meal: BBQ Beans, Coleslaw, Corn on the Cob, Garden Rice, Macaroni and Cheese, Mashed Potatoes, Mean Greens, and Red Beans and Rice. Most kids can find something they like. And the choices are so good for a fast-food restaurant, you may want to order an extra side dish for sharing. Off the kids' menu, the KFC Tender Roast Chicken is an excellent choice, along with a few side dishes.

McDonald's healthiest bet is a Grilled Chicken Deluxe Sandwich (mayo on the side) or a Grilled Chicken Deluxe Salad. An

---

ice-cream cone or McDonaldland cookies are okay for dessert.

Popeye's, like KFC, has a variety of side dishes to go along with its cajun-style fried chicken. Unfortunately, most are high in fat except for Corn on the Cob, Cajun Rice, and Potatoes and Gravy.

Roy Rogers Restaurants have several dishes that would appeal to kids: Grilled Chicken Sandwich, Roast Beef Sandwich, Chicken Soup, and Fried or Roasted Chicken. Healthy side dishes round out the meal: Baked Beans, Baked Potato, or Mashed Potatoes with Gravy.

Subway not only offers great kids' meals, but it's also a good place to share a sandwich with Mom or Dad. Subway uses turkey lunch meats, so their sandwiches are lower in fat than the typical deli sandwich. For cold sandwiches, Ham, Roast Beef, Subway Club, Turkey Breast, Turkey Breast and Ham, Seafood, and Crab or Tuna with light mayonnaise are all good choices. For hot sandwiches, Roasted Chicken Breast, Steak and Cheese Sub, and Subway Melt are all good. Subway also has a variety of salads that have some of the same meat combinations. Low-fat mayonnaise and fat-free salad dressings are available.

Taco Bell is great for those tired of the burger-and-fries scenario. Besides the vegetarian kid's meal mentioned earlier, many other good choices are available with fewer than fifteen grams of fat. Since beans, salsa, and cheese are frequent ingredients, many of Taco Bell's items contain a significant amount of calcium and vitamin A. Good choices include Tacos, Soft Tacos, Grilled Steak Soft Taco, Chicken Gordita Supreme, Fiesta, Bean Burrito, Tostada, and Grilled Chicken Burrito.

Wendy's offers several excellent alternatives to burgers: Chili, Salad Bar, and Baked Potato with Broccoli and Cheese. Their new Stuffed Pitas—a cross between a sandwich and a salad—give parents a break from the burger routine. Also available are Caesar Salad with Grilled Chicken or Grilled Chicken Salad.

Looking at the Numbers

Ever wonder how fried chicken compares with a burger—caloriewise, that is? Or how French fries compare with refried beans? Peek at the comparisons at right.

Fast-Food Calorie Counter

Food	Calories
Arby's:	
Light Roast Beef Deluxe Sandwich	296
Light Roast Turkey Deluxe Sandwich	260
Chick-Fil-A:	
Chargrilled Chicken Sandwich	280
Deluxe Chicken Sandwich	290
Chick-n-Strips (4)	230
Jack in the Box:	
Chicken Teriyaki Bowl	670
Grilled Chicken Fillet	480
KFC:	
BBQ Flavored Chicken Sandwich	256
Tender Roast Drumstick (with skin)	97
Original Recipe Drumstick	140
Original Recipe Breast	400
McDonald's:	
Grilled Chicken Deluxe	440
Big Mac	560
Taco Bell:	
Chili & Cheese Burrito	330
Taco	180
Grilled Steak Soft Taco	230
Grilled Chicken Gordita Supreme	300
Bean Burrito	380
Wendy's:	
Garden Ranch Chicken Pita	480
Broccoli & Cheese Baked Potato	470
Grilled Chicken Sandwich	310
Large Chili	310

Convenience Foods

This chapter answers questions such as:

• *In general, which is a more healthy meal—pizza or frozen dinners for kids?*
• *On Monday nights, I need something I can prepare very quickly and that can be eaten in the car. What might work?*
• *My kids love hot dogs! What makes them such a poor choice?*
• *How should I stock my kitchen so I'm set to go when I need quick but healthy meals?*
• *What are some healthy menus that can be prepared quickly?*

Your son has T-ball practice in forty-five minutes. You don't have time to go out. The eternal question "What's for dinner?" is staring you in the face. What to do? Look no farther than your freezer and pantry for a meal in a flash. Your grocery deli and salad bar can help, too; stores are expanding their selections to cater to the hurried.

This chapter provides a summary of convenience foods and good choices. The convenience foods available are constantly changing, so if your favorite healthy food isn't listed, that doesn't mean it's not a good choice. When comparing nutrition information, keep in mind that serving sizes often vary between brands. Generally speaking, iron is hard to find in convenience foods; most have 6–10 percent of the Daily Value for iron—15 percent is a real find. Consider your family's eating habits and special needs while shopping for convenience foods. For example, if your family eats enough fiber, choose a product that has less fiber but more calcium. If your kids eat a lot of high-sodium foods, choose a product with the least amount of sodium.

Kids' Favorites: How Do They Stack Up Nutritionally?

Pizza

A pizza is quick cooking, it provides a significant amount of calcium—usually 25–30 percent of the daily value, and there probably won't be leftovers for Rover. The fat content can range from moderately high to astronomically high, depending on the toppings. If your kids like vegetables, you can quickly chop a few vegetables and put them on the pizza before you bake it. If you have more time, you can stir-fry some eggplant or zucchini for the adult side of the pizza! Best bets for kids are usually cheese pizzas.

Look for: about 10 grams of fat, at least 10 percent Daily Value for calcium, 15 percent Daily Value for vitamin A, and at least 2 grams of fiber per slice. For a balanced meal, add raw veggies and dip, fresh fruit, and milk.

Thumbs-Up Choices:

DiGiorno Rising Crust Vegetable Pizza
10 grams of fat, 3 grams of fiber per serving, and 15 percent Daily Value for vitamin A

Tombstone Vegetable Pizza for One
4 grams of fiber and 25 percent Daily Value for vitamin A

Value Choice:

Totino's Party Cheese Pizza
14 grams of fat and 2 grams of fiber

Frozen Dinners Aimed at Kids

The baby-sitter is good, but she doesn't cook. The options are: order out for pizza, cook ahead (which kind of takes the fun out of going out), or get one of those cute frozen dinners with a prize inside for your child. Behind the cartoon cover, what is the nutritional impact? The good news is your child will probably eat and enjoy it. The bad news is these dinners are sometimes worse than a

fast-food meal! The Kid Cuisine brand generally has corn or French fries for a vegetable, sometimes applesauce, and pudding or a brownie for dessert. Swanson has become a bit more creative with its Fun Feast. The dessert is sometimes a vanilla or chocolate dairy dessert or a berry fruit freeze that is taken out before cooking.

Look for: meals that offer a fruit or a dairy dessert and less than 16 grams of fat, at least 4 grams of fiber, and more than 15 percent Daily Value for vitamin C, vitamin A, or calcium.

Thumb-Up Choices:

Kid Cuisine Pirate Pizza with Cheese
11 grams of fat, 5 grams of fiber, and 15 percent Daily Value for calcium

Swanson Fun Feast Roarin' Ravioli
10 grams of fat, an impressive 8 grams of fiber, and 50 percent Daily Value for vitamin C

Cook-and-Run Foods

Preschool open house is in half an hour. What can be prepared really quickly and eaten in the car, if necessary?

Burritos:
Ever give those 3-for-$1.00 burritos a second look? Surprisingly, these prepackaged burritos can be good nutrition for the money, depending on the brand.

Look for: 10 grams of fat or less and at least 4 grams of fiber. Add raw baby carrots, fruit, and yogurt for a balanced meal.

Thumbs-Up Choices:

Delsey's Foods Beef Burrito and Bean Burrito
5 and 6 grams of fat, respectively, and a good amount of fiber and iron

For a bit more expensive meal: *Amy's Organic Bean and Rice Burrito* (also available with cheese)
5 grams of fat and 6 grams of fiber

Pockets:
Lean Pockets are a good choice. So are Amy's Organic, now found at some large grocery stores. Ken & Robert's Veggie Pockets are also excellent and come in a variety of flavors, such as Oriental, Tex-Mex, Indian, and Broccoli & Cheddar. They are found mostly at large health-food markets.
Look for: fewer than 10 grams of fat and 20 percent Daily Value for calcium and vitamin C. Add a juice box and a banana for a balanced meal.

Thumbs-Up Choices:

Chicken Broccoli Supreme Lean Pocket
7 grams of fat, 3 grams of fiber, 25 percent Daily Value for calcium, and 30 percent for vitamin C

Amy's Pocketfuls Spinach Feta in a Pocket
7 grams of fat, 45 percent Daily Value for vitamin A, 25 percent for calcium, and 20 percent for iron

Ken and Robert's BBQ Style Veggie Pocket
(Tastes like a sliced barbecued beef sandwich, but it's a healthy combination of wheat and soy.)
8 grams of fat and 5 grams of fiber

The following selections were chosen by my eight-year-old, Nicolas:

Pepperoni Pizza Deluxe Lean Pocket
7 grams of fat, 25 percent Daily Value for calcium, and 30 percent Daily Value for iron

Turkey Ham and Cheese Lean Pocket
11 grams of fat, 20 percent Daily Value for calcium, and 15 percent for iron

Homemade Happy Meals

Your child doesn't have to know that the chicken nuggets or fish sticks you made for her special meal are actually healthy! Bake her some French fries, layer yogurt with frozen strawberries and blueberries in a pretty glass, and she won't even miss the drive thru! Keep these brands on hand:

• Butterball Chicken Requests: battered and baked chicken patties
• Banquet Fat-Free Breast Tenders: compare these with their full-fat counterpart, which has 19 grams of fat per serving!
• VanDeKamps Crisp and Healthy Fish: fast for the whole family
• Morningstar Farms Chik Nuggets, Chik Patties, and Buffalo Wings: meatless

Meal in a Bag

This new breed of fast food is similar to a home-cooked meal, but much quicker. You can create a balanced meal in 10 to 15 minutes—what more could you ask? Some meals in a bag come complete with chicken or meat; others require you to add meat.
Look for: fewer than 10 grams of fat per cup, 25 percent Daily Value for vitamins C

and/or A, and at least 2 grams of fiber. Add a fresh fruit and milk for a complete meal.

Thumbs-Up Choices/Complete Meals:
- Marie Callender's Chicken Teriyaki
- Lean Cuisine Skillet Sensations: Beef Fajita or Herb Chicken and Roasted Potatoes
- Stouffer's Skillet Sensations: Broccoli and Beef or Roasted Turkey
- Birdseye Chicken Voilá: Garlic or Teriyaki
- Cascadian Farms Moroccan Organic Vegetarian Meal
- Aztec Organic Vegetarian Meal

For vegetarians, the last two meals listed above are a real find. They are chock-full of fiber, vitamin A, C, and iron.

Thumbs-Up Choices/Add Meat:
Green Giant Create A Meal, Pasta Accents, and FlavR Pac all have meals in a bag—all you have to do is add meat to a vegetable, a vegetable-grain, or a pasta mixture. To make your job even easier, Tyson Foods now has small boxes of precooked cubes or strips of chicken and beef. In addition, Morningstar Farms Recipe Crumbles—tiny pieces of textured vegetable protein—can take the place of hamburger in recipes.

I recently tried the Green Giant Sweet and Sour Stir Fry, and it was excellent! Just one word of advice—if your family is big on vegetables, you may want to buy two bags of the stir-fry so you can have plenty! There are too many good choices to mention. Most are fat-free or low in fat, except for the ones with creamy sauces. Do watch the sodium, though.

Frozen and Refrigerated Pastas

Frozen and refrigerated pastas, especially those containing cheese—like ravioli and tortellini—also offer a quick meal. The beauty of pasta is that children can eat it plain, while adults can have a more sophisticated meal. For example, you can serve pasta plain, with butter, or with one of the following toppings:
- Marinara sauce
- Fat-free sour cream mixed with marinara sauce
- Salsa
- Sautéed mushrooms or other vegetables
- Pesto sauce, plain or mixed with fat-free sour cream

Look for: 6 or fewer grams of fat, at least 2 grams of fiber, and 15 percent Daily Value for calcium. Add tomato sauce, garlic bread, and fresh fruit for a complete meal.

Thumbs-Up Choices:
All these have 6 or fewer grams of fat and 2 or more grams of fiber:
- Celentano Mini Cheese Ravioli
- Contadina Cheese Tortellini
- Contadina Garden Vegetable Tortellini
- Gina Italian Village Meat Tortellini
- Rosetto Chicken Ravioli

Have Time to Cook, But Don't Feel Like Cooking?

Many family-sized entrées are now available at the grocery store and at warehouse stores like Sam's Club. Although these meals are not exactly fast food, they still save significant amounts of prep time since all you have to do is put them in the oven!

Look for: 16 or fewer grams of fat, 3 grams of fiber, 25 percent Daily Value for calcium, and 25 percent Daily Value for vitamin A and/or C. Add a spinach salad, roll, and fruit sorbet for a balanced meal.

Thumbs-Up Choices:

Ortega Chicken Fajita Bake
An excellent choice, with 11 grams of fat and 45 percent of Daily Value for vitamin C. The only disadvantage is 920 milligrams of sodium per serving.

Prego Seven Cheese Lasagna
A great choice, with 16 grams of fat and 40 percent of Daily Value for calcium.

Prego Fettucini Florentine
A good choice, with 13 gams of fat and 25 percent of Daily Value for calcium.

Amy's Organic Vegetable Lasagna
A good bet, with 8 grams of fat, 4 grams of fiber, 50 percent of Daily Value for vitamin A, 25 percent for vitamin C, 15 percent calcium, and 10 percent iron.

Also available: Black Bean and Vegetable Enchiladas and Cheese Enchiladas

Many grocery stores are expanding their deli departments to provide ready-to-heat meals for families. For example: Albertson's has weekly Quick Fixin' Ideas, which include fairly healthy meals like Chicken Fajitas with Rice and Beans, Chicken Teriyaki with Rice, Pot Roast with Mashed Potatoes, and Stuffed Shells. A family of four can eat for about 10 dollars–cheaper than going out and more nutritious than fast food.

The nice thing is, if you like fajitas and your spouse likes pot roast, you can both be happy. Albertson's and other stores also carry marinated, seasoned, or stuffed chicken, fish, or meat. All you have to do is pop it in a pan or on a grill. Many delis also often have a large selection of salads. Mallards has a line of fresh, ready-to-eat-in-seven-minutes choices– found in the meat department.

Burgers and Hot Dogs

My favorite ultimate fast food is a Gardenburger, popped in the toaster and served on a bun with all the fixings. When we tried the Hamburger Style meatless burger from Garden Chef, my kids exclaimed, "Better than McDonald's!" Enough said. Green Giant, Morningstar Farms, and Fantastic Foods are other companies that make vegetarian burgers. You can find Gardenburgers at most grocery stores, including the national chains A & P, Albertson's, Costco, Cub Foods, Giant, Kroger, Safeway, Sam's Club, and Smith's, plus at natural-food stores.

Look for: 6 or fewer grams of fat and at least 3 grams of fiber per serving.

Thumbs-Up Choice:

Garden Chef Gardenburger

A great choice, with 0 fat, 3 grams of fiber, and 10 percent of Daily Value for calcium and iron. Comes in different flavors, but young kids will probably prefer the Original flavor and Hamburger Style the best.

Hot dogs, nutritionally speaking, are among the worst foods for kids. But does that affect kids' cravings for them? No way! The best option is not to buy hot dogs very often and to buy the low-fat, fat-free, or vegetarian variety. Vegetarian hot dogs are made mostly of soy, have no nitrates, and are fat-free. Some good examples: Lightlife Wonderdogs and Smartdogs, Yves Tofu Weiners, Veggie Chili Dogs, and Jumbo Veggie Dogs. You can now find vegetarian hot dogs at most grocery stores. Morningstar Farms Meat Free Corn Dogs are a favorite with my kids, who don't even know they're not eating meat!

Hot dogs made with meat have plenty of sodium and nitrates—good reasons to keep them to a minimum. The following brands feature fat-free or low-fat hot dogs: Ball Park, Healthy Choice, Hormel, and Oscar Mayer. If you buy regular hot dogs or choose to buy chicken or turkey dogs instead, read the label carefully. Some brands of chicken and turkey dogs have more fat than beef hot dogs!

Look for: 10 or fewer grams of fat per dog. For both burgers and hot dogs, add low-fat cheese and serve with broccoli florets and an orange for a balanced meal.

Pot Pies

Baby boomers may feel a hint of nostalgia when they spot the Chicken Pot Pies, still there after all these years. Look, but don't touch! Pot pies are one of the worst of frozen convenience foods; they contain from 21 to 37 grams of fat and 700 to 1000 milligrams of sodium. However, compared to a fast-food meal, even pot pies probably come out ahead.

Look for: pot pies with the least fat and the most vitamins.

Thumbs-Up Choice:

Banquet Vegetable Cheese Pot Pie with Broccoli

17 grams of fat, 25 percent Daily Value for vitamin A, and 8 percent Daily Value for calcium

Canned Meals for Kids

Once you finished the frozen food and the cereal aisle, you thought you were safe. But no . . . the canned food aisle also has foods vying for your child's attention! Spaghetti O's are still popular with kids, as are newcomers to the can club: Dinosaurs, Spiderman, ABCs, Where's Waldo, Sonic, and Garfield Pasta. The good news: These offer a quick meal that your kid will eat, and they are generally low in fat and high in vitamins. The bad news: They are generally high in sodium.

Look for: 11 or fewer grams of fat, 15 percent Daily Value for iron, and 10 percent Daily Value for Vitamin A. Serve with milk, fruit, and carrot salad for a complete meal.

Macaroni and Cheese

What childhood would be complete without macaroni and cheese? This must be a comfort food for kids, because I have never seen a kid who didn't like it! Not only can you find plain mac-and-cheese dinners, you can also find Bugs Bunny, Numbers, Super Heroes, and Rug Rats shapes! Of course, the specialty mac-and-cheese meals come in smaller boxes for the same price!

Nutritionally speaking, this meal will be high in fat if you prepare it according to package instructions. By adjusting the preparation method, you can cut the fat by two-thirds. In our family, we leave out the margarine, add a bit more milk, and then add either Light Velveeta Cheese or Light American Cheese to beef up the calcium.

Lunch in a Box

Yet another shortcut for parents, Lunchables and similar foods are heavy on the sodium and fat and provide next to nothing in the fruit and vegetable department. For example, a Lunchable Fun Pack with Bologna has 1,210 milligrams of sodium and 27 grams of fat; though it does have 25 percent of the Daily Value for calcium, your child gets that calcium at great nutritional expense! Avoid sending Lunchables (and similar products) that include hot dogs in your child's lunch unless the hot dogs will be reheated before eating. Many prepackaged lunches come with lean deli meat such as ham or turkey, cheese, crackers, a 10-percent juice drink, and sometimes a small Nestlé's Crunch bar or Jell-O pudding.

Look for: products with the least fat and sodium. Send fresh fruit along with it.

Thumbs-Up Choice:
Lunchables Cheese Pizza
15 grams of fat, 40 percent Daily Value for calcium, and 25 percent Daily Value for vitamins A and C

Tuna lunch in a box is another great option. Try the following:
- Bumble Bee Tuna Salad (15 grams fat or fat-free).
- Star Kist Ready Mixed Tuna Salad (6 grams of fat)
- Star Kist Charlie's Tuna Salad Lunch Kit. This is great for the kid who likes to have it his way. It includes a portion of tuna, a packet of low-fat mayonnaise, a packet of relish, and crackers. Your child can create his own tuna salad, and all you need to provide is something to drink and perhaps a yogurt or fresh fruit.

Make Your Own "Lunchbagables"

It's true that when seconds count, it's a blessing to be able to open the fridge, pull out a box, and slip it in your child's backpack. But with just a few more seconds, you could put together a healthier alternative that your child will also enjoy!

Following are some of the lunches I sometimes send with my four-year-old, who doesn't always like sandwiches. (They are also great options if you are out of bread!)

- 1 or 2 sticks of string cheese, 6 to 8 whole-wheat crackers, apple slices, and a juice box
- Graham cracker and peanut butter sandwiches, 1 banana, Kozy Shack Rice Pudding, and a juice box
- 1 Turkey Gobbler (a fat-free turkey link, individually wrapped), 1 stick of string cheese, 6 whole-grain crackers, 1 Del Monte Fruit Cup Mixed Fruit, and a juice box
- 2 slices low-fat American cheese (cut into triangles), 1 to 2 ounces baked tortilla chips, Seneca 100% Natural Applesauce cup, animal crackers to dip, and a juice box

Thumbs-Up Choices for Lunchbagables:

- Fresh fruit like apples, grapes, and oranges, which pack well
- Kozy Shack Puddings and Rice Pudding (These are just like Mom used to make when she had time: They contain only basic ingredients like milk, eggs, and sugar, with no artificial colors or preservatives.)
- Del Monte Fruit Naturals Mixed Fruit or Pineapple Tidbits
- Libby's Natural Lite Diced Peaches or Pears in fruit juice
- Seneca 100% Natural Applesauce (no sugar added)
- Mott's Unsweetened Applesauce
- Yogurt (Vanilla has the least sugar.)
- Yoplait Go-Gurt: yogurt-in-a-tube that's easy to eat and can be frozen

Note: Be sure to include an ice pack to keep perishables cold.

Ramen Noodles

Budget food extraordinaire, these quick-cooking noodles in a package are liked by kids of all ages. However, they are very high in sodium and have more fat than regular pasta because they are cooked in oil before they are packaged. Other soups would be healthier, but you can improve on ramen noodles by adding some finely chopped vegetables and some leftover chicken.

Meal Helpers

Hamburger Helper Chicken and Tuna Helper are generally high in sodium and low in fiber. And even though they might have specks of dehydrated vegetables, you couldn't scrape together even one serving! Tuna Helper may be a great way to get your family to eat more fish; however, if your kids eat vegetables, frozen meals-in-a-bag are better choices. If meal helpers are the only thing that works for your family, make sure to serve a vegetable or salad and fruit and milk along with it.

Look for: meal helpers with the least fat and sodium.

▼

Other Quick Meal Ideas

With frozen food, prepared salads, and vegetables, you don't need to rely on convenience foods all the time for a quick meal.

Try the following suggestions:

- *Pizza:* Quick pizza can be made with English muffins, French bread, pita bread, or even tortillas. Simply have pizza or pasta sauce and shredded mozzarella cheese on hand.
- *Pasta:* Dry pasta generally cooks in eight to ten minutes. During the last few minutes, toss in some frozen vegetables and ham. Drain and top with spiced, crushed tomatoes or pesto sauce.
- *Burritos:* All you need are tortillas, canned beans, and cheese. You can also add salsa or enchilada sauce, lettuce, tomatoes, and low-fat sour cream.
- *Chicken:* Chicken breasts cook quickly. Sauté a little onion and garlic in a pan. Add the chicken and cook for about ten to fifteen minutes, adding a spoon of water every so often to keep the chicken moist. Remove the chicken and make a sauce using pan juices by adding one of the following: fat-free sour cream, marinara sauce, apricot jam and soy sauce, or pesto sauce mixed with fat-free sour cream.
- *Bean soup:* For an easy black bean soup, all you need are a can of black beans and some chicken broth. Purée both in the blender and serve with grated Monterey Jack cheese and tortilla strips.
- *Pasta Salad Niçoise:* Sounds fancy, but all this tasty salad needs is some leftover pasta, tuna, olives, boiled eggs, and leftover green beans. Serve over a bed of lettuce.

▼

The Pantry Necessities

Keep the foods below on hand for meals in a flash.

In Your Cupboard:
- Bulgur (cracked wheat)
- Canned beans: black, kidney, pinto, garbanzo (chickpeas)
- Canned tuna, chicken, salmon
- Contadina Pasta Ready Tomatoes
- Marinara sauce
- Pasta
- Salsa

In Your Refrigerator:
- Chopped garlic
- Eggs
- Fat-free sour cream
- Pesto sauce
- Shredded cheese
- Tortillas

In Your Freezer:
- Bread dough
- Chicken breasts
- Crabmeat
- Frozen or fresh tortellini or ravioli
- Gardenburgers
- Meal-in-a-bag dinners
- Vegetable mixes

▼

Meal-in-a-Flash Menus

Gardenburger on whole-wheat bun
Fresh fruit salad
Yogurt

Cheese ravioli with butter
Steamed baby carrots
Fresh blueberries over pound cake

Scrambled eggs with salsa on corn tortillas
  with cheese
Grapefruit halves

Pasta salad with canned chicken, artichoke
  hearts, and tomatoes
Toasted French bread
Peaches

Sloppy Joe sandwich filling made with
  Green Giant Harvest Burger for Recipes
Whole-grain bun
Shredded coleslaw mix with ranch dressing
Fresh mango half

VanDeKamp's Crisp and Healthy Fish
Canned corn
Tomato slices

Green Giant Meal Starters Sweet and Sour
  with chicken
Rice or bulgur
Vanilla pudding with banana slices

Tossed salad
Macaroni and cheese with canned salmon
Mixed vegetables
Pineapple chunks

French bread pizza
Raw sugar snap peas
Fresh apple with peanut butter

Grilled ham and cheese sandwich
Carrot and raisin salad
Yogurt and strawberry parfait

Beans and franks (soy franks, if preferred)
Raw carrots and broccoli
Cornbread

Lentil soup
Avocado and tomato salad
Whole-wheat rolls
Pear smoothie

Pasta tossed with Pasta Ready Tomatoes,
  Monterey Jack cheese, and pine nuts
Spinach salad with mandarin oranges
Garlic toast
Frozen grapes

Tostadas with beans, salsa, lettuce, and
  cheese
Corn with red and green bell pepper
Applesauce and sugar cookie

Romaine lettuce salad with strawberries,
  chicken, and honey-mustard dressing
Bran muffins
Frozen yogurt with peaches

Macaroni and cheese
Vegetable tray with ranch dip
Microwave-baked apple with cinnamon
  sugar

References

Chapter 2

1. Ogden, C.L. et al. Prevalence of overweight among preschool children in the United States, 1971-1994. *Pediatrics*. 1997 April; 99(4): E1.

2. Update: prevalence of overweight among children, adolescents and adults–United States, 1988-1998. *MMWR Weekly*. 1997 March 7; 46(9): 199–202.

3. Dietz, W.H. Periods of risk in childhood for the development of adult obesity–what do we need to learn? *Journal of Nutrition*. 1997 September; 127(9): 1884s–1886s.

4. Seidman, D.S. et al. A longitudinal study of birth weight and being overweight in late adolescence. *American Journal Dis Child*. 1991; 145: 782–785.

5. Whitaker, R.C. et al. Early adiposity rebound and the risk of adult obesity. *Pediatrics*. 1998 March; 101(3): E5.

6. Deheeger, et al. Individual patterns of food intake in development in children: a 10 months to 8 years of age follow-up study of nutrition and growth. *Physiological Behavior*. 1996 March; 59(3): 403–407.

7. Johnson, S.L. and Birch, L.L. Parents' and children's adiposity and eating style. *Pediatrics*. 1994; 94: 653-661.

8. Van Lenthe et al. Rapid maturating in adolescence results in greater obesity in adulthood: the Amsterdam Growth and Health Study. *American Journal of Clinical Nutrition*. 1996; 64: 18–24.

9. Lloyd, T. et al. Fruit consumption, fitness, and cardiovascular health in female adolescents: the Penn State Young Women's Health Study. *American Journal of Clinical Nutrition*. 1998 April; 67(4): 624–630.

10. Johnson, S.L. et al. Conditioned preferences: young children prefer flavors associated with high dietary fat. *Physiological Behavior*. 1991 December; 50(6): 1245-1251.

11. Fisher, J.O. and Birch, L.L. Fat preferences and fat consumption of 3–5 year old children are related to parental adiposity. *Journal of the American Dietetic Association*. 1995 July; 95(7): 759–764.

Ricketts, C.D. Fat preferences, dietary fat intake and body composition in children. *European Journal of Clinical Nutrition*. 1997 November; 51: 778–81.

12. Tucker, L.A. Body fat percentage of children varies according to their diet composition. *Journal of The American Dietetic Association*. 1997 September; 97(9): 981–986.

13. Maffeis, C. et al. Influence of diet, physical activity and parents' obesity on children's adiposity: a four year longitudinal study. *International Journal of Obesity and Related Metabolic Disorders*. 1998 August; (8): 758–764.

14. AHA Scientific Position, Exercise and Children. American Heart Association. 1998.

15. AHA Scientific Position, Exercise and Children. American Heart Association. 1998.

16. Serdula, M.K. et al. Do obese children become obese adults? A review of the literature. *Preventive Medicine*. 1993 March; 22(2): 167–177.

17. Satter, Ellyn. Childhood obesity demands new approaches. *Obesity and Health*. 1991 May/June: 42–43.

18. Kleiner, S.M. Water: an essential but overlooked nutrient. *Journal of the American Dietetic Association*. 1999; 99: 200–206.

19. Berenson, G.S. et al. Atherosclerosis: a nutritional disease of childhood. *American Journal of Cardiology*. 1998 November 26; 82(10B): 22T–29T.

20. Berenson, G.S. et al. Association between multiple cardiovascular risk factors and atherosclerosis in children and young adults. The Bogalusa Heart Study. *New England Journal of Medicine;* 1998 June 4; 338(23): 1650–1656.

21. Lapinleimu, H. et al. Prospective randomized trial in 1062 infants of diet low in saturated fat and cholesterol. *Lancet*. 1995; 345(8948): 471–476.
Nicklas, T.A. et al. Impact of fat reduction on micronutrient density of children's diets: the CATCH study. *Preventive Medicine*. 1996 July; 25(4): 478–485. *Archives of Pediatric and Adolescent Medicine*. 1997 February; 151(2): 181–188.

Lagstrom, H. Nutrient intakes by young children in a prospective randomized trial of a low-saturated fat, low-cholesterol diet. The STRIP Baby Project. Special Turku Coronary Risk Factor Intervention Project for Babies. *Archives of Pediatric and Adolescent Medicine*. 1997 February; 151(2): 181–188.
Boulton, T.J. and Magareyu, A.M. Effects of differences in dietary fat on growth, energy and nutrient intake from infancy to eight years of age. *Acta Paediatrica*. 1995 February; 84(2): 146–150.

22. Cholesterol in Children; Healthy Eating Is a Family Affair, Parents' Guide. National Institutes of Health, National Heart, Lung, and Blood Institute, NIH publication no. 92-3099. November 1992.

23. AHA Scientific Position, Dietary Guidelines for Children. American Heart Association. 1998.

24. Geleijnse, J.M. Long-term effects of neonatal sodium restriction on blood pressure. *Hypertension*. 1997 April; 29(4): 913–917.

25. Simons-Morton, D.G. Diet and blood pressure in children and adolescents. *Pediatric Nephrology*. 1997 April; 11(2): 244–249.

26. Holliday, M.A. *Pediatric Nephrology*. 1995 October; 9(5): 663–666.

27. Simons-Morton, D.G. et al. Nutrient intake and blood pressure in the dietary intervention study in children. *Hypertension*. 1997 April; 29(4): 930–936.

28. Food, Nutrition, and the Prevention of Cancer: A Global Perspective, American Institute for Cancer Research.

29. Pillow, P.C. et al. Case-control assessment of diet and lung cancer risk in African Americans and Mexican Americans. *Nutrition and Cancer.* 1997; 29(2): 169–173.

De Stefani, E. Influences of fat, cholesterol, and calcium on colorectal cancer. *Nutrition and Cancer.* 1997; 29(1): 83–89.

30. Rose, D.P. Dietary fatty acids and prevention of hormone-responsive cancer. *Proceedings. Society for Experimental Biology Medicine.* 1997 November; 2169(2): 224–233.

Gogos, C.A. Dietary omega-3 fatty acids plus vitamin E restore immunodeficiency and prolong survival for severely ill patients with generalized malignancy: a randomized control trial. *Cancer.* 1998 January 15; 82(2): 395–402.

31. Trichopoulos, D. et al. What causes cancer? *Scientific American.* 1996 September.

32. Influences of fat, cholesterol, and calcium on colorectal cancer. De Stefani, E. *Nutrition and Cancer.* 1997; 29(1): 83–89.

33. Steinmetz, K.A. et al. Vegetables, fruits, and cancer. II. Mechanisms. *Cancer Causes and Control.* 1991; 2: 427–442.

34. La Vecchia, C. Fruits and vegetables and human cancer. *European Journal of Cancer Prevention.* 1998 February; 7(1): 3–8.

Block, G. et al. Fruits, vegetables, and cancer prevention: a review of the epidemiological evidence. *Nutrition and Cancer.* 1992; 18(1): 1–29.

35. Thompson, F.E. and Dennison, B.A. Dietary sources of fats and cholesterol in U.S. children aged 2 through 5 years. *American Journal of Public Health.* 1994 May; 84(5): 799–806.

Chapter 3
1. Gibson, E.L. et al. Fruit and vegetable consumption, nutritional knowledge and beliefs in mothers and children. *Appetite.* 1998 October; 31(2): 205–28.

2. Anderson, J.W. et al. Health benefits and practical aspects of high-fiber diets. *American Journal of Clinical Nutrition.* 1994 May.

3. Matkovic, V. and Ilich, J.Z. Calcium requirements for growth: are current recommendations adequate? *Nutrition Reviews.* 1993; 51(6): 171.

4. Kant, A.K. and Schatzkin, A. Consumption of energy-dense, nutrient-poor foods by the U.S. population: effect on nutrient profiles. *Journal of the American College of Nutrition.* 1994 June; 13(3): 285–291.

Chapter 4
1. Trahms, C. and Pipes, Peggy. *Nutrition in Infancy and Childhood,* 6th edition. WCB-McGraw Hill: 1997; 10–11.

2. Dennison, B.A. et al. Excess juice consumption by preschool-aged children is associated with short stature and obesity. *Pediatrics.* 1997 January; 99(1): 15–22.

3. See note 2 above.

4. Dennison, B.A. Fruit juice consumption by infants and children: a review. *Journal of the American College of Nutrition*. 1996 October; 15(5 Suppl): 4s–11s.

5. Smith, M.M. and Lifshitz, F. Excess fruit juice consumption as a contributing factor in nonorganic failure to thrive. *Pediatrics*. March; 93(3): 438–443.

6. Somer, E. *The Essential Guide to Vitamins and Minerals*. HarperCollins, New York: 1992; 242.

7. Favier, A.E. Hormonal effects of zinc on growth in children. *Biological Trace Element Research*. 1992 January; 32: 383–398.

8. Primary school teachers' beliefs and advice to parents concerning sugar consumption and activity in children. *Psychological Reports*. 1993 February; 72(1): 47–55.

9. Krummel, D.A. et al. Hyperactivity: is candy causal? *Critical Reviews in Food Science and Nutrition*. 1996 January; 36(1–2): 31–47.

10. Wolraich, M.L. et al. The effect of sugar on behavior or cognition in children. A meta-analysis. *Journal of the American Medical Association*. 1995 November 22; 274(20): 1617–1621.

11. Hoover, D.W. and Milich, R. Effects of sugar ingestion expectancies on mother-child interactions. *Journal of Abnormal Child Psychology*. 1994 August; 22(4): 501–515.

12. Mahan, L.K. et al. Sugar "allergy" and children's behavior. *Annals of Allergy*. 1988 December; 61(6): 453–458.

13. Rapoport, J.L., et al. Behavioral effects of caffeine in children. Relationship between dietary choice and effects of caffeine challenge. *Archives of General Psychiatry*. 1984; 41: 1073.

14. Marlowe, M. et al. Main and interaction effects of metallic toxins on classroom behavior. *Journal of Abnormal Child Psychology*. 1985 June; 13(2): 185–198.

15. Somer, E. *The Essential Guide to Vitamins and Minerals*. HarperCollins, New York: 1992.

16. Stare, F.J. et al. Diet and hyperactivity: is there a relationship. *Pediatrics*. 1980 October; 66(4): 521–525.

17. Shaywitz, B.A. et al. Aspartame, behavior, and cognitive function in children with attention deficit disorder. *Pediatrics*. 1994 January; 93(1): 70–75.

18. Trahms, C. and Pipes, P. *Nutrition in Infancy and Childhood,* 6th edition. WCB-McGraw-Hill: 1997; 296.

19. Birch, L.L. et al. Effects of a nonenergy fat substitute on children's energy and macronutrient intake. *American Journal of Clinical Nutrition*. 1993 September; 58(3): 326–333.

Chapter 5

1. Tariq, S.M. et al. Cohort study of peanut and tree nut sensitization by age of four years. *British Medical Journal.* 1996 August 31; 13(7056): 514–517.

2. Chandra, R.D. Five-year follow-up of high-risk infants with family history of allergy who were exclusively breast-fed or fed partial whey hydrolysate, soy, and conventional cow's milk formulas. *Journal of Pediatric Gastroenterology and Nutrition.* 1997 April; 24(4): 442–446.

3. Herrmann, D.E. Prospective study of the atopy preventive effect of maternal avoidance of milk and eggs during pregnancy and lactation. *European Journal of Pediatrics.* 1996 September; 155(9): 770–774.

4. The American Dietetic Association, Koerner, C.B. and Munoz-Furlong, A. *Food Allergies.* John Wiley and Sons, New York: 1998; 23.

5. Marini, A. et al. Effects of a dietary and environmental prevention programme on the incidence of allergic symptoms in high atopic risk infants: three years' follow-up. *Acta Paediatrica Supplement.* 1996 May; 414: 1–21.

Chapter 6

1. American Academy of Pediatrics, Committee on Nutrition. Nutritional aspects of vegetarian diets. *Pediatric Nutrition Handbook,* 3rd edition. American Academy of Pediatrics, Elk Grove Village, Illinois: 1993; 302–313.

2. Messina, Mark and Virginia. *The Dietitian's Guide to Vegetarian Diets.* Aspen Publishers, Gaithersburg, Maryland: 1996; 127.

3. Messina, Mark and Virginia. *The Dietitian's Guide to Vegetarian Diets.* Aspen Publishers, Gaithersburg, Maryland: 1996; 281.

4. Messina, Mark and Virginia. *The Dietitian's Guide to Vegetarian Diets.* Aspen Publishers, Gaithersburg, Maryland: 1996; 277.

5. National Cholesterol Education Program. Highlights of the report of the Expert Panel on Blood Cholesterol Levels in Children and Adolescents. *Pediatrics.* 1992; 89: 495–500.

6. Position of the American Dietetic Association: Vegetarian Diets. *Journal of the American Dietetic Association.* 1996 September.

Chapter 7

1. Kaste, L.M. et al. Coronal caries in the primary and permanent dentition of children and adolescents 1–17 years of age: United States, 1988–1991. *Journal of Dental Research.* 1996; 75: 631.

2. Herod, E.L. The effect of cheese on dental caries: a review of the literature. *Australian Dental Journal.* 1991 April; 36(2): 120–125.
    Jensen, M.E. and Weferl, J.S. Effects of processed cheese on human plaque pH and demineralization and remineralization. *American Journal of Dentistry.* 1990 October; 3(5): 217–223.

3. Petti, S. et al. The effect of milk and sucrose consumption on caries in 6–11 year old Italian school children. *European Journal of Epidemiology*. 1997 September; 13(6): 659–664.

4. Chewing gum and dental health. Literature review. *Revue Belge de Medecine Dentaire*. 1992; 47(3): 67–92.

Bowen, W.H. Food components and caries. *Advanced Dental Research*. July; 8(2): 215–220.

Chapter 8

1. Consumers Union. Worst first: high risk insecticide uses, children's foods and safer alternatives. 1998 September.

2. Consumers Union. Worst first: high risk insecticide uses, children's foods and safer alternatives. 1998 September; chapter 2.

3. Consumers Union. Worst first: high risk insecticide uses, children's foods and safer alternatives. 1998 September; chapter 2.

4. Consumers Union. Do you know what you're eating? An analysis of US government data on pesticide residues in food. 1999 February.

5. Federal Trade Commission. FTC freezes ad claims for thawing trays; pulls the plug on ad claims for thermo-electric coolers. Press Release. 1996 December 9.

6. Hinman, Al and Josephson, K.L. et al. What's the most unsanitary spot in your house? CNN Interactive. 1996 March 5.

Characterization and quantification of bacterial pathogens and indicator organisms in household kitchens with and without the use of a disinfectant cleaner. *Applied Microbiology*. 1997 December; 83(6): 737–750.

7. Food and Drug Administration. On the home front. *FDA Consumer*. 1997 November/December.

University of Nebraska Cooperative Extension in Lancaster County. *FoodTalk E-mail Newsletter*. (http://ianrwww.unl.edu/ianr/lanco/family/FoodTalk.htm).

Doyle, Michael. Telephone interview.

8. U.S. Department of Agriculture, Food Safety and Inspection Service. Focus on cutting board safety. 1997 September.

Food and Drug Administration. On the home front. *FDA Consumer*. 1997 November/December.

9. Food and Drug Administration, Greeley, Ann. *FDA Consumer*. 1997 July/August: 27–28.

10. Lead in water: pipe nightmares? *Consumer Reports Magazine*. 1995 July: 463.

11. Franklin, D. Lead: Still poison after all these years. *Hippocrates*. 1991 September: 33.

Chapter 9

1. Koletzko, S. et al. Role of infant feeding practices in development of Crohn's disease in childhood. *British Medical Journal*. 1989; 298: 1617–1618.

Virtanen, S.M. et al. Infant feeding in Finnish children less than 7 years of age with newly diagnosed IDDM. Childhood Diabetes in Finland Study Group. *Diabetes Care*. 1991; 14: 415–417.

Davis, M.K. et al. Infant feeding in childhood cancer. *Lancet.* 1988; 2(8607): 365–368.

2. Kalkwarf, H.J. and Specker, B.L. Bone mineral loss during lactation and recovery after weaning. *Obstetrics and Gynecology.* 1995; 86: 26–32.

Kalkwarf, H.J. et al. Intestinal calcium absorption of women during lactation and after weaning. *American Journal of Clinical Nutrition.* 1996; 63(4): 526–531.

Newcomb, P.A. et al. Lactation and a reduced risk of premenopausal cancer. *New England Journal of Medicine.* 1994; 330(2): 81–87.

Whittemore, A.S. Characteristics relating to ovarian cancer risk: implications for prevention and detection. *Gynecologic Oncology.* 1994; (3, Pt. 2): S15–S19.

3. Powers, N.G. and Slusser, W. Breastfeeding update 2: clinical lactation management. *Pediatric Review.* 1997; 18(5): 147–161.

4. Gale, C.R. and Martyn, C.N. Breastfeeding, dummy use, and adult intelligence. *Lancet.* 1996 April 20; 347(9008): 1072–1075.

5. Pinyerd, B.J. Strategies for controlling the infant with colic: fact or fiction? *Journal of Pediatric Nursing.* 1992 December; 7(6): 403–410.

6. See note 5 above.

7. Lust, K.D. et al. Maternal intake of cruciferous vegetables and other foods and colic symptoms in exclusively breast fed infants.

Journal of the American Dietetic Association. 1996; 1: 46–48.

8. Chandra, R.K. Five-year followup of high risk infants with family history of allergy who were exclusively breast-fed or fed partial whey hydrolysate soy, and conventional cow's milk formulas. *Journal of Pediatric Gastroenterology and Nutrition.* 1997 April; 24(4): 380–388.

Halken, S. et al. The effect of hypoallergenic formulas in infants at risk of allergic disease. *European Journal of Clinical Nutrition.* 1995 September; 49 Suppl 1: S77–S83.

9. Cohen, R. et al. Comparison of maternal absenteeism and infant illness rates among breastfeeding and formula-feeding women in two corporations. *American Journal of Health Promotion.* 1995; 10(2): 148–153.

Jones, E.G. and Matheny, R.J. Relationship between infant feeding and exclusion rate from child care because of illness. *Journal of the American Dietetic Association.* 1993; 93(9): 809–811.

10. Slusser, W. and Powers, N.G. Breastfeeding update 1: immunology, nutrition, and advocacy. *Pediatric Review.* 1997; 18(4): 111–119.

11. Bruce, R.C. and Kliegman, R.M. Hyponatremic seizures secondary to oral water intoxication in infancy: association with commercial bottled drinking water. *Pediatrics.* 1997 December; 100: 6.

12. Bakerbrink, J.A. et al. Multiple organ failure after ingestion of pennyroyal oil

from herbal tea in two infants. *Pediatrics.* 1996 November; 98(5): 944–947.

Chapter 10
1. American Academy of Pediatrics Work Group on Breastfeeding. Breastfeeding and the use of human milk. *Pediatrics.* December 1997; 100(6): 1035–1039.

Chapter 11
1. American Dietetic Association, Nutrition standards in child-care programs: technical support paper. *Journal of the American Dietetic Association.* 1994 March; 94(3): 324–328.

Chapter 12
1. Consumers Union. Is your kid failing lunch? *Consumer Reports Magazine.* 1998 September.

Chapter 15
1. Bonn, D. Fresh fruit improves lung funcion. *Lancet.* 1997 July 12; 350(9071).

Chapter 17
1. Food Survey Research Group, U.S. Department of Agriculture, Agricultural Research Service. 1996 continuing survey of food intakes by individuals.

Recommended Resources

If you would like more information on health or nutrition, the resources below should be helpful.

General Nutrition

The American Dietetic Association. To find a registered dietitian in your area: www.eatright.org. To listen to a recorded message: 800-366-1655. To talk to a registered dietitian: 900-CALL-AN-RD.

Duyff, Roberta Larson, M.S., R.D., C.F.C.S. *The American Dietetic Association's Complete Food and Nutrition Guide.* John Wiley and Sons, 1996.

Newsletters

Consumer Reports on Health. Phone: 800-234-2188.

Environmental Nutrition. Phone: 800-829-5384.

FDA Consumer. Mail orders: Superintendent of Documents, P.O. Box 371954, Pittsburgh, PA 15250-7954. Phone orders: 202-512-1800. Fax orders: 202-512-2250. Website: ww.fda.gov/fdac/default.htm.

Mayo Clinic Health Letter. Phone: 800-333-9037.

Tufts University Health and Nutrition Letter. Phone: 800-274-7581.

University of California at Berkeley Wellness Letter. Phone: 800-829-9080.

Government Organizations

Environmental Protection Agency. Website: www.epa.gov.

Food and Drug Administration (FDA).

Center for Food Safety and Applied Nutrition. Phone: 800-332-4010. Website: www.vm.cfsan.fda.gov.

Consumer Information Office. Phone: 301-443-3170. Website: www.fda.gov.

Food Information and Seafood Hotline. Phone: 800-332-4010.

National Lead Information Center. Phone: 800-532-3394.

United States Department of Agriculture (USDA). Meat and Poultry Hotline: 800-335-4555.

National Cancer Institute. Phone: 800-4-CANCER. Website: www.cancernet.nci.nih.org.

National Institutes of Health. Phone: 301-496-4000. Website: www.nih.gov/health.

Other Health Organizations

American Cancer Society. Phone: 800-227-2345. Website: www.cancer.org.

American Heart Association. Phone: 800-242-8721. Website: www.amhrt.org.

Consumer Advocacy Groups

Center for Science in the Public Interest. Publisher of *Nutrition Action Healthletter.* Website: www.nutritionaction.org.

Consumers Union. Publisher of *Consumer Reports Magazine*. Website: www.consumersunion.org.

Breastfeeding

Gotsch, Gwen, and Judy Torgus. *The Womanly Art of Breastfeeding*. Plume, 1997.

Huggins, Kathleen. *The Nursing Mother's Companion*. Revised edition. Harvard Common Press, 1999.

Huggins, Kathleen, and Linda Ziedrich. *The Nursing Mother's Guide to Weaning*. Harvard Common Press, 1994.

La Leche League International. Phone: 800-LALECHE. Website: www.lalecheleague.org.

Neifert, Marianne, M.D. *Dr. Mom's Guide to Breastfeeding*. Plume, 1998.

Pryor, Gale. *Nursing Mother, Working Mother: The Essential Guide for Breastfeeding and Staying Close to Your Baby After You Return to Work*. Harvard Common Press, 1997.

Tamaro, Janet. *So That's What They're For! Breastfeeding Basics*. Adams Media Corporation, 1998.

Breastfeeding for Special Needs

Gotsch, Gwen. *Breastfeeding Your Premature Baby*. LaLeche League International, 1999.

Peterson, Debra Stewart. *Breastfeeding the Adopted Baby*. Corona Publishing, 1995.

Baby Care

The American Academy of Pediatrics, et al. *Caring for Your Baby and Young Child: Birth to Age 5*. Bantam Doubleday Dell, 1998.

Brazelton, T. Berry, M.D. *Touchpoints: Your Child's Emotional and Behavioral Development*. Perseus Press, 1994.

Eisenberg, Arlene, Heidi E. Murkoff, and Sandee E. Hathaway. *What to Expect the First Year*. Workman, 1996.

Leach, Penelope. *Your Baby and Child: From Birth to Age Five*. Knopf, 1997.

Sears, William and Martha. *The Baby Book: Everything You Need to Know about Your Baby from Birth to Age Two*. Little, Brown and Company, 1993.

Tracy, Amy E., Dianne I. Maroney, R.N., Judy C. Bernbaum, and Jessi Groothius. *Your Premature Baby and Child*. Berkeley Publishing Group, 1999.

Body Image/Children's Nutrition

Berman, Christine, and Jacki Fromer. *Meals Without Squeals: Child Care Feeding Guide and Cookbook*. Bull Publishing Company, 1997.

Evers, Connie L., M.S., R.D. *How to Teach Nutrition to Kids: An Integrated, Creative Approach to Nutrition Education for Children Ages 6–10*. 24 Carrot Press, 1995.

Ikeda, Joanne P., and Priscilla Naworski. *Am I Fat? Helping Young Children Accept Differences in Body Size: Suggestions for Teachers, Parents and Other Care Providers of Children to Age 10*. ETR Associates, 1993.

Jacobson, Michael F., Ph.D. *What Are We Feeding Our Kids?* Workman Publishing Company, 1994.

Kosharek, Susan M. *If Your Child Is Overweight: A Guide for Parents.* The American Dietetic Association, 1993.

Satter, Ellyn. *Child of Mine: Feeding with Love and Good Sense.* Bull Publishing Company, 1991.

Satter, Ellyn. *How to Get Your Kid to Eat . . . But Not Too Much.* Bull Publishing Company, 1987.

Sports Nutrition

Clark, Nancy. *Nancy Clark's Sports Nutrition Guidebook: 2nd Edition.* Human Kinetics, 1996.

Jennings, Debbi Sowell. *Play Hard, Eat Right: A Parents' Guide to Sports Nutrition for Children.* John Wiley and Sons, 1995.

Vegetarian Eating

The American Dietetic Association. *Being Vegetarian.* John Wiley and Sons, 1998.

Havala, Suzanne. *Simple, Lowfat and Vegetarian.* Vegetarian Resource Group, 1994.

Krizmanic, Judy. *A Teen's Guide to Going Vegetarian.* Puffin, 1994.

Melina, Vesanto, R.D., Brenda Davis, R.D., and Victoria Harrison, R.D. *Becoming Vegetarian: The Complete Guide to Adopting a Healthy Vegetarian Diet.* Book Publishing Company, 1995.

Messina, Virginia, M.P.H., R.D., and Mark, Ph.D. *The Vegetarian Way: Total Health for You and Your Family.* Crown Publishing, 1996.

Shaw, Diana. *The Essential Vegetarian Cookbook: Your Guide to the Best Foods on Earth.* Clarkson Potter, 1997.

Vegetarian Resource Group. Phone: 410-366-8343. Website: www.vrg.org.

Wasserman, Debra. *Conveniently Vegan: Turn Packaged Foods into Delicious Vegetarian Dishes.* Vegetarian Resource Group, 1997.

Wasserman, Debra, and Reed Mangels. *Simply Vegan: Quick Vegetarian Meals.* Vegetarian Resource Group, 1995.

Healthy Cooking
Kids' Cookbooks

American Heart Association. *American Heart Association Kids' Cookbook.* Times Books, 1993.

Berenstain, Stan and Jan. *The Berenstain Bears Cook-It! Breakfast for Mama.* Random House, 1996.

Brennan, Georgeanne and Ethel. *The Children's Kitchen Garden: A Book of Gardening, Cooking, and Learning.* Ten Speed Press, 1997.

Cook, Deanna F. *The Kids' Multicultural Cookbook: Food and Fun around the World.* Williamson Publishing, 1995.

Crist, Vonnie Winslow, and Debra Wasserman. *Leprechaun Cake and Other*

Tales: A Vegetarian Story-Cookbook. Vegetarian Resource Group, 1995.

Katzen, Mollie, and Ann Henderson. *Pretend Soup and Other Real Recipes: A Cookbook for Preschoolers and Up.* Tricycle Press, 1994.

Wilder, Laura Ingalls, and Amy Cotler. *My Little House Cookbook and Apron.* HarperCollins Juvenile Books, 1998.

Cooking for Kids with Special Needs
Hess, Mary Abbott. *The Art of Cooking for the Diabetic.* Signet, 1998.

Hollerorth, Hugo, and Debra Kaplan. *Everyone Likes to Eat: How Children Can Eat Most of the Foods They Enjoy and Still Take Care of Their Diabetes.* John Wiley and Sons, 1993.

National Heart, Lung, and Blood Institute Information Center. Single copy of each booklet below available free. Phone: 301-251-1222. Mail: NHLBI, P.O. Box 30105, Bethesda, MD 20824-0105.

> *Cholesterol in Children: Healthy Eating Is a Family Affair* (parent's guide)
>
> *Eating with Your Heart in Mind* (7-to-10-year-olds)
>
> *Heart Health—Your Choice* (11-to-14-year-olds)

Cooking with Food Intolerances
Hagman, Bette. *The Gluten-Free Gourmet Cooks Fast and Healthy: Wheat-Free with Less Fuss and Fat.* Henry Holt, 1997.

Munoz-Furlong, Anne, ed. *The Food Allergy News Cookbook: A Collection of Recipes from Food Allergy News and Members of the Food Allergy Network.* Chronimed Publishing, 1998.

Updike, Sheri. *The Lactose-Free Cookbook.* Warner Books, 1998.

Zukin, Jane. *Raising Your Child without Milk: Reassuring Advice and Recipes for Parents of Lactose-Intolerant and Milk-Allergic Children.* Prima Publishing, 1995.

Please see Food Allergy Chapter for more resources.

Cooking for Kids
Lansky, Vicki. *Feed Me! I'm Yours.* Meadowbrook Press, 1994.

Nissenberg, Sandra K., and Barbara N. Pearl. *Brown Bag Success: Making Healthy Lunches Your Kids Won't Trade.* John Wiley and Sons, 1997.

Cooking for the Family
Barnard, Melanie, Brooke Dojny, Mindy Hermann, R.D., and Wayne Callaway, M.D. *American Medical Association Family Cookbook: Good Food That's Good for You.* Pocket Books, 1999.

Colorado Dietetic Association. *Simply Colorado: Nutritious Recipes for Busy People.* Colorado Dietetic Association, 1992.

Cooking Light. *Cooking Light Five Star Recipes: The Best of 10 Years.* Leisure Arts, 1997.

Gandia, Madhu, M.S., R.D. *Light and Luscious Cuisine of India: Recipes and Tips for Healthy and Quick Meals*. Piquant Publishing, 1997.

Gollman, Barbara, and Kim Pierce. *The Phytopia Cookbook: A World of Plant-Centered Cuisine*. Phytopia Press, 1998.

Ponichtera, Brenda, R.D. *Quick and Healthy Recipes and Ideas: For People Who Say They Don't Have Time to Cook Healthy Meals*. Scaledown Publishing, 1991.

Ponichtera, Brenda, R.D. *Quick and Healthy Volume II: More Help for People Who Say They Don't Have Time to Cook Healthy Meals*. Scaledown Publishing, 1995.

Tribole, Evelyn, M.S., R.D. *Healthy Homestyle Cooking: 200 of Your Favorite Family Recipes—with a Fraction of the Fat*. Rodale Press, 1994.

Tribole, Evelyn, M.S., R.D. *Stealth Health: How to Sneak Nutrition Painlessly into Your Diet*. Viking Press, 1998.

Index

Recipe Index

Eating Expectantly

by Bridget Swinney, M.S., R.D.

Rated one of the "10 best parenting books of 1993" by
Child Magazine, Eating Expectantly (newly revised
and in its third edition) offers a practical and tasty
approach to prenatal nutrition. Dietitian Bridget
Swinney combines nutritional guidelines for each
trimester with 200 complete menus, 85 tasty recipes,
plus cooking and shopping tips.

Order #1135 $12.00

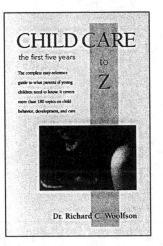

Child Care A to Z

by Dr. Richard C. Woolfson

This easy-to-understand reference contains up-to-date information on 170 topics that every parent needs to know. It is organized alphabetically to help parents find answers to questions about their child's physical, emotional, and intellectual development. Dr. Woolfson is known as the Dr. Spock of the United Kingdom, and his child-care experience is now available to American parents.

Order #1010 $11.00

How to Read Your Child Like a Book

by Lynn Weiss, Ph.D.

This is the first book that helps parents interpret their child's behavior by teaching parents what their child is thinking. Dr. Lynn Weiss, a nationally recognized expert on child development, explains 50 different behaviors of young children from birth to age 6. You will gain new insight and understanding into such behaviors as boundary testing, selfishness, and temper tantrums.

Order #1145 $8.00

Gentle Discipline

by Dawn Lighter, M.A.

Dawn Lighter has written a breakthrough book that will change the way parents think about and practice "discipline." Most parents think of discipline as something to do after children misbehave. Lighter's book provides 50 simple, effective ways to teach children good behavior—so they won't misbehave.

Order #1085 $6.00

Discipline without Shouting or Spanking

by Jerry Wyckoff, Ph.D. and Barbara C. Unell

Do you know all the theories about child rearing but still have trouble coping with some of your child's misbehavior? You'll love this book! It covers the 30 most common forms of misbehavior from whining to throwing temper tantrums. You'll find clear, practical advice on what to do, what not to do, and how to prevent each problem from recurring.

Order #1079 $6.00

Baby & Child Emergency First-Aid Handbook

Edited by Mitchell J. Einzig, M.D.

"This authoritative book is the answer to every parent's fearful question: Will I know what to do if my child has a medical emergency? Concise, easily understood, and clearly illustrated instructions in large print show and tell, step-by-step, what to do and how to do it."

—Morris Green, M.D.
  Professor of Pediatrics, Indiana School of Medicine

Order #1381 $8.00

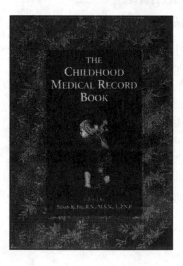

The Childhood Medical Record Book

Edited by Susan K. Fix, R.N., M.S.N., C.P.N.P.

This book offers an easy and convenient way to record the important medical facts for a child, including inoculations, illnesses and injuries, medications and their side effects, operations, allergies, and developmental milestones, such as when a child first stands alone, walks, or talks.

Order #1130 $7.00   hardcover

Baby & Child Medical Care

Edited by Mitchell J. Einzig, M.D.,
and Terril H. Hart, M.D.

Every first-aid or medical problem your child suffers from seems like an emergency. Newly revised and updated, this book provides illustrated step-by-step instructions that show you what to do and tell you when to call your doctor. Its visual approach makes this book much easier to use than Dr. Spock's.

Order #1159 $9.00

First-Year Baby Care

Edited by Paula Kelly, M.D.

One of the leading baby-care books is now totally revised with the most up-to-date medical facts and all new illustrations. Key updates include the latest newborn screening and immunization schedules, new breastfeeding information for working mothers, expanded information on daycare options, updated reference guides to common illnesses, and an update on environmental and safety tips.

Order #1119 $10.00

Practical Parenting Tips

by Vicki Lansky

Here's the #1-selling collection of helpful hints
for parents with babies and small children. It
contains 1,001 parent-tested tips for dealing with
diaper rash, nighttime crying, toilet training,
temper tantrums, and traveling with tots. It will
help parents save time, trouble, and money.

Order #1180 $8.00

Feed Me! I'm Yours

by Vicki Lansky

Now expanded, updated, and revised for the '90s!
This best-selling baby and toddler food cookbook
has sold millions of copies. It's a must-have book
for all new parents. More than 200 child-tested
recipes. Comb-bound for easy use.

"A well-written, humorous combination cookbook
and advice book that makes the job of parenting a
lot easier and enjoyable."
—*Milwaukee Journal*

Order #1109 $9.00

Moms Say the Funniest Things!

by Bruce Lansky

Lansky has collected moms' most popular lines for dealing with "emergencies" like getting the kids out of bed, cleaned, dressed, to school, to the dinner table, undressed, and back to bed. It includes all-time winners like "Put on clean underwear—you never know when you'll be in an accident" and "If God had wanted you to fool around, He would have written the 'Ten Suggestions.'" A fun gift for mom!

Order #4280 $7.00

Dads Say the Dumbest Things!

by Bruce Lansky and K. L. Jones

Lansky and Jones have collected all the greatest lines dads have ever used to get kids to stop fighting in the car, feed the pet, turn off the TV while doing homework, and get home from a date before curfew. It includes winners like "What do you want a pet for—you've got a sister" and "When I said 'feed the goldfish,' I didn't mean feed them to the cat."

Order #4220 $7.00

Grandma Knows Best, But No One Ever Listens!

by Mary McBride

McBride offers much-needed advice for new grandmas on how to

- show baby photos to anyone at any time;
- get out of babysitting or, if stuck, "housebreak" the kids before they wreck the house;

The perfect gift for Grandma. Phyllis Diller says it's "harder to put down than a new grandchild."

Order #4009 $7.00

The Preschooler's Busy Book

by Trish Kuffner

This book contains 365 activities (one for each day of the year) for three- to six-year-olds using things found around the home. It shows parents and daycare providers how to:

• Prevent boredom during even the longest stretches of bad weather, with ideas for indoor play, kitchen activities, and arts and crafts projects;

• Save money by making your own paints, playdough, craft clays, glue, paste, and other arts and crafts supplies;

• Stimulate a child's natural curiosity with fun reading, math, and science activities.

Order #6055 $9.95

Baby Play & Learn

by Penny Warner

Child development expert Penny Warner offers 160 ideas for games and activities that will provide hours of developmental learning opportunities and fun for babies. *Baby Play & Learn* includes:

• A bulleted list of skills that baby is learning through play;

• Step-by-step instructions for each game and activity;

• Illustrations demonstrating how to play many of the games.

Order #1275 $9.00

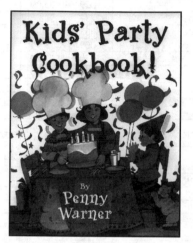

Kids' Party Cookbook!

by Penny Warner

Over 175 reduced-fat recipes with food that's fun and tasty for kids but full of nutrition to please parents. Warner has fun ideas for every meal, including mini-meals, such as Peanut Butter Dogs and Twinkle Sandwiches; creative snacks, such as Aquarium Jello and Prehistoric Bugs; nutritious drinks, such as Beetle Juice and Apple Jazz; creative desserts, such as Spaghetti Ice Cream and Doll-in-the-Cake; holiday fare, such as Candy Cane Parfaits for Christmas and Jack O'Lantern Custard for Halloween. (Ages 8 and up)

Order #2435 $12.00

Mommy's Little Helper Christmas Crafts

by Cynthia MacGregor
Illustrated by Glenn Quist

Now children 3–7 can deck the halls with crafts they made themselves (with just a little help from Mom). Each project comes with easy-to-follow, illustrated instructions for the child. There are directions for Mom, too! These 40 creative crafts are guaranteed to help kids and parents enjoy the holidays with crafts that celebrate the spirit of Christmas.

Order #2445 $8.00

Order Form

Quantity	Title	Author	Order No.	Unit Cost	Total
	Baby & Child Emergency First-Aid Handbook	Einzig, Mitchell	1381	$8.00	
	Baby & Child Medical Care	Einzig/Hart	1159	$9.00	
	Baby Play & Learn	Warner, Penny	1275	$9.00	
	Baby Name Survey Book	Lansky/Sinrod	1270	$9.00	
	Best Baby Name Book	Lansky, Bruce	1029	$5.00	
	Best Baby Shower Book	Cooke, Courtney	1239	$7.00	
	Best Baby Shower Party Games #1	Cooke, Courtney	6063	$3.95	
	Best Baby Shower Party Games #2	Cooke, Courtney	6069	$3.95	
	Child Care A to Z	Woolfson, Richard	1010	$11.00	
	Childhood Medical Record Book	Fix, Susan	1130	$7.00	
	Dads Say the Dumbest Things!	Lansky/Jones	4220	$7.00	
	Discipline without Shouting or Spanking	Wyckoff/Unell	1079	$6.00	
	Eating Expectantly	Swinney, Bridget	1135	$12.00	
	Familiarity Breeds Children	Lansky, Bruce	4015	$7.00	
	Feed Me! I'm Yours	Lansky, Vicky	1109	$9.00	
	First-Year Baby Care	Kelly, Paula	1119	$10.00	
	Gentle Discipline	Lighter, Dawn	1085	$6.00	
	Grandma Knows Best	McBride, Mary	4009	$7.00	
	How to Read Your Child Like A Book	Weiss, Lynn	1145	$8.00	
	Kids' Party Cookbook	Warner, Penny	2435	$12.00	
	Mommy's Little helper Cookbook	MacGregor, C.	2445	$8.00	
	Moms Say the Funniest Things!	Lansky, Bruce	4280	$7.00	
	Maternal Journal	Bennett, Matthew	3171	$10.00	
	Practical Parenting Tips	Lansky, Vicki	1180	$8.00	
	Pregnancy, Childbirth, and the Newborn	Simkin/Whalley/Keppler	1169	$12.00	
	Preschooler's Busy Book	Kuffner, Trish	6055	$9.95	
				Subtotal	
				Shipping and Handling	
			MN residents add 6.5% sales tax		
				Total	

YES! Please send me the books indicated above. Add $2.00 shipping and handling for the first book with a retail price up to $9.99, or $3.00 for the first book with a retail price over $9.99. Add $1.00 shipping and handling for each additional book. All orders must be prepaid. Most orders are shipped within two days by U.S. Mail (7–9 delivery days). Rush shipping is available for an extra charge. Overseas postage will be billed.

Quantity discounts available upon request.

Send book(s) to:

Name _____

Address _____

City _____ State _____ Zip _____

Telephone (_____) _____

Payment via:

☐ Check or money order payable to Meadowbrook Press

☐ Visa (for orders over $10.00 only)   ☐ MasterCard (for orders over $10.00 only)

Account # _____

Signature _____ Exp. Date _____

A FREE Meadowbrook catalog is available upon request.
You can also phone us for orders of $10.00 or more at 1-800-338-2232.

Mail to: Meadowbrook Press
5451 Smetana Drive, Minnetonka, Minnesota 55343

(612) 930-1100   Toll-Free 1-800-338-2232   Fax (612) 930-1940

For more information (and fun) visit our website: www.meadowbrookpress.com